Developing C Language Portable System Call Libraries

Developing C Language Portable System Call Libraries

Matt Weisfeld

A Wiley-QED Publication

John Wiley & Sons, Inc.
New York • Chichester • Brisbane • Toronto • Singapore

Contents

Foreword

The best technical books are the ones that always sit out on your desk. They are the books that are dog-eared and smudged from hard use. *Developing C Language Portable System Call Libraries* is just that type of book!

What? You say, "Prove it!"

Here are four ways:

One—This book gives you twenty fully functional and portable libraries for you to plug into your applications immediately! The thousands of man hours it took to develop these libraries is well worth the price of the book! The code is so timely and useful that several portions of the book have been in both the *C Users Journal* and *Dr. Dobbs' Journal*.

Two—Through Matt's easy-to-follow explanations you will learn the key principles and methods to build your own portable libraries. As a wise man said: "Give a man a fish and you feed him for a day. Teach a man to fish and you feed him for a lifetime!" I especially learned a lot from the chapters on time, environment variables, signals, and the portable user interface.

Three—The book does not shy away from the tough topics. Matt delves right into topics like trapping signals, child processes, and function pointers! Not many books address these, so Matt's in-depth coverage is like a drink of water in the desert.

Four—The book is complete and thorough with every chapter ending with a test program and make files for each platform. And that is no small feat considering the book covers VAX, VMS, HP/UX, SUN SPARC, and Intel Machines. All the major operating systems and compilers have been ported to and tested. Matt leaves no rock unturned!

With reusability at the top of everyone's priority list, you will clear a spot on your desk for *Developing C Language Portable System Call Libraries*!

MICHAEL C. DACONTA
Author of *C Pointers and Dynamic Memory Management*

Acknowledgments

As with any endeavor, this book is the product of more than just one person's efforts. Thus, with great gratitude I express my deepest thanks to the following:

To my wife Sharon, who in many ways should be listed as co-author. Despite all the time pressures associated with job and family, Sharon found time to edit every page of the manuscript and coordinate the details of producing this book. Thanks for keeping me on an even track.

To my daughters Stacy and Stephanie, who perhaps will someday write their own books.

To my grandmother, who kept putting books in my hand until I learned to love them.

To my parents, who continue to support me in whatever I do.

To my sister and brother for putting up with me all these years.

To my friends Chuck Rose, Greg Ordy, Jim Menegay, and the people at ENDOT, Inc., who gave me my start with C and the opportunity to grow with a small startup company. Many of the libraries in this book incorporate techniques I learned while at ENDOT, Inc.

To my friends and supervisors William Hall and Doug Dura, who continually encourage me to explore my professional limits.

To my friends and colleagues at Allen-Bradley, specifically Jim Gross and Mike Gilson, whose technical expertise continues to be a great asset to me.

To Edwin Kerr and everyone at QED, for being very gracious and supportive to a first-time author.

To Mike Daconta and Andy Stamer, who reviewed the initial manuscript and gave me invaluable feedback.

To the people at *The C Users' Journal,* especially Diane Thomas, for being such a class organization.

To the people at *Dr. Dobbs' Journal* for working with me on the article that sparked the idea for this book.

Introduction

The main theme of this book is, as the title suggests, portability. However, readers who view the book strictly in the context of portability may not perceive its underlying purpose. While it is true that the concept of portability is the driving force, the real purpose of this book is to present practical applications and generic libraries that are useful in the real world of C programming. Indeed, having the word portability in the title might be considered limiting. The techniques and applications developed here are useful even if portability is not an issue. Although the concepts and applications are most useful when working on multiple platforms, a programmer working solely on one platform will still find them beneficial.

The approach of building generic libraries is obviously not new. The concept of reusable code is a hot topic today—leading into the realm of object-oriented programming. However, the topic of reusable code that is portable is not often addressed. Great strides have been made in ensuring that the C programming language—more so than any other language—is as portable as possible. Yet, no matter how diligent the efforts in this regard, special problems still exist that keep a language from being totally portable. Most of these problems relate to the operating platform. For example, while VMS and UNIX are multi-tasking, DOS is not. Thus, the creation of concurrent child processes is possible on VMS and UNIX, but not on DOS. Here, the question of portability cannot be addressed by the language—the functionality itself simply does not exist.

Platform specifics are not the only portability problem. Different implementations of C use different command names. In the case of child processes, for instance, in creating a child process, VMS and UNIX use the *fork( )* and *exec( )* commands while DOS uses the *spawn( )* command. This case illustrates the benefits of building portable libraries. By using well-placed ifdefs, a routine can be built that allows the portability issues to be hidden from the programmer. For example, the following structure is used throughout the book:

```
void create_child(void) {

#ifdef DOS

        ...spawn();

#else

        ...fork()/execv();

#endif

}
```

Thus, when the need arises for a portable call to create a child process, the only call necessary is:

```
create_child();
```

While more than this is involved in creating a child process, this short example illustrates how a portable library is built.

The code in this book is library-driven and does not attempt to present a complete product such as a graphics package or a spreadsheet. Each chapter explains and builds a useful library or application—a collection of routines I call a library, although some have only one routine. While you may link these libraries into other programs, and tailor the applications for specific needs, it is my belief that the concept of creating portable libraries may well be more important than the actual code presented here. While the libraries developed here are a useful starting point, there are an unlimited number of libraries waiting to be built.

Simply to take these libraries and use them as is misses the point. The purpose of this book is to define a method that integrates portability into modular libraries. It is left to the reader to tailor these libraries to specific applications, as well as to develop new ones. The libraries presented here are not the only approach available. In short, my main goal is not to say "Here, take these libraries and use them," but to say "Here are some ideas; now develop your own ideas, perhaps incorporating some of these, to satisfy your own programming needs."

In fact, since this book presents a programming philosophy, certain techniques will not meet with universal agreement. For example, though I find it very beneficial to have a common exit routine, some may find this unnecessary. As another example, consider the chapters on user interfaces. In this day and age of windowing environments and sophisticated graphical user interfaces, the value of simple (old technology) user interfaces may seem out of place. However, as long as programmers are still using C outside of GUI environments, there is a need to perform such tasks as retrieving a keystroke and highlighting text on a screen. I have written a number of articles for programming magazines, and, to my surprise, I have received by far the most enthusiastic feedback on an article based on the portable user interface presented in Chapter 18.

My intent here is to build generic and portable applications, not to cover all the technical aspects of portability. While issues such as byte ordering and word size are covered by default in various chapters, the thrust here is to create applications—not get into the gritty details. Since there are already good books available that concentrate on purely technical material, I wanted this book to come from a different perspective.

Each chapter builds on the chapters that precede it. I have, however, attempted to make each chapter stand by itself as much as possible. Therefore, it is possible to go to Chapter 19 on creating a program banner without reading any of the preceding chapters and still find the information understandable and useful. The modular concept of libraries makes this possible. In Chapter 19, a number of other libraries are used; however, they can be linked in without having intimate knowledge of the code itself. For example, the *banner* routine needs the current date and time, which are provided by a previous library. That information can be retrieved by calling the command *get_time( )*. It is enough to know what *get_time( )* returns—you do not need to know how it works. So, even though each chapter stands by itself, there is a specific flow that this book follows. Some routines and applications do require the use of libraries already defined, and the libraries in the first chapters are the basis for ones that come later. However, no library is accessed by another that has not already been explained.

Since the code in this book will run on many different platforms, how the executables are built represent major areas of concern. Each chapter presents the appropriate build scripts, whether they are makefile (UNIX™ and DOS™) or DCL procedures (VMS™). In some libraries the number of object modules surpasses the line length limit of DOS. When this occurs, a file called LISTOBJS is used to store the object names.

One annoying problem that comes into play when porting is the fact that DOS editors place extra escape characters at the end of each line. Thus, any file edited with a DOS editor—at least the ones I used—will include these unwanted characters when transferred to another system. At times this caused some compilers (especially UNIX) many problems. Thus, all code on the disk does not have the DOS format. This does not cause a problem for the DOS compilers. Even the DOS editors accept this format. However, be aware that when a file edited on DOS is ported to another platform, these escape characters may reappear. Since the methods of physically moving code from one platform to another vary significantly, depending on the hardware and the communication products, this topic is not covered in this book.

After inspecting some libraries or applications, it may become apparent that the topic has little to do with portability. While it is true that some libraries presented do not have specific portability problems, they may be necessary for development of future libraries that do. Also, some C compilers provide a wider range of functionality than do others. DOS, for instance, has a richer set of string functions than the other platforms. Even though building equivalent string functions on VMS does not uncover any special portability concerns, the fact that the platforms do not provide the same functionality can be considered a portability issue.

These libraries have been tested to the best of my ability. However, I strongly recommend that they be tested further when used with specific applications.

This book concentrates on the following platforms:

VMS 5.5 VAXstation 3100™

HP/UX 9.0 Apollo series 700™

SUN SPARCstation SLC SunOS Release 4.1.3™
    (cc & gcc V1.39 compilers)

BORLAND C++™ (386 machine)

I tested a late version of the libraries on the Microsoft 7.0™ and Coherent™ platforms on 386 machines (the build procedures are provided). Early versions of the code were ported to the ULTRIX DECstation 3100™ platform (build procedures are not provided).

All platforms are defined on the command line in the build files. Note that when using defines in a VMS DCL file, only the last define is active.

In each chapter there is a short file called *test.c,* to demonstrate how the library in that chapter works. The tests are by no means complete—their main purpose is to provide regression testing so that when one library is changed, nothing else is broken. When porting code to multiple platforms, it is easy for subtle errors to find their way into code. Thus, a regression test is of the utmost importance.

Finally, I would greatly appreciate any feedback, in the form

of questions or problems encountered. I can be reached via QED
or on Compuserve at [71620,2171].

MATT WEISFELD
Lyndhurst, Ohio

The Common Header File

The first order of business is to define the common aspects shared by all the libraries and applications developed in this book. These aspects, incorporated into a common header file, ensure that all programs will function together in a consistent manner. As portability is a primary concern as well, the header file also provides a place where the systems themselves are defined.

The common header file, named *common.h,* is used by every module in this book. Thus it should be the first header file included, with the exception of certain system header files. Returning to the concept of portability, it is imperative that the specific platform—VMS, DOS, or UNIX; ANSI or not—be specified early in each program. The actual platform is defined via the compilation line in the makefile or build procedure. While it could be defined on the first line within *common.h* itself, this could be potentially dangerous if it were not changed when the code was ported from one platform to another. The programs developed here use the following definition standards (an incomplete list):

```
#ifdef VMS
#define ANSI
```

```
#endif
#ifdef BCC
#define ANSI
#endif
#ifdef HPUX
#define UNIX
#define ANSI
#endif
```

Of course, other platforms can easily be added. Again, for portability reasons, this information must be provided early in the compilation process.

Three main operating systems are used for this book: VMS, UNIX (HP-UX), and DOS (BORLAND C++ 3.1). Other platforms to which the libraries in this book were successfully ported include the SUN/SLC (both the SUN C compiler and the GNU C compiler), Microsoft C/C++ 7.0, and Coherent UNIX on a 386 machine. Early versions of the libraries were ported to a DECstation running ULTRIX and the OS9™ real time operating system. The three primary platforms listed above were chosen to represent VMS, DOS, and UNIX. I did not have a version of Curses for Microsoft C/C++ and OS9. However, at least for Microsoft C, the code using Curses should port without much trouble. UNIX presents the most portability issues, since there are many different flavors of UNIX hardware and operating systems.

Other items in the *common.h* file include information that is passed between routines and programs themselves. For example, when you exit a routine, you will usually do so in normal, warning, or error mode. Thus definitions are made to facilitate this process:

```
#define NORMAL  0
#define ERROR   1
#define WARNING 2
```

In some cases it is desirable to differentiate whether a return will exit a routine to a calling routine or actually exit (terminate) the program. There are times when a program is called from a procedure, such as a batch file or DCL procedure, and must return a status. Thus, separate definitions are made to indicate that the program is terminating:

```
#define EXIT_NORMAL   0
#define EXIT_ERROR    1
#define EXIT_WARNING  3
```

These definitions can also be used with the *exit( )* function. Making these consistent among various programs allows them to communicate with each other. For example, if a child process is created, then the child can inform the parent of its status.

The reason that the EXIT_WARNING definition is a 3 rather than a 2 is due to a portability issue. An odd status must be passed back by VMS processes for reasons that are explained in Chapter 2.

Certain data types are not defined in C. For instance, there is no boolean operator. However, there are situations, such as when a flag is used, where it is very useful to have a variable declared as BOOL. Since a boolean variable is a subset of an integer, the following definition is made:

```
#define BOOL int
```

Finally, even though some systems actually define boolean values such as TRUE and FALSE, some do not. Thus, the following definitions are included:

```
#define OFF   0
#define ON    1


#define FALSE 0
#define TRUE  1
```

It is best to place all definitions of this type in a file such as *common.h*. Any programs that need this information can easily access it by simply including this file.

```
/*****************************************************

   FILE NAME   : common.h
   AUTHOR      : Matt Weisfeld

   DESCRIPTION : header common to all libraries

*****************************************************/

#ifdef VMS
#define ANSI
#define VT100
#define LENDIAN
#endif

#ifdef BCC
#define DOS
#define ANSI
#define LENDIAN
#endif

#ifdef MSC
#define DOS
#define ANSI
#define LENDIAN
#endif

#ifdef HPUX
#define UNIX
#define BENDIAN
#ifdef __STDC__
#define ANSI
#endif
#endif

#ifdef SLC
#define SUN
#define NDIFFTIME
#define VT100
#define UNIX
#define BENDIAN
#endif
```

```
#ifdef GCC
#define SUN
#define NDIFFTIME
#define VT100
#define BENDIAN
#define UNIX
#define ANSI
#endif

#ifdef CCC
#define UNIX
#define BENDIAN
#define NDIFFTIME
#endif

#define OFF     0
#define ON      1

#define FALSE   0
#define TRUE    1

#define BOOL int

#define RETURN  0
#define EXIT    1

#define NORMAL    0
#define ERROR     1
#define WARNING   2

#define EXIT_NORMAL   1
#define EXIT_ERROR    3
#define EXIT_WARNING  5

#define STRLEN 130
```

2

A Common Exit Point

The library developed in this chapter holds the distinction of being first for the simple reason that all other libraries and applications ultimately call it. One widely accepted doctrine of sound programming practice is that there should be only one entry and exit point from a program. When a program terminates, at least under normal circumstances, the line of code that issues the *exit( )* command should always be the same.

Some may not agree with the premise of a single exit point—and I am not necessarily stating that the approach taken in this chapter is the only one available to a programmer. However, I find a common exit point to be a valuable programming technique.

2.1 LEAVING AN APPLICATION

There are actually three ways to exit a routine:

- use the *return( )* command
- use the *exit( )* command
- do nothing

Using the *return( )* command passes control back to the calling routine. In the event that the main routine issues a *return( )*, control passes back to the operating system or the parent process. The *exit( )* command terminates a process and returns control to the operating system or parent process. Doing nothing basically defaults to a *return( )* with no return value.

Many ANSI C compilers issue a warning if a *return( )* statement is missing. It is very difficult to track program flow when there are multiple exit points throughout the application. Thus, it is the practice here to end each routine with a *return( )*, thereby avoiding the warning, while using the *exit( )* command in only one place, a routine called *leave( )*.

2.2 THE *leave( )* ROUTINE

The logic for this routine is very simple: call *leave( )* whenever an application's logic requires a program exit. This ensures that there is only one exit point in the process. The *leave( )* function accepts a status variable, so that it can handle the exit properly. The action or actions taken at program termination are up to the individual program design. This implementation simply prints out the status of the exit variable. The functions performed by an exit routine include many possibilities: file closings, temporary file clean-up, restoring system variables, freeing memory, and many others. Using a single exit point ensures the execution of these functions.

In this implementation, *leave( )* recognizes three types of exit conditions: EXIT_NORMAL, EXIT_ERROR, and EXIT_WARNING. The prototype for *leave( )* is:

```
void leave(status)
int status;
```

Thus, any routine can call *leave( )* with one of these simple calls:

```
leave(EXIT_NORMAL)
leave(EXIT_ERROR)
leave(EXIT_WARNING)
```

The following code segment shows the basic form of the *leave*( ) routine:

```
switch (status) {

    case EXIT_NORMAL:
        printf ("EXIT NORMAL\n");
    break;
    case EXIT_WARNING:
        printf ("EXIT WARNING\n");
    break;
    case EXIT_ERROR:
        printf ("EXIT ERROR\n");
    break;

    default:
        printf ("Error: Invalid exit status: %d\n", status);
        status = EXIT_ERROR;
    break;


}

exit(status);
```

A default condition indicates an invalid exit code. After producing an informational message, *leave*( ) exits with EXIT_ERROR. These status variables are for program exit only. There are constants defined in the *common.h* for returning from one routine to another. The use of the constants NORMAL, ERROR, and WARNING are for internal purposes. EXIT_NORMAL, EXIT_ERROR, and EXIT_WARNING indicate an exit status from the program itself that the calling process interprets.

Different operating systems may interpret the exit status differently. For example, when using even number exit values, VMS produces a message similar to:

```
%NONAME-?-NOMSG, Message number 00000006
```

When the even exit values reach 8, access violations occur. Matters like this must be taken into account when defining exit status constants.

2.3 USING THE LEAVE LIBRARY

The test program for the leave library calls *leave( )* with three return values. This value is dependent on input from the user. The three valid inputs are 1 (for normal), 3 (for error), and 5 (for warning). To test the program, enter commands similar to the following:

```
test 1
test 3
test 5
```

Any other input will generate an exit value of 999, which the *leave( )* routine will flag as an error. The program uses *atoi( )* to convert the string values from the *argv* list to integers. Remember that these exit values are up to the programmer and may be tailored to specific needs.

It is even possible to have a standard houskeeping routine that resides in the application program directory that *leave( )* calls using:

```
housekeeping();
```

To use the common exit point routine, link in the *leave* object file with the application. No other action is necessary.

2.4 CONCLUSION

There are many advantages to a common exit point. The sheer size of many applications makes it imperative that program flow remain simple. Knowing the exact point of program termination is a significant step in this direction.

Even though this library is relatively small, it is very important. The value of a single exit point is especially important when problems arise and debugging begins, since it is easier to trace back to the point where *leave( )* is called. The object code generated by compiling *leave.c* is linked into every library and application covered in this book.

```
/***************************************************

   FILE NAME   : test.c
   AUTHOR      : Matt Weisfeld

   DESCRIPTION : test program for leave()

***************************************************/
#include <stdio.h>
#include <stdlib.h>
#include "proto.h"

/*
    Enter all possibilities to test if leave() works
    properly. Also, use an invalid value. Try to
    break the routine. Beware that passing a parameter
    that is not a number may not behave as expected.
*/

main(argc,argv)
int argc;
char **argv;
{

    int value;

    if (argc != 2) {
       printf ("must have two arguments\n");
       leave(EXIT_ERROR);
    }

    /* converting a non-number ascii string may be
       interpreted as a 0. */

    value = atoi(argv[1]);

    printf ("Test the leave routine: value = %d\n", value);
```

```
    switch (value) {

        case EXIT_NORMAL :

            leave (EXIT_NORMAL);

        break;

        case EXIT_WARNING :

            leave (EXIT_WARNING);

        break;

        case EXIT_ERROR :

            leave (EXIT_ERROR);

        break;

        default :

            leave (999); /* bad leave value */

        break;

    }

    return(EXIT_NORMAL);

}

/*##############################################*/


/****************************************************

  FILE NAME   : leave.c
  AUTHOR      : Matt Weisfeld

  DESCRIPTION : common exit point for all
                libraries.

****************************************************/
```

```c
#include <stdio.h>
#include <stdlib.h>
#include "proto.h"

/******************************************************

   ROUTINE NAME : leave()

   DESCRIPTION  : common exit point for all
                  libraries.

   INPUT        : int (status)

   OUTPUT       : exit (status)

******************************************************/
void leave(status)
int status;
{

    switch (status) {

    case EXIT_NORMAL:
       printf ("EXIT NORMAL\n");
    break;
    case EXIT_WARNING:
       printf ("EXIT WARNING\n");
    break;
    case EXIT_ERROR:
       printf ("EXIT ERROR\n");
    break;
    default:
       printf ("Error: Invalid exit status: %d\n", status);
    status = EXIT_ERROR;
    break;
    }

    exit (status);

    return;
}

/*#############################################*/
```

```
/****************************************************

   FILE NAME   : leave.h
   AUTHOR      : Matt Weisfeld

   DESCRIPTION : header file for leave()

****************************************************/
#ifdef ANSI
void leave(int);
#else
void leave();
#endif


/*##############################################*/


/****************************************************

   FILE NAME   : proto.h
   AUTHOR      : Matt Weisfeld

   DESCRIPTION : prototypes for leave()

****************************************************/
#ifdef VMS
#include "[-.common]common.h"
#endif
#ifdef BCC
#include "..\common\common.h"
#endif
#ifdef MSC
#include "..\common\common.h"
#endif
#ifdef HPUX
#include "../common/common.h"
#endif
#ifdef SLC
#include "../common/common.h"
#endif
#ifdef GCC
#include "../common/common.h"
```

```
#endif
#ifdef CCC
#include "../common/common.h"
#endif
#include "leave.h"

/*############################################*/

$! VMS DCL PROCEDURE
$ clr
$ if (P1.eqs."") then GOTO ALL
$ if (P1.eqs."ALL") then GOTO ALL
$ if (P1.eqs."LINK") then GOTO LINK
$ set verify
$ cc/define=VMS 'P1'
$ goto LINK
$ ALL:
$ set verify
$ cc/define=VMS test
$ cc/define=VMS leave
$ LINK:
$ link/executable=test test,leave
$ copy test.exe [weisfeld.exe]
$ set noverify

/*############################################*/

# makefile for BCC/C++ Compiler

OBJS    = test.obj leave.obj
HDRS    = proto.h leave.h ..\common\common.h
FLAGS   = -c -DBCC
COMP    = bcc

test.exe:  $(OBJS)
   $(COMP) $(OBJS)

test.obj: test.c $(HDRS)
   $(COMP) $(FLAGS) test.c

leave.obj: leave.c $(HDRS)
   $(COMP) $(FLAGS) leave.c
```

```
test.c:
leave.c:

leave.h:

/*###############################################*/

# makefile for MSC/C++ Compiler

OBJS     = test.obj leave.obj
HDRS     = proto.h leave.h ..\common\common.h
FLAGS    = /c /DMSC
COMP     = cl

test.exe:  $(OBJS)
    $(COMP) $(OBJS)

test.obj: test.c $(HDRS)
    $(COMP) $(FLAGS) test.c

leave.obj: leave.c $(HDRS)
    $(COMP) $(FLAGS) leave.c

test.c:
leave.c:

leave.h:

/*###############################################*/

# makefile for HPUX C Compiler

OBJS     = test.o leave.o
HDRS     = proto.h leave.h
FLAGS    = -c -DHPUX -Aa
COMP     = cc

test:  $(OBJS)
    $(COMP) -o test $(OBJS)

test.o: test.c $(HDRS)
    $(COMP) $(FLAGS) test.c
```

```
leave.o: leave.c $(HDRS)
    $(COMP) $(FLAGS) leave.c

test.c:
leave.c:

leave.h:

/*############################################*/


# makefile for SUN SLC C Compiler

OBJS    = test.o leave.o
HDRS    = proto.h leave.h
FLAGS   = -c -DSLC
COMP    = cc

test:  $(OBJS)
    $(COMP) -o test $(OBJS)

test.o: test.c $(HDRS)
    $(COMP) $(FLAGS) test.c

leave.o: leave.c $(HDRS)
    $(COMP) $(FLAGS) leave.c

test.c:
leave.c:

leave.h:

/*############################################*/

# makefile for SUN GCC C Compiler

OBJS    = test.o leave.o
HDRS    = proto.h leave.h
FLAGS   = -c -DGCC
COMP    = gcc

test:  $(OBJS)
    $(COMP) -o test $(OBJS)
```

```
test.o: test.c $(HDRS)
    $(COMP) $(FLAGS) test.c

leave.o: leave.c $(HDRS)
    $(COMP) $(FLAGS) leave.c

test.c:
leave.c:

leave.h:


/*##############################################*/


# makefile for CCC Compiler

OBJS     = test.o leave.o
HDRS     = proto.h leave.h
FLAGS    = -c -DCCC
COMP     = cc

test:  $(OBJS)
    $(COMP) -o test $(OBJS)

test.o: test.c $(HDRS)
    $(COMP) $(FLAGS) test.c

leave.o: leave.c $(HDRS)
    $(COMP) $(FLAGS) leave.c

test.c:
leave.c:

leave.h:
```

## 3

Error Handling

Despite good programming intentions, errors are inevitable. As most programmers know all too well, it does not take long for undisciplined error control to get out of hand; therefore, it is well worth the initial investment to develop a robust error handling strategy.

Trapping errors early in any process is extremely important. Allowing a detectable error to propagate throughout a program is a recipe for disaster. It is important to check vigorously for errors and try to anticipate what types of errors might occur.

3.1 ERROR HANDLING STRUCTURES

The first issues to consider when creating an error routine are:

1. the determination of the information required when an error occurs
2. the action that is taken when an error is detected
3. the format by which the error is called

The error handling structure with this information looks like this:

```
typedef struct error_structure {
    int error_number;
    int error_action;
    char *error_string;
}ERROR_STRUCT;
```

This technique is quite simple, but very powerful.

Suppose that an application checks for the following errors:

1. "Out of space" error generated by a *malloc*( )
2. "Unable to fork" error generated by a *vfork*( )
3. Unable to execute a process by an *exec*( )
4. A warning that a macro already exists

Each error (warning) must correspond to a unique number:

```
#define ER_NOSPACE      0      /* no space left for malloc */
#define ER_NOFORK       1      /* could not fork process */
#define ER_NOEXEC       2      /* could not exec process */
#define WR_MACEXISTS    3      /* macro already exists */
...

#define LASTERROR      -1
```

Include the definition of LASTERROR, since future searches will use this to indicate the end of the error list.

The number of errors defined depends on the application. Each error must have a unique, descriptive name that indicates the cause of the problem. In this example, there are two classes of errors, each prefaced by either an ER (fatal error) or WR (warning). The application with which you are working dictates the need for and number of classes. A class called IN (information) is another example of a valid class.

It is possible to group all classes together, as follows:

```
#define ER_NOSPACE      0      /* no space left for malloc */
#define ER_NOFORK       1      /* could not fork process */
#define ER_NOEXEC       2      /* could not exec process */
#define WR_MACEXISTS    3      /* macro already exists */
```

```
#define WR_DEFEXISTS    4    /* definition already exists */
#define IN_FILEEXISTS   5    /* file exists */
#define IN_SPACELOW     6    /* not much space is left */


...


#define LASTERROR      -1
```

However, adding new error definitions causes problems with this approach because renumbering is necessary each time a new class is out of sequence. This becomes quite cumbersome, and the slightly increased clarity is generally not worth the extra effort.

The error codes reside in a file called *er.h*. Each routine that generates an error must include this file. To complete the error definition, another header file called *errdefs.h* identifies the error action and the information presented. A sample *errdefs.h* follows.

```
#include "er.h"

ERROR_STRUCT error_message[] =

/* actual error messages */

{

    /* #0 */
    ER_NOSPACE, EXIT,
    "An attempted space allocation failed in module '%s'.",
    /* #1 */
    ER_NOFORK, EXIT,
    "An attempt to create a new process failed. Status '%d'.",
    /* #2 */
    ER_NOEXEC, EXIT,
    "EXECV of '%s' failed. Status '%d'.",
    /* #3 */
    WR_MACEXISTS, RETURN,
    "Macro '%s' already exists.",
    /* #4 */
    WR_DEFEXISTS, RETURN,
```

```
"Definition '%s' already exists.",
/* #5 */
IN_FILEEXISTS, RETURN,
"File '%s' already exists.",
/* #6 */
IN_SPACELOW, RETURN,
"Space is low, only '%d' left.",


...


/* LAST */
LASTERROR, EXIT, NULL,
};
```

Each error definition in this file corresponds to the error structure defined at the beginning of this chapter. Take *error #1* as an example:

```
/* #1 */
ER_NOFORK, EXIT,
"An attempt to create a new process failed. Status '%d'.",
```

Comments such as the one shown above are helpful as the error list becomes large, allowing a specific number to be located easily. ER_NOFORK is the defined error number contained in the file *er.h*. The second parameter is the error action. In this case, the error action can be one of two possibilities: either exit the program, or return to the spot where the error occurred.

```
#define RETURN  0
#define EXIT    1
```

The error string is basically a message presented in a readable format. Note that the message string contains escape sequences as well as text. Even though the text is predefined, the escape sequences allow the programmer to include runtime information in the error message, such as status or the routine where the error occurred. Also note that the number of escape sequences varies among the message strings.

The *errdefs.h* file will differ for each application. Note that the first line of *errdefs.h* is an *include* of *er.h*. These two files are separate because the information in *errdefs.h* need only reside in the main routine. For example, a routine calling *error( )* needs the following code:

```
#include "er.h"

...

error(ER_NOSPACE, "check");
```

If a routine includes *errdefs.h,* a compilation error may result from defining the error structure twice.

3.2 ERROR HANDLING CODE

The error handling code in *error.c* need not include *errdefs.h* or *er.h;* however, it must have access to the error structure defined in *errdefs.h*. Thus, define the structure as *extern:*

```
extern ERROR_STRUCT error_message[];
```

With the structure now available to the error routine, examine the C code. The main responsibilities of the *error( )* routine are:

1. Determine if the error is valid (as defined in *er.h*).
2. Build the error message.
3. Print the error message.
4. Determine whether to exit or return.

The main portability problem concern is that message strings can include multiple escape sequences. This means that the parameter list passed to *error( )* is variable (just like *printf( )*). A call to *error( )* might have three parameters, such as:

```
error(ER_BADMODE, mode, "banner");
```

A call to *error( )* could have four parameters, such as:

```
error(ER_BADMODE, status, mode, "banner");
```

The problem is that there is no way to know ahead of time how many parameters are coming. Fortunately, the ANSI standard provides a way to handle variable parameter lists, called *va_arg*. Unfortunately, *va_arg* is not portable to nonANSI systems. However, there is a way to simulate *va_arg*, even though it is better to use the ANSI provision when it is available.

Since there are fundamental calling differences between the ANSI and nonANSI versions of this routine, the prototypes do not reside in *proto.h*. The prototypes for *error( )* are as follows:

```
#ifdef ANSI
void error (int current_error, ...)
#else
void error (current_error, p1, p2, p3, p4)
int current_error;
void *p1;
void *p2;
void *p3;
void *p4;
#endif
```

Both versions require that the error number be the first argument. The use of the ellipse (...) in the ANSI function definition signifies that *va_arg* is a variable argument list. Before exploring the actual code of the error routine, a brief description of *va_arg* is in order.

3.3 USING *va_arg*

To utilize the ANSI *va_arg* facility, include the header file *stdarg.h:*

```
#include <stdarg.h>
```

This header file contains macros (possibly functions) that perform the support functions necessary for using variable lists.

Declare a pointer of type *va_list:*

```
va_list args;
```

This statement declares *args* as a pointer to the next argument in the variable list. Initialize the pointer as follows:

```
va_start (args, current_error);
```

This statement initializes the pointer *args* to the first argument after *current_error*. There must always be one permanent argument in the function definition before the variable list—in this instance, the variable *current_error*. To actually retrieve the first argument from the list, use this statement:

```
param = va_arg(args, data_type);
```

The variable *param* is assigned the next item in the list. Similar calls return further arguments in the list. Finally, when the list is exhausted, the *va_end* comand is executed:

```
va_end(args);
```

This statement performs housekeeping, explained later in this chapter.

3.4 INTEGRATING THE CODE

Now that you understand *va_args*, we can integrate it into the error routine. The first line of code creates the actual instance of the error structure:

```
struct error_structure *error_struct;
```

This pointer references the error messages created in *errdefs.h*. The first task is to determine if the error number passed to the error routine from somewhere within the program is a valid error definition, for example, ER_NOSPACE or ER_NOFORK. A simple linear search is performed to confirm the existence of the error. The loop starts by assigning the pointer *error_struct* to the address of the first error definition in the error structure as follows:

```
error_struct = &error_message[0];
```

The loop continues until reaching LASTERROR. Each iteration of the loop increases *error_struct* by the size of the structure:

```
error_struct++;
```

This statement calculates the size of the structure, then increases the pointer by this value. The result is that *error_struct* now points to the next error message. If at any time the current error matches a defined error in the structure, a break statement terminates the loop. If, however, the error does not exist, the program continues through the loop until encountering LASTERROR, which generates an error message reporting an invalid error.

If a valid error contains escape sequences, they expand at this point. The implementation of expanding escape sequences depends on whether or not the system is ANSI.

3.5 NONANSI SYSTEMS

If the system is nonANSI, or does not support *va_args,* then a *sprintf( )* command places the proper information in a buffer descriptively called *buff:*

```
char buff[STRLEN];
```

Remember that an error string may contain escape sequences such as:

```
"Macro '%s' already exists.",
```

To expand the escape sequences, use the *sprintf( )* command:

```
sprintf (buff, error_struct->error_string,p1,p2,p3,p4);
```

In this case, the number of escape sequences is four. More can easily be added by the programmer. Be aware that while this approach works on all the systems to which it was ported in developing this book, portability problems may arise on other systems. Do not take the parameters' passing order on the stack for granted. Passing no parameters may also pose a problem on some systems.

For example, on nonANSI systems this routine has a function definition with *p1,p2,p3,p4*. Calling the error routine without the full complement of parameters may cause a problem if the system fails to pass a NULL in place of the omitted parameter. The bottom line is this: be aware of what each nonANSI system does when it comes to parameter passing of this nature, especially if unexpected results occur.

If the system is ANSI compliant, then *args* contains all the arguments. The final, expanded string is still placed in *buff*. Since *args* contains a variable parameter list, *sprintf*( ) will not work. An ANSI version of *sprintf*( ) for a variable parameter list is *vsprintf*( ). The call to *vsprintf*( ) looks like:

```
vsprintf (buff, error_struct->error_string, args);
```

Remember to use *va_start* and *va_end* when using *vsprintf*( ). The entire section of code is as follows:

```
#ifdef ANSI

va_start(args,current_error);

vsprintf (buff, error_struct->error_string, args);

va_end(args);

#else

sprintf (buff, error_struct->error_string,p1,p2,p3,p4);

#endif
```

In the example above, consider the following the *error_string:*

```
"Macro '%s' already exists."
```

The single parameter 'number' expands to this:

```
"Macro 'number' already exists."
```

The elegance of this solution is that the user does not have to write code to expand the string. The *sprintf( )* or *vsprintf( )* function takes care of it. Thus any escape sequences supported by the C compiler, such as %s, %d, %c, and so on, are valid in the error routine.

3.6 DETERMINING THE ERROR ACTION

After expanding the error message, the error routine determines the program action. Remember that the *error_action* is the second parameter in the *error_structure* after the *error_number:*

```
WR_MACEXISTS, RETURN,
```

In this case the user has specified that when the error, treated here as a warning, is encountered, control returns to the calling program so processing can continue. If the *error_action* is an EXIT, treated as EXIT_ERROR, then program termination occurs. The integer variable *exit_status* holds the action for future use. A simple case statement initiates the proper action. If the *error_action* is illegal—something other than RETURN or EXIT—an error message prints and the action behaves as an EXIT. The case statement prints the actual error message with the following statement:

```
fprintf(stderr,"ERROR (%d):  %s\n",current_error,buff);
```

In this library, an error message consists of the program name, error number, the line number of the detected error and the error message itself. Again, the information reported by *error*( ) remains at the user's discretion.

Depending on the error action defined in the error structure, the routine either calls *leave*( ) or returns control to the point of invocation.

3.7 USING THE ERROR LIBRARY

The test program for the *error* library tests both possible error types: errors and warnings. The first test generates an error that returns to the point of call. The second test generates a warning that does likewise. Finally, a generated error forces a program exit.

To use the error libraries, link the *error* object library with the application. The *er.h* and *errdefs.h* files are required.

3.8 CONCLUSION

Error handling, even though not a pleasant thought, is a very important feature in any program or software project. By developing a sound error handling strategy and making it easy to use, you will ensure that those errors that do occur are easily identified and more readily fixed.

To utilize this library, simply link in the error object file to any application, define the *er.h* and *errdefs.h* files, and—happy error hunting!

```
/****************************************************

   FILE NAME   : test.c
   AUTHOR      : Matt Weisfeld

   DESCRIPTION : test program for error.

****************************************************/
#include <stdio.h>
#include "proto.h"
#include "errdefs.h"
```

```
main()
{

    printf ("Generate an error that will return here.\n");

    error (ER_NOSPACE, "test");

    printf ("Control regained here.\n");

    printf ("Generate a warning that will return here.\n");

    error (WR_MACEXISTS, "mac", 3);

    printf ("Control regained here.\n");

    printf ("Generate an error that will terminate program.\n");

    error (ER_NOFORK, -1);

    return(EXIT_NORMAL);

}

/*###############################################*/


/***************************************************

  FILE NAME   : error.c
  AUTHOR      : Matt Weisfeld

  DESCRIPTION : common error routine for all
                libraries.

***************************************************/
#include  <stdio.h>
#include  "proto.h"
#ifdef ANSI
#include   "stdarg.h"
#endif
#ifdef DOS
```

```
#include  "stdlib.h"
#endif

extern ERROR_STRUCT error_message[];
/****************************************************

  ROUTINE NAME : error()

  DESCRIPTION  : common error routine for all
                 libraries.

  INPUT        : int, ... (variable arg list)

  OUTPUT       : none (return to caller or
                 call leave())

****************************************************/
#ifdef ANSI
void error (int current_error, ...)
#else
void error (current_error, p1, p2, p3, p4)
int current_error;
int *p1;
int *p2;
int *p3;
int *p4;
#endif
{

    struct error_structure *error_struct;

    int exit_status;

    int i;

    char buff[STRLEN];

#ifdef ANSI

    va_list args;

#endif
```

```
    /* loop through error messages until end of list */

    for (error_struct = &error_message[0];
         error_struct->error_number != LASTERROR;
         error_struct++) {

        /* break out of for loop if found */

        if (error_struct->error_number == current_error)
            break;

    }

    /* if we did not find the error, we have an internal error */

    if (error_struct->error_number == LASTERROR) {
        fprintf(stderr, "\nERROR : invalid error\n");
        leave(ERROR);
    }

#ifdef ANSI

    va_start(args, current_error);

    vsprintf (buff, error_struct->error_string, args);

    va_end(args);

#else

    sprintf (buff, error_struct->error_string, p1, p2, p3, p4);

#endif

    /* report the error message */


    switch (error_struct->error_action) {

        case RETURN:
            fprintf(stderr,"ERROR (%d) - %s\n",current_error,buff);
            exit_status = NORMAL;
```

```
        break;
        case EXIT:
            fprintf(stderr,"ERROR (%d) - %s\n",
                current_error,buff);
            exit_status = EXIT_ERROR;
        break;
        default:
            fprintf(stderr, "\nERROR : unknown error action\n");
            exit_status = EXIT_ERROR;
        break;

    }

    if (exit_status == EXIT_ERROR)
        leave(EXIT_ERROR);
    else
        return;

} /* program */

/*###############################################*/


/****************************************************

  FILE NAME    : error.h
  AUTHOR       : Matt Weisfeld

  DESCRIPTION : header file for error()

****************************************************/
#ifdef ANSI
void error (int, ...);
#else
void error ();
#endif

/* internal error structure */

typedef struct error_structure {
    int    error_number;    /* number assigned to error */
    int    error_action;    /* EXIT pilot or return */
```

```
    char   *error_string;   /* text to be printed */
} ERROR_STRUCT;

#define LASTERROR -1

/*###############################################*/


/*****************************************************

  FILE NAME    : er.h
  AUTHOR       : Matt Weisfeld

  DESCRIPTION  : error definitions for error()
                 test.

*****************************************************/
#define ER_NOSPACE   0     /* no space left for malloc */
#define ER_NOFORK    1     /* could not fork process */
#define ER_NOEXEC    2     /* could not exec process */
#define WR_MACEXISTS 3     /* macro already exists */

/*###############################################*/

/*****************************************************

  FILE NAME    : errdefs.h
  AUTHOR       : Matt Weisfeld

  DESCRIPTION  : error descriptions for error()
                 test.

*****************************************************/
#include "er.h"

ERROR_STRUCT error_message[] =

/* actual error messages */

{
```

```
    /* #0 */
    ER_NOSPACE, RETURN,
    "An attempted space allocation failed in module '%s'.",
    /* #1 */
    ER_NOFORK, EXIT,
    "An attempt to create a new process failed. Status '%d'.",
    /* #2 */
    ER_NOEXEC, EXIT,
    "EXECV of '%s' failed. Status '%d'.",
    /* #3 */
    WR_MACEXISTS, RETURN,
    "Macro '%s' already exists in line #%d.",
    /* LAST */
    LASTERROR, EXIT, NULL
};


/*#################################################*/


/****************************************************

  FILE NAME   : proto.h
  AUTHOR      : Matt Weisfeld

  DESCRIPTION : prototypes for error().

****************************************************/
#ifdef VMS
#include "[-.common]common.h"
#include "[-.leave]leave.h"
#endif
#ifdef BCC
#include "..\common\common.h"
#include "..\leave\leave.h"
#endif
#ifdef MSC
#include "..\common\common.h"
#include "..\leave\leave.h"
#endif
#ifdef HPUX
#include "../common/common.h"
```

```
#include "../leave/leave.h"
#endif
#ifdef SLC
#include "../common/common.h"
#include "../leave/leave.h"
#endif
#ifdef GCC
#include "../common/common.h"
#include "../leave/leave.h"
#endif
#ifdef CCC
#include "../common/common.h"
#include "../leave/leave.h"
#endif

#include "error.h"

/*###########################################*/

$ clr
$ if (P1.eqs."") then GOTO ALL
$ if (P1.eqs."ALL") then GOTO ALL
$ if (P1.eqs."LINK") then GOTO LINK
$ set verify
$ cc/define=VMS 'P1'
$ goto LINK
$ ALL:
$   set verify
$ cc/define=VMS test
$ cc/define=VMS error
$ LINK:
$ link/executable=test test,error,[-.leave]leave
$ copy test.exe [weisfeld.exe]
$ set noverify

/*###########################################*/

# makefile for BCC/C++ Compiler

OBJS    = test.obj error.obj
LIBS    = ..\leave\leave.obj
HDRS    = proto.h error.h errdefs.h er.h
```

```
FLAGS    = -c -DBCC
COMP     = bcc

test.exe:  $(OBJS)
   $(COMP) $(OBJS) $(LIBS)

test.obj: test.c $(HDRS)
   $(COMP) $(FLAGS) test.c

error.obj: error.c $(HDRS)
   $(COMP) $(FLAGS) error.c

test.c:
error.c:

error.h:
errdefs.h:
er.h:

/*###########################################*/

# makefile for MSC/C++ Compiler

OBJS     = test.obj error.obj
LIBS     = ..\leave\leave.obj
HDRS     = proto.h error.h errdefs.h er.h
FLAGS    = /c /DMSC
COMP     = cl

test.exe:  $(OBJS)
   $(COMP) $(OBJS) $(LIBS)

test.obj: test.c $(HDRS)
   $(COMP) $(FLAGS) test.c

error.obj: error.c $(HDRS)
   $(COMP) $(FLAGS) error.c

test.c:
error.c:
```

```
error.h:
errdefs.h:
er.h:

/*##########################################*/

# makefile for HPUX C Compiler

OBJS     = test.o error.o
LIBS     = ../leave/leave.o
HDRS     = proto.h error.h errdefs.h er.h
FLAGS    = -c -DHPUX
COMP     = cc

test:   $(OBJS)
    $(COMP) -o test $(OBJS) $(LIBS)

test.o: test.c $(HDRS)
    $(COMP) $(FLAGS) test.c

error.o: error.c $(HDRS)
    $(COMP) $(FLAGS) error.c

test.c:
error.c:

error.h:
errdefs.h:
er.h:

/*##########################################*/

# makefile for SUN SLC C Compiler

OBJS     = test.o error.o
LIBS     = ../leave/leave.o
HDRS     = proto.h error.h errdefs.h er.h
FLAGS    = -c -DSLC
COMP     = cc

test:   $(OBJS)
    $(COMP) -o test $(OBJS) $(LIBS)
```

```
test.o: test.c $(HDRS)
    $(COMP) $(FLAGS) test.c

error.o: error.c $(HDRS)
    $(COMP) $(FLAGS) error.c

test.c:
error.c:

error.h:
errdefs.h:
er.h:

/*##############################################*/

# makefile for SUN GCC C Compiler

OBJS     = test.o error.o
LIBS     = ../leave/leave.o
HDRS     = proto.h error.h errdefs.h er.h
FLAGS    = -c -DSLC
COMP     = gcc

test:   $(OBJS)
    $(COMP) -o test $(OBJS) $(LIBS)

test.o: test.c $(HDRS)
    $(COMP) $(FLAGS) test.c

error.o: error.c $(HDRS)
    $(COMP) $(FLAGS) error.c

test.c:
error.c:

error.h:
errdefs.h:
er.h:

/*##############################################*/
```

```
# makefile for CCC C Compiler

OBJS     = test.o error.o
LIBS     = ../leave/leave.o
HDRS     = proto.h error.h errdefs.h er.h
FLAGS    = -c -DCCC
COMP     = cc

test:   $(OBJS)
    $(COMP) -o test $(OBJS) $(LIBS)

test.o: test.c $(HDRS)
    $(COMP) $(FLAGS) test.c

error.o: error.c $(HDRS)
    $(COMP) $(FLAGS) error.c

test.c:
error.c:

error.h:
errdefs.h:
er.h:
```

3.9 SELECTED REFERENCE

Kernighan, Brian W. and Dennis M. Ritchie. *The C Programming Language,* 2nd ed. Englewood Cliffs, N.J.: Prentice Hall, 1988, pp. 155, 174.

4

Timekeeping

Dealing with time functions seems very basic. However, almost every system has its own idiosyncrasies which make portable timekeeping anything but trivial. Because of this, portable libraries that produce standard time outputs are quite helpful.

The real guts of this chapter begin in the "C Time Functions" section. I begin here by first presenting an overview of time definitions because I always found it confusing when terms like epochs were used to define computer time functions and I did not know what an epoch was. If you are aware of the meanings of this and similar terms, skip to the "C Time Functions" section. If not, absorbing some background information about the development of timekeeping is definitely in order.

4.1 A BRIEF OVERVIEW OF TIME

Depending on whom you believe, time began on January 1, 1970 at 00:00:00, January 1, 4713 B.C. at noon, or some other equally arbitrary date. Given these varied hypotheses, it is easy to see why timekeeping becomes confusing. Since a common time reference is very important to many computer applications, it is necessary to understand how time is actually kept and what all these different dates mean.

One thing is certain—accurate time keeping was needed long before computers came onto the scene. Many scientific applications, especially those used in astronomy, require very precise time measurements. Astronomic calculations are sometimes quite complex and take quite a bit of time to perform. Though today computers speed up these operations, it is still important to understand the theory behind timekeeping.

4.2 THE CALENDAR

Almost all time measurements relate to astronomical phenomena. The aspects of time that we take for granted, such as days, weeks, months and years, are all defined by nature. Days correspond to the rotation of Earth about its axis. The month is a rough approximation of the moon's revolution around Earth. Weeks are defined by the seven- to eight-day phases of the moon: new, first quarter, full, last quarter. Finally, the year is the length of time (called a tropical year) that Earth takes to complete a circuit around the sun.

The basis by which we humans relate to long periods of time is the calendar. One of the first calendars, developed for Julius Caesar in about 45 B.C., was based on an Egyptian calendar. The main problem for calendar makers , and for timekeeping in general, is the fact that nature did not see fit to make the heavenly bodies revolve and spin in whole numbers. For example, Earth takes 365.2422 days to circle the sun. To address this problem, the Julian Calendar introduced the concept of the leap year. The leap year added an extra day every fourth year to the month of February. With this construct in place, an average year became 365.25 days long—a much better approximation than before, but still slightly longer than the actual year. The leap year is necessary for very practical reasons. Astronomers are not the only ones who require accurate timekeeping. Farmers need a fairly accurate calendar to guide them in their planting and harvesting. A calendar that becomes even a little inaccurate over time poses a subtle yet serious problem. Simply imagine if the Northern Hemisphere were to experience summer in November!

Even the improvements made by the Julian calendar proved to be inadequate. By the 16th century the vernal equinox predicted by the Julian Calendar was off by ten days when compared to the actual vernal equinox. Pope Gregory commissioned a new calendar to correct the problems the Julian calendar presented. The resulting Gregorian calendar eliminated the leap year for every year that was divisible by 100 (but not by 400). To bring the two vernal equinoxes in line with each other, he also eliminated ten days from the Julian calendar. Thus years like 1800, 1900 (but not 2000), and so on, do not have a leap day inserted. Skipping leap years three times every four centuries and subtracting ten days greatly improved the accuracy of the calendar. The new average year length, as shown in the equations below, is 365.2425 days, very close to the actual figure.

```
(400*365)+100-3 = 146097
146097/400      = 365.2425
```

4.3 TIME DEFINITIONS

Most astronomical measurements, and thus many computer measurements, are based on the concept of an epoch. In fact, computer timing functions were inspired by astronomers, who needed far better timekeeping tools than were readily available. The Second College Edition of The American Heritage Dictionary definition for an *epoch* is: an instant in time that is arbitrarily selected as a point of reference. The key word is "arbitrary." The beginning of an epoch is defined by the user, for whatever purpose the user finds appropriate. Thus, January 1, 1970 is as good a date to start an epoch as any.

The reason why an epoch is important is that everything is measured in relation to it. One of the most important terms in timekeeping is the Julian day. The *Julian day* is the number of days, including a fraction, since the beginning of an epoch. Thus, 20.75 Julian days equals 20 days and 18 hours after the commencement of the epoch.

For astronomical purposes, the epoch by which Julian days are measured is noon, January 1, 4713 B.C. from the point of the

Greenwich meridian. Note that the epoch began at noon, half a day out of synchrony with the traditional day, which starts at midnight. Local time, the time in your neck of the woods, is calculated by factoring in the local time zone with respect to the Greenwich meridian, which is time zone 0. Even the term B.C. is confusing. Generally, it is accepted that there was no year 0. The year 1 A.D. immediately followed the year 1 B.C. However, astronomers consider the year prior to 1 A.D. as the year 0. Any years before this are represented with negative numbers. Thus, the year 2 B.C. corresponds to the astronomical year -1.

Another problem for calendar makers is the fact that the sun and the stars do not move in unison across the sky. While the stars remain relatively fixed in the sky, the sun actually moves within the backdrop of the stars—since Earth revolves around the sun. This means that the measurement of a day in relation to the stars, called the sidereal day, is slightly out of synchronization with the solar or civil day. A 24-hour sidereal day is about 23 hours 56 minutes in a solar day. The civil day is measured from the Greenwich meridian (longitude 0) and is called Universal Time or Greenwich Mean Time (GMT).

Modern technology provides an even more accurate measurement of time. The international atomic time (TAI), kept at the Bureau International l' Heure in Paris, measures time by using the atom. Clocks synchronized to this standard are said to follow Coordinated Universal Time (UTC), which is to keep within 0.9 seconds. For all practical purposes, UTC is the same as UT and GMT.

4.4 C TIME FUNCTIONS

With epochs, Greenwich Mean Time and Coordinated Universal Time defined, the timing mechanisms of today's computers can be explored. In fact, almost all computer timing operations depend on these terms.

There are basically two types of computer timekeeping: calendar time and processor time. Calendar time is simply the passing of actual time. Processor time is the amount of CPU time that a specific process consumes. Both are calculated with respect to the current epoch.

The calendar time has many applications that are not always obvious: file access rights and modifications, certain status information, user log-ins, time stamping of data files, and many others. Measuring processor time aids in computer resource management and computer benchmarks.

C represents time in three basic structures:

```
time_t        calendar time
clock_t       elapsed processor time
struct tm     calendar time broken down
```

4.4.1 Determining Calendar Time

Most platforms support versions of the functions *time( )* and *localtime( )* that behave in a consistent manner. The function *time( )* returns, in seconds, the time elapsed since the beginning of the epoch, 00:00:00, January 1, 1970. This may seem like an awfully large number, and it is; however, it is the most efficient way to represent the current time. Unfortunately, unless a user can perform incredible mathematical calculations on the fly, this raw data is not very helpful.

Despite the fact that *time( )* is available on most platforms, the procedure for calling it is not always the same. In all cases, the value returned by the *time( )* function is of type *time_t,* which is basically a data item of type long. However, whereas most platforms call *time( )* as follows,

```
time_t time_val;

time(&time_val);
```

BORLAND C++ has the format:

```
time_val = time(NULL);
```

Actually, though using the first form with BORLAND C++ will not cause an error, it does produce inconsistent results on some occasions. The best policy is to use the format recommended by the BORLAND C++ reference manual and described above.

4.4.2 *localtime( )*

To convert the information obtained by calling *time( )* into a more useful format, the *localtime( )* function is used. This function converts the output from the *time( )* command, or a user provided value of the same format, into hours, minutes, seconds, A.M. or P.M., weekday, month, and year. This format is also referred to as broken-down time. To use these functions, the header file *time.h* must be included in the program module.

The following structure is used by the function *localtime( )*:

```
struct tm {     /* broken down time */
        int     tm_sec, tm_min, tm_hour;
        int     tm_mday, tm_mon, tm_year;
        int     tm_wday, tm_yday, tm_isdst;
};
```

The fields within this structure are as follows:

```
tm_sec          seconds
tm_min          minutes
tm_hour         hours (24)
tm_mday         day of the month (1-31)
tm_mon          month (0-11)
tm_year         year (last two digits)
tm_wday         day of the week (0-6)
tm_yday         day of the year (0-365)
tm_isdst        daylight savings time (always 0)
```

The format returned by the *localtime( )* function is somewhat less cryptic than the value returned by the function *time( )*, but not much. To convert the information into a more readable format, a bit of processing needs to be done. *Note:* successive calls to *localtime( )* will overwrite the information already in the structure.

4.4.3 *asctime( )*

Most C compilers provide a function called *asctime( )*. This function takes the output from *localtime( )* and produces a string like:

```
Mon Dec 21 11:15:31 1992
```

asctime( ) returns a string pointer:

```
struct tm *time_structure;

char * buffer;

buffer = asctime(time_structure);
```

4.4.4 *ctime*( )

The function *ctime*( ) provides the same functionality as the command:

```
asctime(localtime(time_structure));
```

Thus, in most cases, the following command is used to obtain the character time string:

```
char *buffer;

buffer = ctime(&time_val);
```

4.4.5 *ftime*( )

While the time command returns its output in seconds, the *ftime*( ) command gives the programmer greater granularity. The output from *ftime*( ) includes time in milliseconds, the local timezone, and a flag that indicates whether daylight savings time is in use.

The *ftime*( ) command is very standard, differing only with VMS where the structure definition is as follows:

```
timeb_t btime;
```

All other platforms use the format:

```
struct timeb btime;
```

The structure in both cases looks like:

```
struct timeb {
      long time;
      short millitm;
      short timezone;
      short dstflag;
};
```

The time field represents the value as it is returned by the *time( )* function. By using *millitm,* the program can measure time in millisecond increments. Using *timezone* gives the time zone of the current location, the difference between GMT and local time in hours. The flag *dstflag* indicates whether or not daylight savings time is in use. For VMS, the fields *timezone* and *dstflag* are always 0.

4.5 DETERMINING PROCESSOR TIME

Capturing CPU time is another necessary time function. This value is used for benchmarks as well as other computer time measurements. Two ways of gathering this information exist: the *clock( )* command and the *times( )* command. Whereas *clock( )* is supported by all platforms except Coherent, *times( )* is supported only on platforms that are multitasking.

4.5.1 *clock( )*

The *clock( )* command returns the time elapsed between two events measured in CPU time. On UNIX and VMS, the value returned by *clock( )* includes all the times from any child processes. Be aware that the platforms may not define a process in the same manner. VMS treats process time as the current login process.

The value of CLK_TCK, a constant provided by most systems, depends on the processor. To convert the return value of *clock( )* to seconds, divide it by the value CLK_TCK. Here are the various system definitions for CLK_TCK:

VMS	`#define CLK_TCK 100`
HP/UX	`#define CLK_TCK 1000000`
DOS	`#define CLK_TCK 18.2`
SUN/SLC	`#define CLK_TCK 1000000 /* not defined by system */`

In the case of DOS, a timing mechanism on the chip calls *int 08h* approximately 18.2 times a second. Some systems also define the macro CLOCKS_PER_SEC, which is equivalent to CLK_TCK, to conform with the ANSI standard.

The time returned by *clock*( ) is relative to the previous call to *clock*( ). The bottom line is that the results from one call to *clock*( ) must be compared with another to get any meaningful results; the values are not absolute. On UNIX systems, the value returned by *clock*( ) wraps around every 2147 seconds—about 36 minutes. Thus *clock*( ) cannot be used for timing long processes.

4.5.2 *times*( )

The *times*( ) command reports the accumulated times of the current process as well as its terminated child processes. This function is not available on DOS, since DOS does not support multitasking environments.

For UNIX, the following header must be included:

```
#include <sys/times.h>
```

UNIX uses the following structure:

```
struct tms {
      clock_t tms_utime;  /* user time */
      clock_t tms_stime;  /* system time */
      clock_t tms_cutime; /* child user time */
      clock_t tms_cstime; /* child system time */
}

struct tms buffer;
```

VMS uses the structure:

```
struct tbuffer_t {
        clock_t proc_user_time;     /* user time */
        clock_t proc_system_time;   /* system time */
        clock_t child_user_time;    /* child user time */
        clock_t child_system_time;  /* child system time */
}

tbuffer_t buffer;
```

In both cases the call is made using:

```
times(&buffer);
```

VMS does not differentiate between user and system time. Thus all system times are returned as 0. All times are expressed in 10-millisecond units.

The *times( )* command will not work when compiled with the ANSI flag defined for the HP/UX system, so be sure not to use the -Aa flag.

4.6 PORTABLE TIME COMMANDS

As stated before, the command *time( )* returns a fairly standard value across platforms. However, since the calling convention is slightly different in BORLAND C++, a portable library called *get_time( )* is needed to hide this difference. The short routine for *get_time( )* follows:

```
/* structure to hold timer values */

time_t get_time()
{

        time_t time_val;

#ifdef BCC
        time_val = time(NULL);
#else
```

```
        time(&time_val);
#endif

        return (time_val);

}
```

In both BORLAND C++ and other platforms, the return value is of type *time_t*. Only the calling conventions differ.

C provides the function *difftime( )* to calculate the difference between two distinct *time_t* values. The prototype is as follows:

```
double get_difftime(time_val1, time_val2)
time_t time_val1;
time_t time_val2;
```

However, not all systems provide the function *difftime( )*. In general, nonANSI systems do not have this function, nor do some ANSI-based compilers, such as the GNU C compiler running on the SUN SLC. When *difftime( )* is available, the code looks like:

```
dtime = difftime(time_val2,time_val1);
```

When the *difftime( )* function does not exist, the following code is used:

```
dtime = (double) time_val2 - (double)time_val1;
```

Always use the system *difftime( )* command when it is available. Since systems usually have system dependent features, using code written specifically for the platform is the best policy. The return value from *difftime( )* is a double representing the time between two *time_t* values.

4.6.1 Time String Functions

C provides a number of time functions that produce output in string formats that actually resemble English. The C functions *asctime( )* and *ctime( )* both work the same on all platforms. However, due to the difference in the calling function to *time( )*, portable libraries are developed.

The function *asctime( )* requires three steps. First, the Julian day is obtained by calling *time( )*. Then, this value is converted into broken-down time by calling *localtime( )*. Finally, the broken-down time is used to build a string by calling *asctime( )*. The code looks like this:

```
void get_asctime(string)
char *string;
{

        struct tm *time_structure;

        time_t time_val;

        time_val = get_time();

        time_structure = localtime(&time_val);

        return(asctime(time_structure)) ;
}
```

The *get_ctime( )* function is quite similar to *get_asctime( )*. In fact, the relationship is in the same vein as the relationship between *asctime( )* and *ctime( )*. A call to *get_ctime( )* is the same as:

```
get_asctime(localtime(&time_val));
```

4.6.2 User Formatted Time Strings

If the string provided by *asctime( )* and *ctime( )* is in the desired format, the programmer need go no further. However, if a different format is called for, additional processing is needed. Suppose that the time information needs to look like:

```
Monday, August 10, 1992.  1:06:14 P.M.
```

To produce this output, the following user structures are defined:

```
/* array for month display */

static char  *month[12] = {
      "January", "February", "March", "April", "May",
      "June", "July",
      "August", "September", "October", "November",
      "December"};

/* array for weekday display */

static char *weekday[7] = {
      "Sunday", "Monday", "Tuesday", "Wednesday",
      "Thursday",
      "Friday", "Saturday"};

/* array for AM/PM display */

static char *hour[2] = {"AM","PM"};
```

In this way, the strings in the structures are accessed by using the information provided by *localtime*( ). For example:

```
weekday[time_structure->tm_wday]
month[time_structure->tm_mon]
```

Since the time is provided in military time, a simple comparison is performed to determine whether the time is A.M. or P.M. If the time is greater than 12, then 12 is subtracted and the AM/PM flag is set to the appropriate offset to be used in the hour structure. A *sprintf*( ) function is used to build the actual date string and place the result as follows.

```
sprintf (string,"%s, %s %2d, 19%2d. %2d:%02d:%02d %s.",
              weekday[time_structure->tm_wday],
              month[time_structure->tm_mon],
              time_structure->tm_mday,
              time_structure->tm_year,
              time_structure->tm_hour,
```

```
                    time_structure->tm_min,
                    time_structure->tm_sec,
                    hour[meridian]);
```

This string is then available to the remainder of the program.

A function for converting a broken-down time structure to a string, called *get_broken_down( )* has the following prototype:

```
char *get_broken_down(time_structure)
struct tm *time_structure;
```

Any time a programmer builds a time string, this function will most likely be needed.

The function *get_strtime( )* requires no input—it simply uses the current time to format a string:

```
char *get_strtime()
```

However, there are times when a *time_t* value other than the current time needs to be converted to a similar format. The function *cvt_strtime( )* is provided for this purpose:

```
char *cvt_strtime(time_val)
time_t time_val;
```

The code is identical to *get_strtime( )*, except that the function accepts a *time_t* value as input.

4.6.3 Processor Time

The function *get_clock( )* is provided to return the current value of processor time. This routine is very short:

```
long get_clock()
{

#ifndef CCC
        clock_t ticks;

        if ( (ticks = clock() ) == -1)
```

```
#endif
                return (NOTAVAILABLE);

        return(ticks/TICKS);
}
```

Note that the *clock*( ) function is not available on Coherent. Thus *ifdefs* must be used in the code for that platform to account for its absence.

On systems that support multitasking, the function *times*( ) is provided to break down both processor and user time into parent and child times. Since DOS is not multitasking, *times*( ) is not available on that platform. Furthermore, as shown in the following code, VMS and UNIX have different structures for this function:

```
#ifdef VMS
        tbuffer_t buffer;
#endif
#ifdef UNIX
        struct tms buffer;
#endif
```

Since the structures for all platforms are not uniform, a new structure called PROCESS_TIMES is created as follows:

```
typedef struct {
        double uparent;
        double sparent;
        double uchild;
        double schild;
} PROCESS_TIMES;
```

The address of this structure is passed to the *get_times*( ) routine:

```
int get_times(process_times)
PROCESS_TIMES *process_times;
```

For example, for user time:

```
#ifdef VMS
tbuffer_t buffer;
times(&buffer);

process_times->uparent=
      (double)buffer.proc_user_time/(double)PROC_TIME;
#endif

#ifdef UNIX
struct tms buffer;
times(&buffer);

process_times->uparent=
      (double)buffer.proc_user_time/(double)PROC_TIME;
#endif
```

The constant PROC_TIME is used to adjust for the different platforms:

VMS	1000
HPUX	CLK_TCK
SUN	60

VMS reports the times in milliseconds. HPUX uses the system defined CLK_TCK. SUN reports time in 1/60ths of a second. The function *get_times( )* places the appropriate information into this structure based on the platform in use. If *times( )* does not exist, a warning is passed back via the *status* variable.

4.6.4 More Time Granularity

The library *get_ftime( )* is a function providing much more granularity than the other time functions. Again, the various platforms have different structures:

```
#ifdef VMS
      timeb_t btime;
#else
      struct timeb btime;
#endif
```

To make these differences transparent, the following structure is defined:

```
typedef struct {
        time_t localtime;
        unsigned short millitm;
        short timezone;
        short dstflag;
} FTIMES;
```

The prototype for the function *get_ftime*( ) is:

```
void get_ftime(ftimes)
FTIMES *ftimes;
```

The pointer to a structure of this type is passed to *get_ftimes*( ), which calls *ftime*( ) as follows:

```
ftime(&btime);

ftimes->localtime=btime.time;
ftimes->millitm=btime.millitm;
ftimes->timezone=btime.timezone;
ftimes->dstflag=btime.dstflag;
```

4.7 USING THE TIMEKEEPING LIBRARY

The test program for *timelibs* is developed a bit differently than the other libraries. Because of the number of functions in the library and their relative complexity, each function has its own test routine. The major issues in these libraries are the data structures. Some routines require that specific structures be declared to gather the information. Refer back to the previous sections in this chapter for information on specific routines.

One portability problem in this test program is the fact that Microsoft C does not have the *pause*( ) command, used to simulate elapsed time for some of the functions. In the case of Microsoft or any other platform that does not have the *pause*( ) command, a simple *for* loop is used, with the PAUSE value set in a *define* statement.

Keeping time with these libraries is as easy as linking the *timelibs* library with the relevant applications. The most important point to keep in mind is the means—structure, character pointer, and so on—by which the time information is returned. Also, if a character string is passed to one of the routines, be certain that it is understood whether or not the string will actually be changed.

4.8 CONCLUSION

Because of the large number of time functions and the complexity of some of their outputs, each test was placed in a routine of its own. The libraries built here provide a good foundation for timekeeping within a C program. As always, specific applications have specific needs, and this is truer in timekeeping than in most other computer applications. You may therefore find that your specific needs will require altering these libraries or building completely new ones. For instance, astronomers may benefit from many of the features presented in this chapter, but will no doubt need much more functionality to calculate the positions of heavenly bodies and the timing of astronomical events. For the majority of timing applications, however, these routines will do quite well.

```
/****************************************************

   FILE NAME   : test.c
   AUTHOR      : Matt Weisfeld

   DESCRIPTION : test file for time libraries

****************************************************/

#include <stdio.h>
#ifdef BCC
#include <dos.h>
#include <conio.h>
#endif
#include "proto.h"
#include "errdefs.h"
```

```
#define PAUSE 10000000
main()
{

        test_get_difftime();

        test_get_asctime();

        test_get_ctime();

        test_get_strtime();

        test_cvt_strtime();

        test_get_ftime();

        test_get_clock();

        test_get_times();

        printf ("\n");

        leave(EXIT_NORMAL);

        return(EXIT_NORMAL);

}

/* test the portable library get_difftime() */

void test_get_difftime()
{
        time_t time_val1, time_val2;
        double dtime;

        printf ("\nTEST GET_TIME & GET_DIFFTIME\n");

        time_val1 = get_time();

        do_sleep();

        time_val2 = get_time();
```

```
        if ( (dtime=get_difftime(time_val1, time_val2)) != -1)
                printf ("difftime = %f\n", dtime);
        else
                error (ER_TIMECORR, "difftime()");

        return;
}

/* test the portable library get_asctime() */

void test_get_asctime()
{

        printf ("\nTEST GET_ASCTIME\n");

        printf ("test: string = %s\n", get_asctime());

        return;
}

/* test the portable library get_ctime() */

void test_get_ctime()
{

        printf ("\nTEST GET_CTIME\n");

        printf ("test: string = %s\n", get_ctime());

        return;
}

/* test the portable library get_strtime() */

void test_get_strtime()
{

        time_t time_val1;
        char *ptr;

        printf ("\nTEST GET_STRTIME\n");
```

```
        time_val1 = get_time();

        ptr = cvt_strtime(time_val1);

        printf ("test: string = %s\n", ptr);


        return;
}

/* test the portable library cvt_strtime() */

void test_cvt_strtime()
{
        time_t time_val1;
        char *ptr;

        printf ("\nTEST CVT_STRTIME\n");

        time_val1 = get_time();

        ptr = cvt_strtime(time_val1);

        printf ("test: string = %s\n", ptr);

}

/* test the portable library get_ftime() */

void test_get_ftime()
{

        FTIMES ftimes;

        printf ("\nTEST GET_FTIME\n");
        get_ftime(&ftimes);

        printf ("localtime = %s\n",
        cvt_strtime(ftimes.localtime));
        printf ("millitm   = %u\n", ftimes.millitm);
        printf ("timezone  = %d\n", ftimes.timezone);
        printf ("dstflag   = %d\n", ftimes.dstflag);
}
```

```
/* test the portable library get_clock() */

void test_get_clock()
{
        unsigned long i,j;

#ifndef CCC
        clock_t start, end;
#endif
        printf ("\nTEST GET_CLOCK\n");

        if ( (start = get_clock()) == NOTAVAILABLE)
                error (WR_NOTAVAIL, "clock()");
        for (i=0;i<PAUSE;i++) j=j+1;
        if ( (end = get_clock()) == NOTAVAILABLE)
                error (WR_NOTAVAIL, "clock()");

        printf ("CPU seconds = %ld\n", end-start);

        return;
}

/* test the portable library get_times() */

void test_get_times()
{

        PROCESS_TIMES process_times;

        printf ("\nTEST GET_TIMES\n");

        if (get_times(&process_times)==WARNING) {
                error(WR_NOSUPPORT, "get_times()");
                printf ("Warning should return here.\n");
        } else {
                printf ("parent user times (seconds) = %f\n",
                        process_times.uparent);
                printf ("parent system times (seconds) = %f\n",
                        process_times.sparent);
                printf ("child user times (seconds) = %f\n",
                        process_times.uchild);
```

```
            printf ("child system times (seconds) = %f\n",
                    process_times.schild);
        }

        return;
}

/* make a sleep function since MSC does not have one */

void do_sleep()
{

#ifndef MSC
        sleep(3);
#else
        for (i=0;i<PAUSE;i++) j=j+1;
#endif
}

/*#########################################*/


/***************************************************

   FILE NAME   : timelibs.c
   AUTHOR      : Matt Weisfeld

   DESCRIPTION : library for portable time
                 functions.

***************************************************/

#include <stdio.h>
#include "proto.h"
#include "er.h"
#ifdef BCC
#include <stdlib.h>
#include <string.h>
#include <dos.h>
#endif
```

```
#define AM 0
#define PM 1

/* array for month display */

static char  *month[12] = {
             "January", "February", "March", "April",
             "May", "June", "July",
             "August", "September", "October", "November",
             "December"};

/* array for weekday display */

static char *weekday[7] = {
             "Sunday", "Monday", "Tuesday", "Wednesday",
             "Thursday",
             "Friday", "Saturday"};

/* array for AM/PM display */

static char *hour[2] = {"AM","PM"};

/****************************************************

  ROUTINE NAME : get_time()

  DESCRIPTION  : produce portable output for the
                 time() function.

  INPUT        : none

  OUTPUT       : value of time_t

****************************************************/
/* structure to hold timer values */

time_t get_time()
{

      time_t time_val;

#ifdef BCC
      time_val = time(NULL);
```

```
#else
        time(&time_val);
#endif

        return (time_val);

}

/***************************************************

   ROUTINE NAME : get_asctime()

   DESCRIPTION  : produce portable output for the
                  asctime() function.

   INPUT        : none

   OUTPUT       : value of char * (time string)

***************************************************/
char *get_asctime()
{

        struct tm *time_structure;

        time_t time_val;

        time_val = get_time();

        time_structure = localtime(&time_val);

        return (asctime(time_structure));

}

/***************************************************

   ROUTINE NAME : get_ctime()

   DESCRIPTION  : produce portable output for the
                  ctime() function.
```

```
    INPUT        : none

    OUTPUT       : value of char * (time string)

**************************************************/
char *get_ctime()
{

        time_t time_val;

        time_val = get_time();

        return (ctime(&time_val));

}


/**************************************************

  ROUTINE NAME : get_strtime()

  DESCRIPTION  : produce time string in the
                 format:
           Sunday, January 31, 1993  1:04:54 PM.

    INPUT        : none

    OUTPUT       : value of char * (time string)

**************************************************/
char *get_strtime()
{

        struct tm *time_structure;

        time_t time_val;

        time_val = get_time();

        time_structure = localtime(&time_val);

        return (get_broken_down(time_structure));

}
```

```
/****************************************************

   ROUTINE NAME : cvt_strtime()

   DESCRIPTION  : convert time_t format to string
                    in the format:
              Sunday, January 31, 1993  1:04:54 PM.

   INPUT        : value of char *, time_t

   OUTPUT       : char * (time string)

****************************************************/
char *cvt_strtime(time_val)
time_t time_val;
{

      struct tm *time_structure;

      /* get time information */

      time_structure = localtime(&time_val);

      return (get_broken_down(time_structure));

}
/****************************************************

   ROUTINE NAME : get_broken_down()

   DESCRIPTION  : convert a tm broken down struct
                    to a string in the format:
              Sunday, January 31, 1993  1:04:54 PM.

   INPUT        : tm * (broken down struct)

   OUTPUT       : char * (time string)

****************************************************/
char *get_broken_down(time_structure)
struct tm *time_structure;
{
```

```
        int meridian;

        /* use static to keep around when routine ends */

        static char str_time[STRLEN];

        if (time_structure->tm_hour > 12)
        {
              time_structure->tm_hour =
           (time_structure->tm_hour)-12;
           meridian = PM;
        }else
           meridian = AM;

        /* build the time information */

        sprintf (str_time,"%s, %s %2d, 19%2d. %2d:%02d:%02d %s.",
                    weekday[time_structure->tm_wday],
                    month[time_structure->tm_mon],
                    time_structure->tm_mday,
                    time_structure->tm_year,
                    time_structure->tm_hour,
                    time_structure->tm_min,
                    time_structure->tm_sec,
                    hour[meridian]);

        return (str_time);

}

/****************************************************

  ROUTINE NAME : get_clock()

  DESCRIPTION  : produce portable output for the
                 clock() function.

  INPUT        : none

  OUTPUT       : long (number of ticks)

****************************************************/
```

```
long get_clock()
{


#ifndef CCC
      clock_t ticks;

      if ( (ticks = clock()) == -1)
#endif
            return (NOTAVAILABLE);

      return(ticks/TICKS);


}

/**************************************************

  ROUTINE NAME : get_difftime()

  DESCRIPTION  : produce portable output for the
                 difftime() function.

  INPUT        : p1 - time_t
               : p2 - time_t

  OUTPUT       : double (p2-p1)

**************************************************/
double get_difftime(time_val1, time_val2)
time_t time_val1;
time_t time_val2;
{

      double dtime;

      /* time_val2 cannot be greater than time_val1 */

      if (time_val2 < time_val1)
          return(-1);

#ifdef NDIFFTIME
      dtime = (double)time_val2 - (double)time_val1;
```

```
#else
        dtime = difftime(time_val2,time_val1);
#endif
        return(dtime) ;


}

/*****************************************************

   ROUTINE NAME : get_times()

   DESCRIPTION  : produce portable output for the
                  times() function.

   INPUT        : PROCESS_TIMES * (pointer to
                  process times structure)

   OUTPUT       : int (status)

*****************************************************/
int get_times(process_times)
PROCESS_TIMES *process_times;
{

        int status;

#ifdef VMS
    tbuffer_t buffer;
    times (&buffer);

        process_times->uparent =
            (double)buffer.proc_user_time/(double)PROC_TIME;
        process_times->sparent =
            (double)buffer.proc_system_time/(double)PROC_TIME;
        process_times->uchild =
            (double)buffer.child_user_time/(double)PROC_TIME;
        process_times->schild =
            (double)buffer.child_system_time/(double)PROC_TIME;
        status = NORMAL;

#endif
#ifdef UNIX
```

```
        struct tms buffer;
        times (&buffer);

            process_times->uparent =
                (double)buffer.tms_utime/(double)PROC_TIME;
            process_times->sparent =
                (double)buffer.tms_stime/(double)PROC_TIME;
            process_times->uchild =
                (double)buffer.tms_cutime/(double)PROC_TIME;
            process_times->schild =
                (double)buffer.tms_cstime/(double)PROC_TIME;
        status = NORMAL;
#endif

#ifdef DOS
        status = WARNING;
#endif

        return (status);


}

/**************************************************

  ROUTINE NAME : get_ftime()

  DESCRIPTION  : produce portable output for the
                 ftime() function.

  INPUT        : FTIMES * (pointer to ftime
                              structure)

  OUTPUT       : none

**************************************************/
void get_ftime(ftimes)
FTIMES *ftimes;
{

#ifdef VMS
        timeb_t btime;
#else
```

```
        struct timeb btime;
#endif

        ftime(&btime);

        ftimes->localtime=btime.time;
        ftimes->millitm= btime.millitm;
        ftimes->timezone=btime.timezone;
        ftimes->dstflag=btime.dstflag;

        return;

}

/*#########################################*/


/****************************************************

   FILE NAME   : timelibs.h
   AUTHOR      : Matt Weisfeld

   DESCRIPTION : header file for time libraries

****************************************************/

#include <time.h>

/* define the number of ticks for each processor */

#ifdef VMS
#define TICKS CLK_TCK
#define PROC_TIME 1000
#endif

#ifdef DOS
#define TICKS CLK_TCK
#endif

#ifdef HPUX
#define TICKS CLOCKS_PER_SEC
#define PROC_TIME CLK_TCK
#endif
```

```
#ifdef SUN    /* sun report time in microseconds */
#define TICKS 1000000
#define PROC_TIME 60
#endif

/* necessary include files */

#ifdef UNIX
#include <sys/times.h>
#include <sys/timeb.h>
#include <sys/types.h>
#endif

#ifdef DOS
#include <sys\timeb.h>
#endif

/* portable structures for time commands */

typedef struct g_times {
       double uparent;
       double sparent;
       double uchild;
       double schild;
} PROCESS_TIMES;

typedef struct f_times {
       time_t localtime;
       unsigned short millitm;
       short timezone;
       short dstflag;
} FTIMES;

/* prototypes */

#ifdef ANSI
void do_sleep(void);
void test_get_difftime(void);
void test_get_asctime(void);
void test_get_ctime(void);
void test_get_strtime(void);
void test_cvt_strtime(void);
void test_get_ftime(void);
```

```
void test_get_times(void);
void test_get_clock(void);
void get_ftime(FTIMES *);
char *get_asctime(void);
char *get_strtime(void);
char *cvt_strtime(time_t);
char *get_broken_down(struct tm *);
char  *get_ctime(void);
int get_times(PROCESS_TIMES *);
long get_clock(void);
double get_difftime(time_t, time_t);
time_t get_time(void);
#else
void test_get_difftime();
void test_get_asctime();
void test_get_ctime();
void test_get_strtime();
void test_cvt_strtime();
void test_get_ftime();
void test_get_times();
void test_get_clock();
void get_ftime();
void do_sleep();
char *get_asctime();
char *get_strtime();
char *cvt_strtime();
char *get_broken_down();
char  *get_ctime();
int get_times();
long get_clock();
double get_difftime();
time_t get_time();
#endif

#define NOTAVAILABLE -1

/*###############################################*/


/**************************************************

   FILE NAME   : errdefs.h
   AUTHOR      : Matt Weisfeld
```

```
   DESCRIPTION : error descriptions for time
                 libraries.

**************************************************/
#include "er.h"

ERROR_STRUCT error_message[] =

/* actual error messages */

{

     /* #0 */
     WR_NOSUPPORT, RETURN,
     "'%s' is not supported on this platform.",
     /* #1 */
     WR_NOTAVAIL, RETURN,
     "Return value from '%s' is not available.",
     /* #2 */
     ER_TIMECORR, EXIT,
     "A time value from '%s' is corrupted.",
     LASTERROR, EXIT,NULL
};


/*##############################################*/


/**************************************************

  FILE NAME   : er.h
  AUTHOR      : Matt Weisfeld

  DESCRIPTION : error definitions for time
                libaries.

**************************************************/
#define WR_NOSUPPORT  0  /* OS does not support feature */
#define WR_NOTAVAIL   1  /* return value unavailable from
                            system */
#define ER_TIMECORR   2  /* a time value is corrupted */

/*##############################################*/
```

```
/*****************************************************

   FILE NAME   : proto.h
   AUTHOR      : Matt Weisfeld

   DESCRIPTION : prototype file for time
                 libraries.

*****************************************************/
#ifdef VMS
#include "[-.common]common.h"
#include "[-.leave]leave.h"
#include "[-.error]error.h"
#endif

#ifdef BCC
#include "..\common\common.h"
#include "..\leave\leave.h"
#include "..\error\error.h"
#endif

#ifdef MSC
#include "..\common\common.h"
#include "..\leave\leave.h"
#include "..\error\error.h"
#endif

#ifdef HPUX
#include "../common/common.h"
#include "../leave/leave.h"
#include "../error/error.h"
#endif

#ifdef SLC
#include "../common/common.h"
#include "../leave/leave.h"
#include "../error/error.h"
#endif

#ifdef GCC
#include "../common/common.h"
#include "../leave/leave.h"
```

```
#include "../error/error.h"
#endif

#ifdef CCC
#include "../common/common.h"
#include "../leave/leave.h"
#include "../error/error.h"
#endif


#include "timelibs.h"

/*###############################################*/

$! VMS DCL PROCEDURE
$ clr
$ if (P1.eqs."") then GOTO ALL
$ if (P1.eqs."ALL") then GOTO ALL
$ if (P1.eqs."LINK") then GOTO LINK
$ set verify
$ cc/define=VMS 'P1'
$ goto LINK
$ ALL:
$                        set verify
$ cc/define=VMS test
$ cc/define=VMS timelibs
$ LINK:
$ link/executable=test test,timelibs,[-.leave]leave,
[-.error]error
$ copy test.exe [weisfeld.exe]
$ set noverify

/*###############################################*/

# makefile for BCC/C++ Compiler

OBJS    = test.obj timelibs.obj
LIBS    = ..\leave\leave.obj ..\error\error.obj
HDRS    = proto.h timelibs.h errdefs.h er.h
FLAGS   = -c -DBCC
COMP    = bcc
```

```
test.exe:  $(OBJS)
        $(COMP) $(OBJS) $(LIBS)

test.obj: test.c $(HDRS)
        $(COMP) $(FLAGS) test.c

timelibs.obj: timelibs.c $(HDRS)
        $(COMP) $(FLAGS) timelibs.c

test.c:
timelibs.c:

timelibs.h:
errdefs.h:
er.h:

/*#############################################*/

# makefile for MSC/C++ Compiler

OBJS     = test.obj timelibs.obj
LIBS     = ..\leave\leave.obj ..\error\error.obj
HDRS     = proto.h timelibs.h errdefs.h er.h
FLAGS    = /c /DMSC
COMP     = cl

test.exe:  $(OBJS)
        $(COMP) $(OBJS) $(LIBS)

test.obj: test.c $(HDRS)
        $(COMP) $(FLAGS) test.c

timelibs.obj: timelibs.c $(HDRS)
        $(COMP) $(FLAGS) timelibs.c

test.c:
timelibs.c:

timelibs.h:
errdefs.h:
er.h:
```

```
/*##############################################*/

# makefile for HPUX C Compiler

OBJS    = test.o timelibs.o
LIBS    = ../leave/leave.o ../error/error.o
HDRS    = proto.h timelibs.h errdefs.h er.h ../leave/leave.h \
          ../error/error.h
FLAGS   = -c -DHPUX
COMP    = cc

test:  $(OBJS)
       $(COMP) -o test $(OBJS) $(LIBS)

test.o: test.c $(HDRS)
       $(COMP) $(FLAGS) test.c

timelibs.o: timelibs.c $(HDRS)
       $(COMP) $(FLAGS) timelibs.c

test.c:
timelibs.c:

timelibs.h:
errdefs.h:
er.h:

../error/error.h:
../leave/leave.h:

/*##############################################*/

# makefile for SUN SLC C Compiler

OBJS    = test.o timelibs.o
LIBS    = ../leave/leave.o ../error/error.o
HDRS    = proto.h timelibs.h errdefs.h er.h ../leave/leave.h \
          ../error/error.h
FLAGS   = -c -DSLC
COMP    = cc
```

```
test:   $(OBJS)
        $(COMP) -o test $(OBJS) $(LIBS)

test.o: test.c $(HDRS)
        $(COMP) $(FLAGS) test.c

timelibs.o: timelibs.c $(HDRS)
        $(COMP) $(FLAGS) timelibs.c

test.c:
timelibs.c:

timelibs.h:
errdefs.h:
er.h:

../error/error.h:
../leave/leave.h:

/*##############################################*/

# makefile for SUN GCC C Compiler

OBJS    = test.o timelibs.o
LIBS    = ../leave/leave.o ../error/error.o
HDRS    = proto.h timelibs.h errdefs.h er.h ../leave/leave.h \
          ../error/error.h
FLAGS   = -c -DGCC
COMP    = gcc

test:   $(OBJS)
        $(COMP) -o test $(OBJS) $(LIBS)

test.o: test.c $(HDRS)
        $(COMP) $(FLAGS) test.c

timelibs.o: timelibs.c $(HDRS)
        $(COMP) $(FLAGS) timelibs.c

test.c:
timelibs.c:
```

```
timelibs.h:
errdefs.h:
er.h:

../error/error.h:
../leave/leave.h:

/*############################################*/

# makefile for CCC Compiler

OBJS    = test.o timelibs.o
LIBS    = ../leave/leave.o ../error/error.o
HDRS    = proto.h timelibs.h errdefs.h er.h ../leave/leave.h \
          ../error/error.h
FLAGS   = -c -f -DCCC
COMP    = cc

test:  $(OBJS)
       $(COMP) -f -o test $(OBJS) $(LIBS)

test.o: test.c $(HDRS)
       $(COMP) $(FLAGS) test.c

timelibs.o: timelibs.c $(HDRS)
       $(COMP) $(FLAGS) timelibs.c

test.c:
timelibs.c:

timelibs.h:
errdefs.h:
er.h:

../error/error.h:
../leave/leave.h:
```

4.9 SELECTED REFERENCE

Duffet-Smith, Peter. *Practical Astronomy with Your Calculator,* 3rd
    ed. Cambridge: Cambridge University Press, 1988.

5

Advanced String Manipulation

Many libraries, portable or not, are large, often complex applications. However, generally the small libraries performing the most common functions get the most use. While most C compilers and ANSI C itself provide for many of these widely used, common functions, it is often necessary to develop a personal library of additional functions. Whenever code is likely to be reused, whether within a single application or across several, it is a prime candidate for inclusion in a library. This is particularly true in relation to string operations. String operations, which can normally be identified by the prefix *str*, are the subject of many prewritten library functions. There are functions to copy strings (*strcpy*), to concatenate strings (*strcat*), and so on.

Two main types of string functions will be discussed here. The first type consists of functions that actually operate on a string and produce a resulting string that is different from the original. For example, when a function converts a string to all uppercase letters, the new string will most likely be modified unless all characters in the string are already uppercase. The second type of string functions involves no modification of the string itself, but instead returns information about the content of the string. For example, the C function *isalpha*( ) determines if an individual character is a letter (a-z or A-Z). In all cases, it is important to verify that the string passed to the routine is a valid character pointer.

5.1 STRING CONVERSIONS

Many character operations are directly applicable to strings, since strings are simply a collection of characters. For example, the function *tolower( )* converts a character to lowercase as follows:

```
c1 = tolower(c2);
```

However, many compilers do not provide a function to convert an entire string to lowercase. To perform this commonly required function, the programmer must write code in the following manner:

```
for (i=0;string[i]!='\0';i++) {

    string[i] = tolower(string[i]);

}
```

A library function called *strtolower( )*, is created to allow a program access to this code with the following call:

```
char *buffer;

buffer = strtolower("HELLO");
```

The library code needed to accomplish this is quite compact:

```
char *strtolower(char *string)
{

    int i;
    char *buffer;

    if (string == NULL) {
        printf ("Error: input string is NULL\n");
```

```
            return (NULL);
    }

    if ((buffer = malloc(strlen(string)+1)) == NULL) {
        printf ("Error: out of memory. Process
        terminated.\n");
        return (NULL);
    }

    for (i=0;string[i]!='\0';i++) {

        buffer[i] = tolower(string[i]);

    }

        buffer[i] = '\0';

    return(buffer);

}
```

In most cases involving strings, it is best not to change the original string. A better choice is to create a new string and pass its pointer back. Note that the new string is created by using *malloc( )* to obtain the necessary space. It is unwise simply to create a string within the library as follows:

```
char buffer[STRLEN];
```

This is a poor procedure because the space in this case is technically available only while the routine is actually active. Once the return is executed, the routine no longer exists. In fact, the space containing the string *buffer* may still exist, but only if the space is not reused. It is possible to create *buffer* as static; however, this is still not as desirable as using *malloc( )*. Another advantage of *malloc( )* is that it uses only the space required. An alternative method is to pass two strings: a source and a destination. In this way, the original string will again remain unchanged.

Similar functions are created to convert a string to upper-case:

```
char *strtoupper(char *string)
{

     int i;
     char *buffer;

     if (string == NULL) {
         printf ("Error: input string is NULL\n");
         return (NULL);
     }

     if ((buffer = malloc(strlen(string)+1)) == NULL) {
         printf ("Error: out of memory. Process
         terminated.\n");
         return (NULL);
     }

     for (i=0;string[i]!='\0';i++) {

         buffer[i] = toupper(string[i]);

     }

       buffer[i] = '\0';

     return(buffer);

}
```

5.2 STRING INSPECTION

The character function *isalpha( )* mentioned earlier is easily extrapolated to a string function, *stralpha( )*:

```
int stralpha(char *string)
{

     int i;
     int flag = 1;
```

```
    if (string == NULL) {
        printf ("Error: input string is NULL\n");
        return (NULL);
    }

    for (i=0;string[i]!='\0';i++) {

        if ( !isalpha(string[i]) ) {

            flag = 0;
            break;

        }
    }

    return(flag);

}
```

In this routine, the string itself remains unchanged. A loop similar to the one used in the previous string functions is entered. However, instead of checking to see if a character needs to be changed, the intent here is to identify whether or not the character is a letter. Regardless of the outcome, the character is not modified. To accomplish this verification, a flag is defined. The flag, initially set to one, will be turned off if any of the characters fail the test:

```
if ( !isalpha(string[i]) ) {

    flag = 0;
    break;

}
```

There are many different variations on this theme. Simply look at any C compiler reference manual and flip through the pages dealing with character operations. In addition, many other string functions are listed in the code at the end of this chapter.

5.3 STRING INITIALIZATION

Besides the ideas for string functions that may be gleaned from C reference manuals, you will find that daily experience generates other ideas. One function that is very useful and easy to write is a string initialization mechanism. Due to the manner in which C handles strings, it is quite possible to have garbage in a string. Thus, it is very helpful, even necessary, to initialize the string to known values. For example, consider the following string definition:

```
char buffer[STRLEN];
```

This string is defined to have 130 characters; however, most values that are assigned to this allotted space will not add up to exactly 130, as in the following command:

```
strcpy(buffer, "hello there");
```

This string occupies 12 characters in the buffer (11 for the characters and one for '\0'), and the remaining characters are extraneous. Thus, to initialize this string only the first 12 characters need be considered. With this in mind, the string initialization routine is written as follows:

```
int strinit(char *string, char c)
{

    int i;

    if (string == NULL) {
        printf ("Error: input string is NULL\n");
        return (NULL);
    }

    for (i=0;string[i]!='\0';i++) {

        string[i] = c;

    }
```

```
    return(i);


}
```

This routine returns the number of characters initialized. It is particularly useful when a string needs to be blanked. Simply set the character to spaces:

```
strinit (string, ' ');
```

5.4 CHARACTER REPLACEMENT

Another function in the same vein performs character replacement. Assume there is a requirement that a string not contain spaces, and the following string exists with a space:

```
"hello there"
```

If the solution is to convert any space to a dash (-), then the following routine, *strrep( )*, is used:

```
int strrep(char *string, char old, char new)
{

    int i;
    int count;

    if (string == NULL) {
        printf ("Error: input string is NULL\n");
        return (NULL);
    }

    for (i=0,count=0;string[i]!='\0';i++) {

        if (string[i] == old) {
            string[i] = new;
            count++;
        }

    }
```

```
        return(count);

}
```

This routine returns the number of characters modified.

5.5 COUNTING CHARACTERS IN A STRING

Finally, another string function may be written to count the number of times a certain characters occurs within a string. It is sometimes necessary to know information of this nature in a parsing situation, for example. If spaces are used to delineate tokens, then knowing the number of spaces will identify the number of tokens. Consider the following string:

```
string[80] = "print file1 file2 file3";
```

This line contains 3 spaces and thus four tokens. To determine such information, call the function *strcount*( ) as follows:

```
blanks = strcount(string, ' ');
```

using the following routine:

```
int strcount(char *string, char c)
{

    int i;
    int count;

    if (string == NULL) {
        printf ("Error: input string is NULL\n");
        return (NULL);
    }

    for (i=0,count=0;string[i]!='\0';i++) {

        if (string[i] == c) count++;

    }
```

```
    return(count);


}
```

5.6 USING THE STRING LIBRARY

The string libraries are tested in the file *test.c*. Test strings are built using the string buffers *string, string1*, and *string2*. The character pointer buffer is used when only a character pointer is returned. The code is commented to explain each test as well as the *printf( )*s embedded in the code. Errors are called when invalid conditions are passed back from the library functions.

Using the string libraries is very straightforward. Simply link the *strlibs* object library with the relevant application. When using these libraries, be aware of the return value of the function. Make sure you know when a pointer is being returned as opposed to when a parameter is being passed.

5.7 CONCLUSION

Since not all platforms support the same degree of string handling, libraries such as these are necessary. The routines described here are certainly not all-inclusive. Many more useful string functions are yet to be written.

```
/**************************************************

   FILE NAME   : test.c
   AUTHOR      : Matt Weisfeld

   DESCRIPTION : test program for string
                 libraries.

**************************************************/
#include <stdio.h>
#include <string.h>
#include "proto.h"
#include "errdefs.h"
#ifdef DOS
#include <alloc.h>
#endif
```

```
main()
{
        char string[STRLEN];
        char *string1;
        char string2[STRLEN];
        char *buffer;

        string1 = (char *) malloc(strlen("hello there")+1);

        strcpy (string1, "hello there");

        printf ("string1 = %s\n", string1);

        /* test strtoupper */

        if ( (buffer = strtoupper(string1)) == NULL)
                error(ER_NOSPACE, "strtoupper");

        printf ("after upper: %s\n", buffer);

        /* test strtolower */

        strcpy (string2, "HELLO THERE");

        printf ("string2 = %s\n", string2);

        if ( (buffer = strtolower(string2)) == NULL)
                error(ER_NOSPACE, "strtolower");

        printf ("after lower: %s\n", buffer);

        /* test stralnum */

        strcpy (string, "hello");

        if (stralnum(string)) {
                printf ("isalnum\n");
        } else {
                printf ("is not isalnum\n");
        }
```

```
strcpy (string, "there123");

if (stralnum(string)) {
      printf ("isalnum\n");
} else {
      printf ("is not isalnum\n");
}

strcpy (string, "there@@@");

if (stralnum(string)) {
      printf ("isalnum\n");
} else {
      printf ("is not isalnum\n");
}

/* test stralpha */

strcpy (string, "hello");

if (stralpha(string)) {
      printf ("isalpha\n");
} else {
      printf ("is not isalpha\n");
}

strcpy (string, "hello1");

if (stralpha(string)) {
      printf ("isalpha\n");
} else {
      printf ("is not isalpha\n");
}

/* test strdigits */

strcpy (string, "999.9");
printf ("%s " , string);
if (strfloat(string)) {
      printf ("isfloat\n");
} else {
      printf ("is not isfloat\n");
}
```

```
strcpy (string, "9.99.9");
printf ("%s " , string);
if (strfloat(string)) {
      printf ("isfloat\n");
} else {
      printf ("is not isfloat\n");
}

strcpy (string, "999");
printf ("%s " , string);
if (strinteger(string)) {
      printf ("isinteger\n");
} else {
      printf ("is not isinteger\n");
}

strcpy (string, "99x9");
printf ("%s " , string);
if (strinteger(string)) {
      printf ("isinteger\n");
} else {
      printf ("is not isinteger\n");
}

/* test strcount */

strcpy (string, "test");

printf ("# of t's in %s = %d\n", string, strcount(string,
't'));

/* test strrep */

printf ("letters replaced = %d\n", strrep (string, 't',
'x'));

printf ("after replace: string = %s\n", string);

/* test strinit */

printf ("before init: string = %s\n", string);
```

```
        strinit(string, 'x');

        printf ("after init: string = %s\n", string);

        leave(EXIT_NORMAL);

        return(EXIT_NORMAL);;

}

/*###########################################*/


/*************************************************

   FILE NAME   : strlibs.c
   AUTHOR      : Matt Weisfeld

   DESCRIPTION : string libraries

*************************************************/
#include <stdio.h>
#include <stdlib.h>
#include <ctype.h>
#include <string.h>
#include "proto.h"
#include "er.h"
#ifdef DOS
#include <alloc.h>
#endif


/*************************************************

   ROUTINE NAME : strtoupper()

   DESCRIPTION  : convert string to all upper
                  case.

   INPUT        : char * (raw string)

   OUTPUT       : char * (converted string)

*************************************************/
```

```
char *strtoupper(string)
char *string;
{

        int i;
        char *buffer;

        if (string == NULL) {
                printf ("Error: input string is NULL\n");

                return (NULL);
        }

        if ((buffer = malloc(strlen(string)+1)) == NULL) {
                printf ("Error: out of memory. Process
                terminated.\n");
                return (NULL);
        }

        for (i=0;string[i]!='\0';i++) {

                buffer[i] = toupper(string[i]);

        }

         buffer[i] = '\0';

        return(buffer);

}

/****************************************************

  ROUTINE NAME : strtolower()

  DESCRIPTION  : convert string to all lower
                   case.

  INPUT        : char * (raw string)

  OUTPUT       : char * (converted string)

  ****************************************************/
```

```
char *strtolower(string)
char *string;
{

      int i;
      char *buffer;

      if (string == NULL) {
            printf ("Error: input string is NULL\n");

            return (NULL);
      }

      if ((buffer = malloc(strlen(string)+1)) == NULL) {
            printf ("Error: out of memory. Process
            terminated.\n");
            return (NULL);
      }

      for (i=0;string[i]!='\0';i++) {

            buffer[i] = tolower(string[i]);

      }

       buffer[i] = '\0';

      return(buffer);

}


/**************************************************

  ROUTINE NAME : strcnvtupp()

  DESCRIPTION  : convert string to all upper
                 case (operates on input string).

  INPUT        : char * (raw string)

  OUTPUT       : char * (converted string)

**************************************************/
```

```c
void strcnvtupp(string)
char *string;
{

  int i;

  if (string == NULL) {
    printf ("Error: input string is NULL\n");
    return;
  }

  for (i=0;string[i]!='\0';i++) {

    string[i] = toupper(string[i]);

  }

  return;

}

/*****************************************************

  ROUTINE NAME : strcnvtlow()

  DESCRIPTION  : convert string to all lower
                 case (operates on input string).

  INPUT        : char * (raw string)

  OUTPUT       : char * (converted string)

*****************************************************/
void strcnvtlow(string)
char *string;
{

  int i;

  if (string == NULL) {
    printf ("Error: input string is NULL\n");
    return;
  }
```

```
   for (i=0;string[i]!='\0';i++) {

      string[i] = tolower(string[i]);

   }

   return;

}


/****************************************************

   ROUTINE NAME : stralnum

   DESCRIPTION  : determine if a string is all
                  alpha-numerics.

   INPUT        : char * (raw string)

   OUTPUT       : int (BOOLEAN value)

*****************************************************/
int stralnum(string)
char *string;
{

      int i;
      int flag = 1;

      if (string == NULL) {
             printf ("Error: input string is NULL\n");

             return (NULL);
      }

      for (i=0;string[i]!='\0';i++) {

             if ( !isalnum(string[i]) ) {

                    flag = 0;
                    break;
```

```
                    }
            }

        return(flag);

}

/*****************************************************

  ROUTINE NAME : stralpha

  DESCRIPTION  : determine if a string is all
                 alpha.

  INPUT        : char * (raw string)

  OUTPUT       : int (BOOLEAN value)

*****************************************************/
int stralpha(string)
char *string;
{

        int i;
        int flag = 1;

        if (string == NULL) {
                printf ("Error: input string is NULL\n");

                return (NULL);
        }

        for (i=0;string[i]!='\0';i++) {

                if ( !isalpha(string[i]) ) {

                        flag = 0;
                        break;

                }
        }
```

```
                return(flag);

}


/**************************************************

   ROUTINE NAME : strascii

   DESCRIPTION  : determine if a string is all
                  ascii.

   INPUT        : char * (raw string)

   OUTPUT       : int (BOOLEAN value)

***************************************************/
int strascii(string)
char *string;
{

        int i;
        int flag = 1;

        if (string == NULL) {
                printf ("Error: input string is NULL\n");

                return (NULL);
        }

        for (i=0;string[i]!='\0';i++) {

                if ( !isascii(string[i]) ) {

                        flag = 0;
                        break;

                }
        }

        return(flag);

}
```

```
/*****************************************************

   ROUTINE NAME : strcntrl

   DESCRIPTION  : determine if a string contains
                  a control character.

   INPUT        : char * (raw string)

   OUTPUT       : int (BOOLEAN value)

*****************************************************/
int strcntrl(string)
char *string;
{

      int i;
      int flag = 1;

      if (string == NULL) {
            printf ("Error: input string is NULL\n");

            return (NULL);
      }

      for (i=0;string[i]!='\0';i++) {

            if ( !iscntrl(string[i]) ) {

                  flag = 0;
                  break;

            }
      }

      return(flag);

}
```

```
/*****************************************************

   ROUTINE NAME : strinteger

   DESCRIPTION  : determine if a string is all
                  integers.

   INPUT        : char * (raw string)

   OUTPUT       : int (BOOLEAN value)

*****************************************************/
int strinteger(string)
char *string;
{

      int i;
      int flag = 1;

      if (string == NULL) {
            printf ("Error: input string is NULL\n");

            return (NULL);
      }

      for (i=0;string[i]!='\0';i++) {

            if ( !(isdigit(string[i])) ) {
                  flag = 0;
                  break;
            }

      }

      return(flag);

}
```

```c
/******************************************************

   ROUTINE NAME : strfloat

   DESCRIPTION  : determine if a string is all
                  floats.

   INPUT        : char * (raw string)

   OUTPUT       : int (BOOLEAN value)

******************************************************/
int strfloat(string)
char *string;
{

      int i;
      int flag = 1;
      int point_count = 0;

      if (string == NULL) {
            printf ("Error: input string is NULL\n");

            return (NULL);
      }

      for (i=0;string[i]!='\0';i++) {

            if (string[i] == '.') {
                  point_count++;
                  if (point_count >1)
                        flag = 0;
            } else {
                  if ( !(isdigit(string[i])) ) {
                        flag = 0;
                        break;
                  }
            }
      }

      return(flag);

}
```

```
/**************************************************

   ROUTINE NAME : strgraph

   DESCRIPTION  : determine if a string is all
                  printable characters.

   INPUT        : char * (raw string)

   OUTPUT       : int (BOOLEAN value)

**************************************************/
int strgraph(string)
char *string;
{

      int i;
      int flag = 1;

      if (string == NULL) {
            printf ("Error: input string is NULL\n");

            return (NULL);
      }

      for (i=0;string[i]!='\0';i++) {

            if ( !isgraph(string[i]) ) {

                  flag = 0;
                  break;

            }
      }

      return(flag);

}
```

```
/*****************************************************

   ROUTINE NAME : strlower

   DESCRIPTION  : determine if a string is all
                  lower case.

   INPUT        : char * (raw string)

   OUTPUT       : int (BOOLEAN value)

***************************************************/
int strlower(string)
char *string;
{

     int i;
     int flag = 1;

     if (string == NULL) {
          printf ("Error: input string is NULL\n");

          return (NULL);
     }

     for (i=0;string[i]!='\0';i++) {

          if ( !islower(string[i]) ) {

               flag = 0;
               break;

          }
     }

     return(flag);

}
```

```
/*****************************************************

   ROUTINE NAME : strupper

   DESCRIPTION  : determine if a string is all
                  upper case.

   INPUT        : char * (raw string)

   OUTPUT       : int (BOOLEAN value)

*****************************************************/
int strupper(string)
char *string;
{
        int i;
        int flag = 1;

        if (string == NULL) {
                printf ("Error: input string is NULL\n");

                return (NULL);
        }

        for (i=0;string[i]!='\0';i++) {

                if ( !isupper(string[i]) ) {

                        flag = 0;
                        break;

                }
        }

        return(flag);

}
```

```
/******************************************************

   ROUTINE NAME : strprint

   DESCRIPTION  : determine if a string is all
                  printable characters.

   INPUT        : char * (raw string)

   OUTPUT       : int (BOOLEAN value)

******************************************************/
int strprint(string)
char *string;
{

      int i;
      int flag = 1;

      if (string == NULL) {
             printf ("Error: input string is NULL\n");

             return (NULL);
      }

      for (i=0;string[i]!='\0';i++) {

             if ( !isprint(string[i]) ) {

                    flag = 0;
                    break;

             }
      }

      return(flag);

}
```

```
/**************************************************

   ROUTINE NAME : strpunct

   DESCRIPTION  : determine if a string is all
                  punctuation characters.

   INPUT        : char * (raw string)

   OUTPUT       : int (BOOLEAN value)

**************************************************/
int strpunct(string)
char *string;
{

      int i;
      int flag = 1;

      if (string == NULL) {
            printf ("Error: input string is NULL\n");

            return (NULL);
      }

      for (i=0;string[i]!='\0';i++) {

            if ( !ispunct(string[i]) ) {

                  flag = 0;
                  break;

            }
      }

      return(flag);

}
```

```
/********************************************************

   ROUTINE NAME : strspace

   DESCRIPTION  : determine if a string is all
                    spaces.

   INPUT        : char * (raw string)

   OUTPUT       : int (BOOLEAN value)

********************************************************/
int strspace(string)
char *string;
{

      int i;
      int flag = 1;

      if (string == NULL) {
            printf ("Error: input string is NULL\n");

            return (NULL);
      }

      for (i=0;string[i]!='\0';i++) {

            if ( !isspace(string[i]) ) {

                  flag = 0;
                  break;

            }
      }

      return(flag);

}
```

```
/****************************************************

   ROUTINE NAME : strxdigit

   DESCRIPTION  : determine if a string is all
                  hex digits.

   INPUT        : char * (raw string)

   OUTPUT       : int (BOOLEAN value)

****************************************************/
int strxdigit(string)
char *string;
{

      int i;
      int flag = 1;

      if (string == NULL) {
            printf ("Error: input string is NULL\n");

            return (NULL);
      }

      for (i=0;string[i]!='\0';i++) {

            if ( !isxdigit(string[i]) ) {

                  flag = 0;
                  break;

            }
      }

      return(flag);

}
```

```
/*****************************************************

   ROUTINE NAME : strinit

   DESCRIPTION  : initialize a string to char c.

   INPUT        : char *, char

   OUTPUT       : int (# of chars initialized)

*****************************************************/
int strinit(string, c)
char *string;
int c;
{

      int i;

      if (string == NULL) {
             printf ("Error: input string is NULL\n");

             return (NULL);
      }

      for (i=0;string[i]!='\0';i++) {

             string[i] = c;

      }

      return(i);

}

/*****************************************************

   ROUTINE NAME : strrep

   DESCRIPTION  : replace all old chars with new.

   INPUT        : char *, char, char

   OUTPUT       : int (# of chars initialized)

*****************************************************/
```

```
int strrep(string, old, new)
char *string;
int old;
int new;
{

      int i;
      int count;

      if (string == NULL) {
             printf ("Error: input string is NULL\n");

             return (NULL);
      }

      for (i=0,count=0;string[i]!='\0';i++) {

             if (string[i] == old) {
                    string[i] = new;
                    count++;
             }
      }

      return(count);

}

/****************************************************

  ROUTINE NAME : strcount

  DESCRIPTION  : count how many times a char
                 appears in a string.

  INPUT        : char *, char

  OUTPUT       : int (# of chars initialized)

****************************************************/
int strcount(string, c)
char *string;
int c;
{
```

```
        int i;
        int count;

        if (string == NULL) {
                printf ("Error: input string is NULL\n");

                return (NULL);
        }

        for (i=0,count=0;string[i]!='\0';i++) {

                if (string[i] == c) count++;

        }

        return(count);

}

/*###########################################*/


/****************************************************

   FILE NAME   : strlibs.h
   AUTHOR      : Matt Weisfeld

   DESCRIPTION : header file for string libraries.

****************************************************/
#ifdef ANSI
char *strtoupper(char *);
char *strtolower(char *);
void strcnvtupp(char *);
void strcnvtlow(char *);
int stralnum(char *);
int stralpha(char *);
int strasci(char *);
int strcntrl(char *);
int stralnum(char *);
int strinteger(char *);
int strfloat(char *);
```

```
int strgraph(char *);
int strlower(char *);
int strprint(char *);
int strpunct(char *);
int strspace(char *);
int strupper(char *);
int strxdigit(char *);
int strinit(char *, int);
int strcount(char *, int);
int strrep(char *, int, int);
#else
char *strtoupper();
char *strtolower();
void strcnvtupp();
void strcnvtlow();
int stralnum();
int stralpha();
int strasci();
int strcntrl();
int stralnum();
int strinteger();
int strfloat();
int strgraph();
int strlower();
int strprint();
int strpunct();
int strspace();
int strupper();
int strxdigit();
int strinit();
int strcount();
int strrep();
#endif

#define NOMEM -1

/*###########################################*/
```

```
/******************************************************

   FILE NAME    : errdefs.h
   AUTHOR       : Matt Weisfeld

   DESCRIPTION  : error descriptions for strlibs
                  test.

******************************************************/
#include "er.h"

ERROR_STRUCT error_message[] =

/* actual error messages */

{

  /* #0 */
  ER_NOSPACE, EXIT,
  "Bad malloc or NULL string in module '%s'.",
  /* LAST */
  LASTERROR, EXIT, NULL,
};

/*##########################################*/


/******************************************************

   FILE NAME    : er.h
   AUTHOR       : Matt Weisfeld

   DESCRIPTION  : error definitions for strlibs
                  test.

******************************************************/
#define ER_NOSPACE  0      /* no space left for malloc */

/*##########################################*/
```

```
/****************************************************

  FILE NAME   : proto.h
  AUTHOR      : Matt Weisfeld

  DESCRIPTION : prototypes for string libraries.

****************************************************/
#ifdef VMS
#include "[-.common]common.h"
#include "[-.leave]leave.h"
#include "[-.error]error.h"
#endif
#ifdef BCC
#include "..\common\common.h"
#include "..\leave\leave.h"
#include "..\error\error.h"
#endif
#ifdef MSC
#include "..\common\common.h"
#include "..\leave\leave.h"
#include "..\error\error.h"
#endif
#ifdef HPUX
#include "../common/common.h"
#include "../leave/leave.h"
#include "../error/error.h"
#endif
#ifdef SLC
#include "../common/common.h"
#include "../leave/leave.h"
#include "../error/error.h"
#endif
#ifdef GCC
#include "../common/common.h"
#include "../leave/leave.h"
#include "../error/error.h"
#endif
#ifdef CCC
#include "../common/common.h"
#include "../leave/leave.h"
#include "../error/error.h"
```

```
#endif
#include "strlibs.h"

/*###############################################*/

$! VMS DCL PROCEDURE
$ clr
$ if (P1.eqs."") then GOTO ALL
$ if (P1.eqs."ALL") then GOTO ALL
$ if (P1.eqs."LINK") then GOTO LINK
$ set verify
$ cc/define=VMS 'P1'
$ goto LINK
$ ALL:
$      set verify
$ cc/define=VMS test
$ cc/define=VMS strlibs
$ LINK:
$ link/executable=test test,strlibs,[-.leave]leave,[-
.error]error
$ copy test.exe [weisfeld.exe]
$ set noverify

/*###############################################*/

# makefile for BCC/C++ Compiler

OBJS      = test.obj strlibs.obj
LIBS      = ..\leave\leave.obj ..\error\error.obj
HDRS      = proto.h strlibs.h errdefs.h er.h
FLAGS     = -c -DBCC
COMP      = bcc

test.exe:  $(OBJS)
       $(COMP) $(OBJS) $(LIBS)

test.obj: test.c $(HDRS)
       $(COMP) $(FLAGS) test.c

strlibs.obj: strlibs.c $(HDRS)
       $(COMP) $(FLAGS) strlibs.c
```

```
test.c:
strlibs.c:

strlibs.h:
errdefs.h:
er.h:


/*###########################################*/

# makefile for MSC/C++ Compiler

OBJS     = test.obj strlibs.obj
LIBS     = ..\leave\leave.obj ..\error\error.obj
HDRS     = proto.h strlibs.h errdefs.h er.h
FLAGS    = /c /DMSC
COMP     = cl

test.exe:  $(OBJS)
       $(COMP) $(OBJS) $(LIBS)

test.obj: test.c $(HDRS)
       $(COMP) $(FLAGS) test.c

strlibs.obj: strlibs.c $(HDRS)
       $(COMP) $(FLAGS) strlibs.c

test.c:
strlibs.c:

strlibs.h:
errdefs.h:
er.h:


/*###########################################*/

# makefile for HPUX C compiler

OBJS     = test.o strlibs.o
LIBS     = ../leave/leave.o ../error/error.o
HDRS     = proto.h strlibs.h errdefs.h er.h ../leave/leave.h \
           ../error/error.h
```

```
FLAGS    = -c -DHPUX -Aa
COMP     = cc

test:   $(OBJS)
        $(COMP) -o test $(OBJS) $(LIBS)

test.o: test.c $(HDRS)
        $(COMP) $(FLAGS) test.c

strlibs.o: strlibs.c $(HDRS)
        $(COMP) $(FLAGS) strlibs.c

test.c:
strlibs.c:

strlibs.h:
errdefs.h:
er.h:

/*###############################################*/

# makefile for SUN SLC C compiler

OBJS     = test.o strlibs.o
LIBS     = ../leave/leave.o ../error/error.o
HDRS     = proto.h strlibs.h errdefs.h er.h ../leave/leave.h \
           ../error/error.h
FLAGS    = -c -DSLC
COMP     = cc

test:   $(OBJS)
        $(COMP) -o test $(OBJS) $(LIBS)

test.o: test.c $(HDRS)
        $(COMP) $(FLAGS) test.c

strlibs.o: strlibs.c $(HDRS)
        $(COMP) $(FLAGS) strlibs.c

test.c:
strlibs.c:
```

```
strlibs.h:
errdefs.h:
er.h:

/*############################################*/

# makefile for SUN GCC C compiler

OBJS    = test.o strlibs.o
LIBS    = ../leave/leave.o ../error/error.o
HDRS    = proto.h strlibs.h errdefs.h er.h ../leave/leave.h \
          ../error/error.h
FLAGS   = -c -DGCC
COMP    = gcc

test:   $(OBJS)
        $(COMP) -o test $(OBJS) $(LIBS)

test.o: test.c $(HDRS)
        $(COMP) $(FLAGS) test.c

strlibs.o: strlibs.c $(HDRS)
        $(COMP) $(FLAGS) strlibs.c

test.c:
strlibs.c:

strlibs.h:
errdefs.h:
er.h:

/*############################################*/

# makefile for CCC compiler

OBJS    = test.o strlibs.o
LIBS    = ../leave/leave.o ../error/error.o
HDRS    = proto.h strlibs.h errdefs.h er.h ../leave/leave.h \
          ../error/error.h
FLAGS   = -c -DCCC
COMP    = cc
```

```
test:    $(OBJS)
        $(COMP) -o test $(OBJS) $(LIBS)

test.o: test.c $(HDRS)
        $(COMP) $(FLAGS) test.c

strlibs.o: strlibs.c $(HDRS)
        $(COMP) $(FLAGS) strlibs.c

test.c:
strlibs.c:

strlibs.h:
errdefs.h:
er.h:
```

6

Accessing File Information

When you work with files, most transactions involve reading information stored in the file or writing information to the file. This is not surprising since it is the purpose most people associate with a file. However, the contents of a file are not the only information available to the programmer. A wealth of information is available about the structure of the file, which opens up many programming possibilities. This chapter therefore investigates applications that use the function *stat*( ) to gather information about a file.

6.1 DIRECTORY LISTINGS

A directory listing is an example of an operation that, while not concerned with the file's contents, nevertheless provides a great deal of valuable information. For example, the VMS DCL command

```
$ dir/full test.exe
```

produces the following output:

```
Directory SYS$SYSDEVICE:[ACCOUNT.EXE]

TEST.EXE;3    File ID: (10755,3,0)        Size:        152/153
Owner:        [WEISFELD]
Created:      22-OCT-1992 21:28:50.58
Revised:      22-OCT-1992 21:28:51.35 (1)
Expires:      <None specified>
Backup:       <No backup recorded>
File organization:  Sequential
File attributes:    Allocation: 153, Extend: 0, Global
                    buffer count: 0,
                    No version limit, Contiguous best try
Record format:      Fixed length 512 byte records
Record attributes:  None
RMS attributes:     None
Journaling enabled: None
File protection:    System:RWED, Owner:RWED, Group:RE,
                    World:
Access Cntrl List:  None

Total of 1 file, 152/153 blocks.
```

This listing provides information which may be necessary for a program, such as file size, file protections, file ownership, and file access times.

6.2 FILE EXISTENCE

The preceding listing also verifies that the file actually exists—a point which may seem trivial but is often quite important. A number of situations may arise in which a program needs to verify a file's existence. An example is that of searching a path for a file name. One way to determine whether a file exists is to attempt to open it. However, there is overhead associated with this approach.

A better way is to use the *stat( )* command. Even though *stat( )* is not part of the ANSI definition, most systems support some version of this command. The prototype is as follows:

```
#include <stat.h>

int stat (char *filename, struct stat buffer);
```

To use *stat( )* to determine if a file actually exists, the following syntax is employed:

```
if (stat(filename, &buff) == -1) {
      file_exists = FALSE;
} else {
      file_exists = TRUE;
}
```

Basically, if the file exists, *stat( )* returns a 0. If the operation fails, a -1 is returned, and the assumption must be made that the file does not exist. Be aware that while this is normally a valid assumption, it may not always hold true. For example, the file may actually exist in the directory list, yet be corrupted in such a way that *stat( )* returns a -1. In any event, the file is not usable, and the assumption is therefore reasonable even if not totally accurate.

Unfortunately, some systems do not support *stat( )*. In these cases, the *fopen( )* approach will suffice:

```
if ( (fopen(filename, "r")) == NULL )
      file_exists = FALSE;
else
      file_exists = TRUE;
```

A routine called *fexists( )* is created to determine if a file does indeed exist. The entire routine is as follows:

```
int fexists(filename)
char *filename;
{

      struct stat buff;
      int file_exists;

#ifdef  NSTAT    /* if the system does not support stat */

      if ( (fopen(filename, "r")) == NULL )
            file_exists = FALSE;
      else
            file_exists = TRUE;
```

```
#else

        if (stat(filename, &buff) == -1) {
                file_exists = FALSE;
        } else {
                file_exists = TRUE;
        }

#endif

        return (file_exists);

}
```

The command is used in the following manner:

```
if ( fexists(filename) == TRUE )

        ... file exists

else

        ... file does not exist
```

One portability issue is that of the file name itself. If the program is executed in the directory where the file resides, then only the file name is necessary. However, if the file is not in the current directory, the full path must be provided.

6.3 FILE INFORMATION

Even though *fexists( )* uses *stat( )* in a very practical way, it does not take advantage of any of the information that *stat( )* provides beyond inspecting the return code. In fact, *stat( )* actually returns a wealth of information about a file.

The structure *buff* in the *fexists( )* example is used to hold the *stat( )* information.

```
struct stat buff;
```

The following list represents information that is fairly standard across platforms and is used in the test program to print out various file information.

DEVICE   buff.st_dev

VMS returns a string, while other platforms return an integer.

FILE ID   buff.st_ino

VMS returns a series of three integers:

buff.st_ino[0], buff.st_ino[1], buff.st_ino[2

The other platforms return a single integer.

FILE TYPE   buff.st_mode

The file type is gleaned from *buff.st_mode* by using predefined flags provided by your specific platform. For a complete list of these flags, consult the appropriate reference manual.

FILE PROTECTION   buff.st_mode

The file protection mode uses a format similar to that of the file type. However, instead of performing a comparison, *buff.st_mode* is tested simply to see if the bit is turned on.

USER ID   buff.st_uid

All platforms return an integer.

GROUP ID   buff.st_gid

All platforms return an integer.

FILE SIZE   buff.st_size

All platforms return an integer.

```
LAST MODIFIED        buff.st_mtime
```

All platforms provide a time in *time_t* format. Thus a string representation is obtained by using the time string libraries.

```
FILE CREATED         buff.st_ctime
```

All platforms provide a time in *time_t* format. A string representation is obtained by using the time string libraries.

```
RECORD FORMAT        buff.st_fab_rfm
```

Provided by VMS, this function returns a character.

```
RECORD ATTRIBUTES    buff.st_fab_rat
```

Provided by VMS, this function returns a character.

```
FIXED HEADER SIZE    buff.st_fab_fsz
```

Provided by VMS, this function returns a character.

```
RECORD SIZE          buff.st_fab_mrs
```

Provided by VMS, this function returns an integer.

The one field that requires further explanation is *st_mode*. This field is actually a bit mask. To access the information in this bit mask, the following masks are defined in *stat.h:*

```
S_IFMT       type of file
S_IFDIR      directory
S_IFCHR      character special
S_IFBLK      block special
S_IFREG      regular
S_IFMPC      multiplexed character special
S_IFMPB      multiplexed block special
S_SUID       set user id on execution
S_ISGID      set group id on execution
S_ISVTX      save swapped text even after use
S_IREAD      read permission, owner
```

```
S_IWRITE      write permission, owner
S_IEXEC       execute/search permission, owner
```

These definitions are bit flags, which are compared with *buff.st_mode* to identify specific file attributes. The first 7 definitions represent the type of file—regular, directory, and so forth. To determine which flags are set, a command like the following must be used:

```
if ( (S_IFMT & buff.st_mode) == S_IFDIR)
       printf ("directory  \n");
if ( (S_IFMT & buff.st_mode) == S_IFCHR)
       printf ("special character  \n");
if ( (S_IFMT & buff.st_mode) == S_IFBLK)
       printf ("block special  \n");
if ( (S_IFMT & buff.st_mode) == S_IFREG)
       printf ("regular  \n");
```

A bitwise AND is performed between *buff.st_mode* and the constant S_IFMT.

The rest of the definitions do not have a defined format to compare to. However, they are checked as follows:

```
if ( S_IREAD & buff.st_mode)
       printf ("READ\n");
if ( S_IWRITE & buff.st_mode)
       printf ("WRITE\n");
if ( S_IEXEC & buff.st_mode)
       printf ("EXECUTE\n");
```

6.4 THE *finfo*( ) COMMAND

Writing a portable program to print out this file information, while not really difficult, can get quite involved as many allowances need to be made for each different system. The routine for doing so presented here, *finfo*( ), utilizes information that is largely shared by all platforms.

To call *finfo*( ), use the following syntax:

```
int finfo(char *filename)
```

Calling *finfo*( ) with the command

```
finfo(test.exe) /* VMS */
```

produces the following output:

```
FILENAME          : test.exe

DEVICE            : _DKA300
FILE ID           : (10809,8,0)
FILE TYPE         : regular
FILE PROTECTION   : (OWNER):READ/WRITE/EXECUTE
USER_ID           : 8388737
GROUP_ID          : 128
FILE SIZE (bytes) : 77824
LAST MODIFIED     : Friday, October 23, 1992. 7:38:32 AM.
FILE CREATED      : Friday, October 23, 1992. 7:38:32 AM.
RECORD FORMAT     : 1
RECORD ATTRIBUTES : 0
FIXED HEADER SIZE : 0
RECORD SIZE       : 512
```

The information provided by each system is explained in its respective reference manual. However, many values are provided simply to maintain a semblance of compatibility with the original UNIX implementations. For example, three different time values are included: access time, modification time, and creation time. On some systems, all three times are always the same. In fact, on most systems at least two are always the same.

In the listing previously presented, the file was a regular file. A directory would produce the following output:

```
FILENAME          : try.dir

DEVICE            : _DKA300
FILE ID           : (10814,5,0)
FILE TYPE         : directory
FILE PROTECTION   : (OWNER):READ/WRITE/EXECUTE
USER_ID           : 8388737
GROUP_ID          : 128
```

```
FILE SIZE (bytes) : 512
LAST MODIFIED     : Friday, October 23, 1992. 7:44:21 PM.
FILE CREATED      : Friday, October 23, 1992. 7:44:21 PM.
RECORD FORMAT     : 2
RECORD ATTRIBUTES : 8
FIXED HEADER SIZE : 0
RECORD SIZE       : 512
```

An executable file produces the following output on a DOS machine:

```
FILENAME          : test.exe

DEVICE            : 2
FILE ID           : 0
FILE TYPE         : regular
FILE PROTECTION   : (OWNER):READ/WRITE/
USER_ID           : 0
GROUP_ID          : 0
FILE SIZE (bytes) : 31742
LAST MODIFIED     : Wednesday, February 3, 1993. 8:23:28 PM.
FILE CREATED      : Wednesday, February 3, 1993. 8:23:28 PM.
```

The output for a text file on HP-UX is:

```
FILENAME          : statlibs.c

DEVICE            : 119543296
FILE ID           : 9769
FILE TYPE         : regular
FILE PROTECTION   : (OWNER):READ/WRITE/
USER_ID           : 202
GROUP_ID          : 20
FILE SIZE (bytes) : 4639
LAST MODIFIED     : Wednesday, February 3, 1993. 8:21:44 PM.
FILE CREATED      : Wednesday, February 3, 1993. 8:21:44 PM.
```

6.5 USING THE FILE STATUS LIBRARY

The test program for *statlibs* is very compact. To run the test, simply enter the name of a program file as the first parameter.

For example, for VMS the file information for the test executable is found with the following command:

```
$ test test.exe
```

First, the test program uses *fexists( )* to determine if the file actually exists. If it does not, an error is produced. If it does, *finfo( )* is called and the file information is output to the screen.

6.6 CONCLUSION

There are two other commands related to *stat( )*. Both use the same structure and produce the same output. Whereas *stat( )* takes as input a file name of type char *, the command *fstat( )* takes a file descriptor as input, and the command *lstat( )*, available on UNIX systems, takes a symbolic link as input. Since their functionality is the same, these two commands are not explored here.

The *stat( )* family of commands provides much more information about a file than its contents. One of the many applications where *stat( )* is very useful is a make program which must determine the last time the file was modified. Another is checking the permissions on a file. For additional ideas you may find it very helpful to check the various platform user manuals. Using *stat( )* provides great insight into the workings of a file.

```
/****************************************************

   FILE NAME   : test.c
   AUTHOR      : Matt Weisfeld

   DESCRIPTION : test program for statlibs

****************************************************/
#include <stdio.h>
#include <string.h>
#include "proto.h"
#include "errdefs.h"

main(argc,argv)
int argc;
```

```
char **argv;
{

        char filename[50];

        if (argc != 2)
                error (ER_INVARGS);

        strcpy (filename,argv[1]);

        if (fexists(filename)== TRUE)
                finfo(filename);
        else
                error (ER_NOFILE, filename);

        leave(EXIT_NORMAL);

        return(EXIT_NORMAL);

}

/*##########################################*/


/*****************************************************

  FILE NAME   : statlibs.c
  AUTHOR      : Matt Weisfeld

  DESCRIPTION : libraries for file status

*****************************************************/
#include <stdio.h>
#include <string.h>
#include "proto.h"

/*****************************************************

  ROUTINE NAME : finfo()

  DESCRIPTION  : print file information

  INPUT        : char * (filename)
```

```
    OUTPUT        : int (status)

**************************************************/
int finfo(filename)
char *filename;
{

        FILE *fp;

        int status;

        char command[STRLEN];

        char *access_time;
        char *modify_time;
        char *creation_time;

        struct stat buff;

        int file_exists;

/*

        This output can go to a file if desired:

        fp = fopen("file.out", "w");
*/

        fp = stdout;

        strcpy (command, filename);

        fprintf (fp,"FILENAME            : %s ", command);

        if (stat(command, &buff) == -1) {
                fprintf (fp,"DOES NOT EXIST.\n");
                return (-1);
        } else {
                fprintf (fp,"\n");
        }

        fprintf (fp,"\n");

#ifdef VMS
        fprintf (fp,"DEVICE         : %s\n", buff.st_dev);
```

```
#else
      fprintf (fp,"DEVICE    2 : %d\n", buff.st_dev);
#endif

#ifdef VMS
      fprintf (fp,"FILE ID      : (%d,%d,%d)\n", buff.st_ino[0],
                                    buff.st_ino[1], buff.st_ino[2]);
#else
      fprintf (fp,"FILE ID      : %d\n", buff.st_ino);
#endif

      fprintf (fp,"FILE TYPE    : ");

      if ( (S_IFMT & buff.st_mode) == S_IFDIR)
            fprintf (fp,"directory  \n");
      if ( (S_IFMT & buff.st_mode) == S_IFCHR)
            fprintf (fp,"special character  \n");
#ifndef MSC
      if ( (S_IFMT & buff.st_mode) == S_IFBLK)
            fprintf (fp,"block special  \n");
#endif
      if ( (S_IFMT & buff.st_mode) == S_IFREG)
            fprintf (fp,"regular  \n");
#ifdef VMS
      if ( (S_IFMT & buff.st_mode) == S_IFMPC)
            fprintf (fp,"mult char spec  \n");
      if ( (S_IFMT & buff.st_mode) == S_IFMPB)
            fprintf (fp,"mult block spec  \n");
#endif
#ifndef DOS
      if ( S_ISUID & buff.st_mode)
            fprintf (fp,"set user id  \n");
      if ( S_ISGID & buff.st_mode)
            fprintf (fp,"set group id  \n");
      if ( S_ISVTX & buff.st_mode)
            fprintf (fp,"save swapped text  \n");
#endif

      fprintf (fp,"FILE PROTECTION  : (OWNER):");
      if ( S_IREAD & buff.st_mode)
            fprintf (fp,"READ/");
      if ( S_IWRITE & buff.st_mode)
```

```
                fprintf (fp,"WRITE/");
        if ( S_IEXEC & buff.st_mode)
                fprintf (fp,"EXECUTE");
        fprintf (fp,"\n");

        /* st_atime is always the same as st_mtime, so no
        use printing */
        modify_time = cvt_strtime(buff.st_mtime);
        creation_time = cvt_strtime(buff.st_ctime);

        fprintf (fp,"USER_ID          : %u\n", buff.st_uid);
        fprintf (fp,"GROUP_ID         : %u\n", buff.st_gid);
        fprintf (fp,"FILE SIZE (bytes) : %u\n", buff.st_size);
        fprintf (fp,"LAST MODIFIED    : %s\n", modify_time);
        fprintf (fp,"FILE CREATED     : %s\n", creation_time);

#ifdef VMS
        fprintf (fp,"RECORD FORMAT    : %x\n", buff.st_fab_rfm);
        fprintf (fp,"RECORD ATTRIBUTES : %x\n", buff.st_fab_rat);
        fprintf (fp,"FIXED HEADER SIZE : %x\n", buff.st_fab_fsz);
        fprintf (fp,"RECORD SIZE      : %u\n", buff.st_fab_mrs);
#endif

        return (0);


}

/***************************************************

  ROUTINE NAME : fexists()

  DESCRIPTION  : determine if a file exists

  INPUT        : char * (filename)

  OUTPUT       : int (status)

***************************************************/
int fexists(filename)
char *filename;
```

```
{

        struct stat buff;
        int file_exists;

#ifdef NSTAT

        if ( (fopen(filename, "r")) == NULL )
                file_exists = FALSE;
        else
                file_exists = TRUE;

#else

        if (stat(filename, &buff) == -1) {
                file_exists = FALSE;
        } else {
                file_exists = TRUE;
        }

#endif

        return (file_exists);

}

/*#############################################*/


/****************************************************

   FILE NAME   : proto.h
   AUTHOR      : Matt Weisfeld

   DESCRIPTION : prototypes for syslibs

****************************************************/
#ifdef VMS
#include <stat.h>
#endif

#ifdef UNIX
```

```
#ifdef SUN
#include <sys/stat.h>
#else
#include </usr/include/sys/stat.h>
#endif

#endif

#ifdef DOS
#include <sys/types.h>
#include <sys/stat.h>
#endif

#ifdef ANSI
int finfo(char *);
int fexists(char *);
FILE *open_file(char *, char *);
#else
int finfo();
int fexists();
FILE *open_file();
#endif

/*###############################################*/


/***************************************************

   FILE NAME   : er.h
   AUTHOR      : Matt Weisfeld

   DESCRIPTION : error definitions for stat
                 libaries.

***************************************************/
#define ER_INVARGS  0      /* invalid number of arguments
*/
#define ER_NOFILE   1      /* file does not exist */

/*###############################################*/


/***************************************************
```

```
      FILE NAME    : errdefs.h
      AUTHOR       : Matt Weisfeld

    DESCRIPTION : error descriptions for stat
                  libraries.

****************************************************/
#include "er.h"

ERROR_STRUCT error_message[] =

/* actual error messages */

{

      /* #0 */
      ER_INVARGS, EXIT,
      "Invalid number of arguments.",
      /* #1 */
      ER_NOFILE, EXIT,
      "File '%s' does not exist.",
      LASTERROR, EXIT,NULL,
};


/*###############################################*/


/***************************************************

    FILE NAME    : proto.h
    AUTHOR       : Matt Weisfeld

    DESCRIPTION : prototype file for stat
                  libraries.

****************************************************/

#ifdef VMS
#include "[-.common]common.h"
#include "[-.leave]leave.h"
#include "[-.error]error.h"
```

```
#include "[-.timelibs]timelibs.h"
#endif

#ifdef BCC
#include "..\common\common.h"
#include "..\leave\leave.h"
#include "..\error\error.h"
#include "..\timelibs\timelibs.h"
#endif

#ifdef MSC
#include "..\common\common.h"
#include "..\leave\leave.h"
#include "..\error\error.h"
#include "..\timelibs\timelibs.h"
#endif

#ifdef HPUX
#include "../common/common.h"
#include "../leave/leave.h"
#include "../error/error.h"
#include "../timelibs/timelibs.h"
#endif

#ifdef SLC
#include "../common/common.h"
#include "../leave/leave.h"
#include "../error/error.h"
#include "../timelibs/timelibs.h"
#endif

#ifdef GCC
#include "../common/common.h"
#include "../leave/leave.h"
#include "../error/error.h"
#include "../timelibs/timelibs.h"
#endif

#ifdef CCC
#include "../common/common.h"
#include "../leave/leave.h"
#include "../error/error.h"
```

```
#include "../timelibs/timelibs.h"
#endif

#include "statlibs.h"

/*###########################################*/

$! VMS DCL PROCEDURE
$ clr
$ if (P1.eqs."") then GOTO ALL
$ if (P1.eqs."ALL") then GOTO ALL
$ if (P1.eqs."LINK") then GOTO LINK
$ set verify
$ cc/define=VMS 'P1'
$ goto LINK
$ ALL:
$      set verify
$ cc/define=VMS test
$ cc/define=VMS statlibs
$ LINK:
$ link/executable=test test,statlibs,
[-.timelibs]timelibs,[-.leave]leave,[-.error]error
$ copy test.exe [weisfeld.exe]
$ set noverify

/*###########################################*/

# makefile for BCC/C++ Compiler

OBJS    = test.obj statlibs.obj
LIBS    = ..\leave\leave.obj ..\error\error.obj
          ..\timelibs\timelibs.obj
HDRS    = proto.h statlibs.h errdefs.h er.h
FLAGS   = -c -DBCC
COMP    = bcc

test.exe:  $(OBJS)
       $(COMP) $(OBJS) $(LIBS)

test.obj: test.c $(HDRS)
       $(COMP) $(FLAGS) test.c
```

```
statlibs.obj: statlibs.c $(HDRS)
      $(COMP) $(FLAGS) statlibs.c

test.c:
statlibs.c:

statlibs.h:
errdefs.h:
er.h:

/*#############################################*/

# makefile for MSC/C++ Compiler

OBJS      = test.obj statlibs.obj
LIBS      = ..\leave\leave.obj ..\error\error.obj
            ..\timelibs\timelibs.obj
HDRS      = proto.h statlibs.h errdefs.h er.h
FLAGS     = /c /DMSC
COMP      = cl

test.exe:  $(OBJS)
      $(COMP) $(OBJS) $(LIBS)

test.obj: test.c $(HDRS)
      $(COMP) $(FLAGS) test.c

statlibs.obj: statlibs.c $(HDRS)
      $(COMP) $(FLAGS) statlibs.c

test.c:
statlibs.c:

statlibs.h:
errdefs.h:
er.h:

/*#############################################*/

# makefile for HPUX C Compiler
```

```
OBJS      = test.o statlibs.o
LIBS      = ../leave/leave.o ../error/error.o
            ../timelibs/timelibs.o
HDRS      = proto.h statlibs.h errdefs.h er.h
FLAGS     = -c -DHPUX

COMP      = cc

test:   $(OBJS)
        $(COMP) -o test $(OBJS) $(LIBS)

test.o: test.c $(HDRS)
        $(COMP) $(FLAGS) test.c

statlibs.o: statlibs.c $(HDRS)
        $(COMP) $(FLAGS) statlibs.c

test.c:
statlibs.c:

statlibs.h:
errdefs.h:
er.h:


/*################################################*/

# makefile for SUN SLC C Compiler

OBJS      = test.o statlibs.o
LIBS      = ../leave/leave.o ../error/error.o
            ../timelibs/timelibs.o
HDRS      = proto.h statlibs.h errdefs.h er.h
FLAGS     = -c -DSLC
COMP      = cc

test:   $(OBJS)
        $(COMP) -o test $(OBJS) $(LIBS)

test.o: test.c $(HDRS)
        $(COMP) $(FLAGS) test.c

statlibs.o: statlibs.c $(HDRS)
        $(COMP) $(FLAGS) statlibs.c
```

```
test.c:
statlibs.c:

statlibs.h:
errdefs.h:
er.h:

/*###########################################*/

# makefile for SUN GCC C Compiler

OBJS      = test.o statlibs.o
LIBS      = ../leave/leave.o ../error/error.o
            ../timelibs/timelibs.o
HDRS      = proto.h statlibs.h errdefs.h er.h
FLAGS     = -c -DGCC
COMP      = gcc

test:   $(OBJS)
        $(COMP) -o test $(OBJS) $(LIBS)

test.o: test.c $(HDRS)
        $(COMP) $(FLAGS) test.c

statlibs.o: statlibs.c $(HDRS)
        $(COMP) $(FLAGS) statlibs.c

test.c:
statlibs.c:

statlibs.h:
errdefs.h:
er.h:

/*###########################################*/

# makefile for CCC Compiler
```

```
OBJS      = test.o statlibs.o
LIBS      = ../leave/leave.o ../error/error.o
            ../timelibs/timelibs.o
HDRS      = proto.h statlibs.h errdefs.h er.h
FLAGS     = -c -DCCC
COMP      = cc

test:   $(OBJS)
        $(COMP) -o test $(OBJS) $(LIBS)

test.o: test.c $(HDRS)
        $(COMP) $(FLAGS) test.c

statlibs.o: statlibs.c $(HDRS)
        $(COMP) $(FLAGS) statlibs.c

test.c:
statlibs.c:

statlibs.h:
errdefs.h:
er.h:
```

7

Parsing Libraries

Nearly all computer applications require input, and that input may come from a file or from the terminal. In either case, extracting the necessary information from input is a critical programming task that is especially important to consider when creating compilers and interpreters. The process of reading the input and breaking it up into meaningful information that can be utilized by a computer program is called *parsing*. The pieces of information extracted by the parsing routine are called *tokens*.

A variety of parsing schemes can be utilized to process input. One of the simplest schemes, *white space parsing*, assumes that all tokens are surrounded by white space: blanks, tabs, and so forth. This line of valid C code

```
sum = sum + 1
```

reveals the following 5 tokens when parsed in this manner:

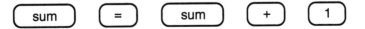

The C programming language does not use white space parsing to delineate tokens, but instead uses *context sensitive parsing*. The following line, which has no whitespace at all, is also valid C code:

```
sum=sum+1;
```

Being context sensitive, parsing in C is based on the syntax and construction of the language, and not on the characters surrounding each token. Context sensitive parsing is much more powerful than the white space scheme illustrated above. However, a language such as C requires that strict grammar rules be designed and adhered to. Realistically, most programmers are not going to tackle the job of writing a compiler as sophisticated as C, Pascal, or other high-level languages. The simplicity of white space parsing provides this approach with a power of its own, and thus it will be utilized throughout this book.

7.1 THE *getline( )* FUNCTION

Besides the token, the line is another important parsing unit. For example, consider the following short user program:

```
sum = 10
y = 2

sum   =   sum   +   y

print sum
EOF
```

The EOF signifies the end of the file. This file contains 6 lines (not including EOF). Note that blank lines are included in the line count. Though not visible to the eye, there is information in a blank line that is very important to the parsing routines. The control characters '\n' are used to terminate each line and signify a carriage return. The file actually looks like this:

```
sum = 10\n
y = 2\n
```

```
\n
sum  =  sum  +  y\n
\n
print sum\n
EOF
```

In fact, the file may also contain a line feed escape sequence, but for parsing purposes here only the new line sequence is considered. Note that even the blank lines contain a newline sequence. This pair of characters always signals the end of the line, and anything that follows will be on a new line.

An ANSI C function called *strtok( )* can perform some of the same functions that will be developed and presented here, but *strtok( )* is not always portable. In addition, the routines detailed here are not very complicated and provide the programmer the luxury of tailoring them to meet specific needs. The *strtok( )* function will be discussed later in this chapter.

The first function to be used is the *getline( )* function. Basically, *getline( )* reads in characters from a data stream until it encounters a new line character sequence. The code to handle this is very compact:

```
while ( (c=getc(fp)) != EOF && c != '\n') s[i++] = c;
```

This *while* loop places an entire line into the character string *s*. The loop will only terminate on encountering a new line sequence or an EOF. It is important that the code does check for EOF, since it is not a given that closing a file will automatically generate a new line. It is also important that the *getc( )* clause be on the left side of this equation. If the code looked like

```
while ( (c != '\n' && c=getc(fp)) != EOF) s[i++] = c;
```

the old value of c would be compared to the newline.

The *while* loop will not include the new line sequence at the end of the string. This is a design decision. If the newline is required at the end of the string, the *while* loop can be rewritten to accomodate it, or a simple additional line of code will do the trick:

```
if (c == '\n')
    s[i++] = c;
```

7.2 THE *get_token*( ) FUNCTION

While the line is an important parsing construct, it is the token that provides information about the line's actual contents. After the line is read into the program, it must be broken down into its component parts. To do this, the function *get_token*( ) is called. The prototype for *get_token*( ) is:

```
int get_token (char *token, char **t_pos)
```

The function's format is:

```
status = get_token(token, &line_ptr);
```

The parameter *token* is a character string that will hold the token passed back from the *get_token*( ) routine. The parameter *line_ptr* is the line that will be used to obtain the next token. An example will help illustrate how the routine is used. Consider the line:

```
print all files
```

After this line is read into a character string called *line*, a pointer called *line_ptr* is set to the beginning of *line:*

```
char line[80];

char *line_ptr;

line_ptr = line;
```

The first time *get_token*( ) is called, token should contain the string 'print'. The second time it is called, token should contain the string 'all', and so on, until the new line sequence is encountered.

The internals of the *get_token*( ) routine are straightforward.

Again, white space is what delineates a token. Stripping the white space from the beginning of a token is the first order of business. This is accomplished with a simple while loop:

```
while (isspace(**t_pos)) (*t_pos)++; /* skip leading
whitespace */
```

The first character that is not white space is the first character of the next token. Only one character is considered a special case: a double quote ("). Remember that the parsing routines recognize white space as the delineator for the token. However, what happens when a space is actually part of the token? For example, a field for name must handle the following possibility:

```
Mary Jane
```

Using only white space to parse this would break the name into two separate tokens. To prevent this, a token can be surrounded by double quotes as follows:

```
"Mary Jane"
```

This forces the *get_token( )* routine to read the string as one token. In short, once a double quote is encountered, everything up to the second double quote is considered part of the token. If there is no second double quote, an error will be generated when the new line sequence or EOF is encountered.

A special case within the special case of the double quotes is the following token:

```
""
```

This is a NULL string. There are some instances when it is desirable to have a NULL string. If two double quotes are found back-to-back, the token passed back will contain only a NULL.

If a double quote condition does not exists, the token can be read in with a simple *while* statement.

```
while ( !isspace(**t_pos) && **t_pos != '\0') {

    token[size++] = *((*t_pos)++);

}
```

This statement will continually place the next character into the character string token until it encounters a white space or NULL. Remember that the tokens are being read from a character string, and a character string is terminated by a NULL.

The final action taken by *get_token*( ) is to assure that the token is terminated with a NULL. Since there is a NULL only at the end of the line (constituting the last token in the line), all tokens that make up the line must have a NULL added.

When *get_token*( ) returns to the calling function, it returns an integer representing the size of the token. If there are no tokens left in the line, a length of zero is passed back.

As indicated earlier in the chapter, ANSI C provides a function called *strtok*( ) that has some of the functionality provided by *get_token*( ). However, not all nonANSI systems provide *strtok*( ). The calling procedures for *strtok*( ) are as follows:

```
#include <string.h>

char *strtok(char *s1, const char *s2);
```

The parameter *s1* is a character string that represents the string to be parsed. The parameter *s2* is also a string and contains the parsing delineation characters. To parse this string, *strtok*( ) must be called in a specific sequence. Assume that the character string *s1* is defined as:

```
char *ptr; static char  s1[] = " print all names";
```

To parse this string, *strtok*( ) is called the initial time as follows:

```
ptr = strtok(s1, " ");
```

The initial call to *strtok*( ) searches the string for the first character that is not one of the characters defined in the second parameter. In effect, this command strips off white space as did the *while* loop presented before. In this case, if no blank is found, a NULL is returned. If the character is found, then this is the start of the first token. Subsequent calls to *strtok*( ) follow this format:

```
ptr = (NULL, " ");
```

If a blank is not found, the token continues until the end of the line. If a blank is found, it is overwritten by a NULL which terminates the next token. If no tokens are left, then a NULL pointer is returned. The *strtok*( ) command maintains its own pointer to keep track of its position in the string.

The use of *strtok*( ) can save some time and coding. However, since it is an ANSI construct, it is not portable to nonANSI systems.

7.3 USING THE PARSING LIBRARY

The test program for *parslibs* first opens a file called *file.txt* to get the information to process. A *while* loop is entered that retrieves one line at a time using *getline*( ) until EOF is reached. Each line is parsed into its tokens using *get_token*( ). The character pointer *ptr* is used to keep place in the line. All tokens are returned into the character string token.

To use the parsing libraries, simply link the *parslibs* object library with your application program. The major problem to watch out for is the use of the string pointers, as in any application. If one of the pointers goes beyond its boundaries, the routines become unpredictable.

7.4 CONCLUSION

Parsing is a very fundamental programming technique. The C programming language (at least the ANSI standard) provides some help in this area. If the C parsing routines provide the appropriate functionality, use these functions instead. However, building portable, custom parsing routines can make your life much easier when you need special functionality.

```c
/*******************************************************

   FILE NAME   : test.c
   AUTHOR      : Matt Weisfeld

   DESCRIPTION : test program for parsing
                 libraries.

*******************************************************/
#include <stdio.h>
#include <stdlib.h>
#include "proto.h"
#include "errdefs.h"

main()
{

     FILE *fp;

     char *ptr;

     char line[STRLEN];

     char token[STRLEN];

     int linenum=0,tokennum=0;

     /* test getline & get_token */

     if ( (fp = fopen ("file.txt", "r")) == NULL){
          error (ER_NOTOPEN, "file.txt");
     }

     while ( (getline (fp, line)) != EOF) {
          printf ("\nline [%d] = %s\n", ++linenum, line);

          tokennum = 0;

          ptr = line;

          while ( (get_token (token, &ptr)) !=0 )
               printf ("token[%d] = %s\n", ++tokennum,
               token);
```

```
        }

        fclose (fp);

        leave(EXIT_NORMAL);

        return(EXIT_NORMAL);

}

/*##############################################*/


/**************************************************

   FILE NAME   : parselib.c
   AUTHOR      : Matt Weisfeld

   DESCRIPTION : parsing routines.

**************************************************/
#include <stdio.h>
#include <ctype.h>

/**************************************************

   ROUTINE NAME : get_token()

   DESCRIPTION  : return a token from a line

   INPUT        : char * (token)

                : char **t_pos (line)

   OUTPUT       : int (num of chars in token)

**************************************************/
int get_token (token, t_pos)
char token[];
char **t_pos;
{
```

```
int    size = 0;

/* skip leading whitespace */
while (isspace(**t_pos)) (*t_pos)++;

switch (**t_pos) {

case '"':

        (*t_pos)++;

        if (**t_pos == '"') {
                token[size++] = '\0';
                (*t_pos)++;
                return(size);
        }

        while ((**t_pos) != '"' && **t_pos !='\0') {
                token[size++] = *((*t_pos)++);
        }

        (*t_pos)++;

        if (**t_pos == '\0')
                size = -1;

break;

default:

        while ( !isspace(**t_pos) && **t_pos != '\0') {


                if (**t_pos == '\\') {
                        (*t_pos)++;
                        token[size++] = *((*t_pos)++);
                } else
                        token[size++] = *((*t_pos)++);
        }

break;
```

```
        }

token[size] = '\0';     /* null-terminate the token  */

return size;            /* return token size         */

}

/****************************************************

  ROUTINE NAME : getline  ()

  DESCRIPTION  : return a line from a file.

  INPUT        : FILE * (file)

               : char * (line)

  OUTPUT       : int (line size)

****************************************************/
int getline(fp, s)
FILE *fp;
char s[];
{

      int c,i;

      i = 0;

      /* read line until EOF or a newline is found */

      while ( (c=getc(fp)) != EOF && c != '\n')
            s[i++] = c;

      if (c == '\n')
            s[i++] = c;

      s[i] = '\0';                  /* terminate string */

      if (c == EOF)                 /* EOF */
            i = EOF;
```

```
        return(i);                     /* return line size */

}


/*##############################################*/


/***************************************************

  FILE NAME    : parselib.h
  AUTHOR       : Matt Weisfeld

  DESCRIPTION : header for parselib.c

***************************************************/
#ifdef ANSI
int get_token (char *, char **);
int getline(FILE *, char *);
#else
int get_token ();
int getline();
#endif

/*##############################################*/


/***************************************************

  FILE NAME    : er.h
  AUTHOR       : Matt Weisfeld

  DESCRIPTION : error definitions for parse
               libaries.

***************************************************/
#define ER_NOTOPEN  0      /* can't open file */

/*##############################################*/
```

```
/*************************************************

  FILE NAME   : errdefs.h
  AUTHOR      : Matt Weisfeld

  DESCRIPTION : error descriptions for time
                libraries.

**************************************************/
#include "er.h"

ERROR_STRUCT error_message[] =

/* actual error messages */

{

    /* #0 */
    ER_NOTOPEN, ERROR,
    "Can't open file '%s'.",
    LASTERROR, EXIT,NULL,
};



/*###############################################*/


/*************************************************

  FILE NAME   : proto.h
  AUTHOR      : Matt Weisfeld

  DESCRIPTION : prototype file for parse
                libraries.

**************************************************/
#ifdef VMS
#include "[-.common]common.h"
#include "[-.leave]leave.h"
#include "[-.error]error.h"
#endif
```

```c
#ifdef BCC
#include "..\common\common.h"
#include "..\leave\leave.h"
#include "..\error\error.h"
#endif

#ifdef MSC
#include "..\common\common.h"
#include "..\leave\leave.h"
#include "..\error\error.h"
#endif

#ifdef HPUX
#include "../common/common.h"
#include "../leave/leave.h"
#include "../error/error.h"
#endif

#ifdef SLC
#include "../common/common.h"
#include "../leave/leave.h"
#include "../error/error.h"
#endif

#ifdef GCC
#include "../common/common.h"
#include "../leave/leave.h"
#include "../error/error.h"
#endif

#ifdef CCC
#include "../common/common.h"
#include "../leave/leave.h"
#include "../error/error.h"
#endif

#include "parslibs.h"

/*#############################################*/
```

```
$! VMS DCL PROCEDURE
$ clr
$ if (P1.eqs."") then GOTO ALL
$ if (P1.eqs."ALL") then GOTO ALL
$ if (P1.eqs."LINK") then GOTO LINK
$ set verify
$ cc/define=VMS 'P1'
$ goto LINK
$ ALL:
$     set verify
$ cc/define=VMS test
$ cc/define=VMS parslibs
$ LINK:
$ link/executable=test test,parslibs,[-.leave]leave,
[-.error]error
$ copy test.exe [weisfeld.exe]
$ set noverify


/*###########################################*/

# makefile for BCC/C++ Compiler

OBJS     = test.obj parslibs.obj
LIBS     = ..\leave\leave.obj ..\error\error.obj
HDRS     = proto.h errdefs.h parslibs.h er.h
FLAGS    = -c -DBCC
COMP     = bcc

test.exe:  $(OBJS)
      $(COMP) $(OBJS) $(LIBS)

test.obj: test.c $(HDRS)
      $(COMP) $(FLAGS) test.c

parslibs.obj: parslibs.c $(HDRS)
      $(COMP) $(FLAGS) parslibs.c

test.c:
parslibs.c:

parslibs.h:
```

```
/*###############################################*/

# makefile for MSC/C++ Compiler

OBJS     = test.obj parslibs.obj
LIBS     = ..\leave\leave.obj ..\error\error.obj
HDRS     = proto.h errdefs.h parslibs.h er.h
FLAGS    = /c /DMSC
COMP     = cl

test.exe:  $(OBJS)
      $(COMP) $(OBJS) $(LIBS)

test.obj: test.c $(HDRS)
      $(COMP) $(FLAGS) test.c

parslibs.obj: parslibs.c $(HDRS)
      $(COMP) $(FLAGS) parslibs.c

test.c:
parslibs.c:

parslibs.h:

/*###############################################*/

# makefile for HPUX C COMpiler

OBJS     = test.o parslibs.o
LIBS     = ../leave/leave.o ../error/error.o
HDRS     = proto.h errdefs.h parslibs.h er.h
FLAGS    = -c -DHPUX -Aa
COMP     = cc

test.exe:  $(OBJS)
      $(COMP) -o test $(OBJS) $(LIBS)

test.o: test.c $(HDRS)
      $(COMP) $(FLAGS) test.c

parslibs.o: parslibs.c $(HDRS)
      $(COMP) $(FLAGS) parslibs.c
```

```
test.c:
parslibs.c:

parslibs.h:


/*##############################################*/

# makefile for SUN SLC C COMpiler

OBJS    = test.o parslibs.o
LIBS    = ../leave/leave.o ../error/error.o
HDRS    = proto.h errdefs.h parslibs.h er.h
FLAGS   = -c -DSLC
COMP    = cc

test.exe:  $(OBJS)
       $(COMP) -o test $(OBJS) $(LIBS)

test.o: test.c $(HDRS)
       $(COMP) $(FLAGS) test.c

parslibs.o: parslibs.c $(HDRS)
       $(COMP) $(FLAGS) parslibs.c

test.c:
parslibs.c:

parslibs.h:


/*##############################################*/

# makefile for SUN GCC C COMpiler

OBJS    = test.o parslibs.o
LIBS    = ../leave/leave.o ../error/error.o
HDRS    = proto.h errdefs.h parslibs.h er.h
FLAGS   = -c -DGCC
COMP    = gcc

test.exe:  $(OBJS)
       $(COMP) -o test $(OBJS) $(LIBS)
```

```
test.o: test.c $(HDRS)
        $(COMP) $(FLAGS) test.c

parslibs.o: parslibs.c $(HDRS)
        $(COMP) $(FLAGS) parslibs.c

test.c:
parslibs.c:

parslibs.h:



/*###############################################*/

# makefile for CCC compiler

OBJS    = test.o parslibs.o
LIBS    = ../leave/leave.o ../error/error.o
HDRS    = proto.h errdefs.h parslibs.h er.h
FLAGS   = -c -DCCC
COMP    = cc

test.exe:  $(OBJS)
        $(COMP) -o test $(OBJS) $(LIBS)

test.o: test.c $(HDRS)
        $(COMP) $(FLAGS) test.c

parslibs.o: parslibs.c $(HDRS)
        $(COMP) $(FLAGS) parslibs.c

test.c:
parslibs.c:

parslibs.h:
```

7.5 SELECTED REFERENCE

Kernighan, Brian W. and Dennis M. Ritchie. *The C Programming Language*, 2nd ed. Englewood Cliffs, N.J.: Prentice Hall, 1988, p. 29.

## 8

Random Number Generation

Many applications, such as simulations, require random number generation. (Because this book assumes basic knowledge of random number theory, this concept will not be elaborated on here.) While the process of producing random numbers is fairly straightforward, it is nonetheless useful to build a library for this purpose. Despite the fact that there is really no way to produce truly random numbers, the approximations produced by these libraries are more than sufficient for most purposes.

8.1 RANDOM NUMBERS WITHIN A RANGE

The majority of random number applications require that a random number be produced within a range. For instance, it may be determined that a simulation has a distribution of 0 to 100. Thus, the random numbers generated must be between 0 and 100.

Computers are not particularly suited for random number generation. While the arrival of customers at a store may be genuinely random, due to the randomness of human nature, computers are very structured machines that are better equipped to handle structured, repeatable behavior. Thus a computer simulation of customer arrivals cannot exactly mimic the true arrival patterns of nature. However, the pseudorandom numbers created by the computer do match real random numbers closely enough so that they are more than adequate for most situations.

One characteristic of pseudorandom numbers provides a benefit not inherent in actual random numbers: repeatability. In most cases, pseudorandom numbers are calculated from a seed. Thus if the same seed is provided, the order of numbers produced will always be the same. This allows the same sequence of numbers to be used in multiple simulations, while other parameters may be varied to accumulate multiple sets of test data.

8.2 *srand( )* AND *rand( )*

A discussion of the actual code required to generate pseudorandom numbers should make these concepts clearer. All platforms use versions of two functions for this purpose. These functions are called *srand( )* and *rand( )*. The seed can be any valid integer—in this case, we use 32767:

```
#define SEED 32767
```

The seed is set by calling *srand( )*:

```
srand(SEED);
```

This initializes the random number generator. The function *srand( )* differs depending on the platform. UNIX has the following prototype:

```
int srand(int);
```

DOS and VMS have another form:

```
void srand(unsigned);
```

In all cases, no return value is expected.

The actual random numbers are generated by the *rand( )* function, which has the following format:

```
int rand (void);
```

A call to *rand( )* returns the next pseudorandom number in the sequence. In VMS, a call will produce a number in the range 0–((2^31)-1) with a period of 2^31. The HP-UX machine produces numbers in the range 0–((2^15)-1) with a period of 2^32. BORLAND produces numbers in the same range and the same period as HP-UX. A period is the quantity of numbers that are generated before the sequence repeats. A simulation would have to be quite large before such repetition occurred.

8.3 NUMBER RANGES

The problem with *rand( )* is that the numbers that it produces are raw and almost certainly not useful in this form. Fortunately, there is a simple technique to convert these raw numbers into numbers that fall within a desired range—the modula operator (%).

Suppose that the required range is between 0 and 9. If any integer is divided by 10, the resulting remainder will always be between 0 and 9. Establishing this range is accomplished by coding the following:

```
int random_num (range)
int range;
{

    int rnd, num;

    rnd = rand();

    num = rnd%range;

    return (num);

}
```

The variable *num* contains the remainder, a number within the desired range. This simple routine is all that is needed to produce sufficiently random numbers.

8.4 USING THE RANDOM NUMBER LIBRARY

The test program for *randlibs* uses a range value of 100 to produce five random numbers. The application must call the *srand( )* function prior to generation of the numbers. The seed value of 32767 is defined in *randlibs.h*. This value could just as easily be defined in the application program itself. Note that no matter how many times the program is run, the sequence of numbers is always the same. Try running the program on different platforms to compare results. Using the *randlibs* library is as simple as linking it with the application program.

8.5 CONCLUSION

The act of generating random numbers is not that difficult. However, the implementations of the different platforms are slightly different. To overcome these differences, as well as to simplify the process in general, these libraries provide a valuable service.

```c
/****************************************************

   FILE NAME   : test.c
   AUTHOR      : Matt Weisfeld

   DESCRIPTION : test  program for randlibs

****************************************************/
#include <stdio.h>
#include "proto.h"
#include "errdefs.h"

main()
{


        int i;
        int x;

        int range=100;
```

```
        srand (SEED);

        for (i=0;i<5;i++) {

                printf ("\n#####\n");

                if ( (x = random_num(range)) == -1) {
                        error (ER_NOZERO);
                }

                printf ("x = %d\n",x);

        }

        leave (EXIT_NORMAL);

        return(EXIT_NORMAL);

}

/*#############################################*/


/****************************************************

  FILE NAME    : randlibs.c
  AUTHOR       : Matt Weisfeld

  DESCRIPTION : generate random numbers

****************************************************/
#include <stdio.h>
#include <stdlib.h>
#include <math.h>
#include "proto.h"
/****************************************************

  ROUTINE NAME : random_num()

  DESCRIPTION  : get a random number within a
                 range
```

```
   INPUT        : int (range)

   OUTPUT       : int (random num)

***************************************************/
int random_num (range)
int range;
{

     int rnd;

     if (range == 0) {
             printf ("Error: can't have a zero\n");
             return (-1);
     }

     rnd = rand();

     return (rnd%range);

}

/*#############################################*/


/***************************************************

   FILE NAME   : randlibs.h
   AUTHOR      : Matt Weisfeld

   DESCRIPTION : header file for randlibs.c

***************************************************/
#define SEED 32767


#ifdef ANSI

#ifndef VMS
#ifndef GCC
void srand(unsigned);
#endif
#else
```

```
int srand(int);
#endif

int rand (void);
int random_num(int);

#else

#ifndef VMS
#ifndef SLC
void srand();
#endif
#else
int srand();
#endif
int rand ();
int random_num();
#endif


/*#############################################*/


/***************************************************

   FILE NAME    : er.h
   AUTHOR       : Matt Weisfeld

   DESCRIPTION : error definition for randlibs

***************************************************/
#define ER_NOZERO   0      /* zero not allowed */

/*#############################################*/


/***************************************************

   FILE NAME    : errdefs.h
   AUTHOR       : Matt Weisfeld

   DESCRIPTION : error strings for randlibs.c

***************************************************/
```

```c
#include "er.h"

ERROR_STRUCT error_message[] =

/* actual error messages */

{

        /* #0 */
        ER_NOZERO, EXIT,
        "A zero is not allowed in this context.",
        /* LAST */
        LASTERROR, EXIT,
};


/*####################################################*/


/****************************************************

   FILE NAME    : proto.h
   AUTHOR       : Matt Weisfeld

   DESCRIPTION : prototype file for random number
                 libraries.

****************************************************/
#ifdef VMS
#include "[-.common]common.h"
#include "[-.leave]leave.h"
#include "[-.error]error.h"
#endif

#ifdef BCC
#include "..\common\common.h"
#include "..\leave\leave.h"
#include "..\error\error.h"
#endif

#ifdef MSC
#include "..\common\common.h"
```

```
#include "..\leave\leave.h"
#include "..\error\error.h"
#endif

#ifdef HPUX
#include "../common/common.h"
#include "../leave/leave.h"
#include "../error/error.h"
#endif

#ifdef SLC
#include "../common/common.h"
#include "../leave/leave.h"
#include "../error/error.h"
#endif

#ifdef GCC
#include "../common/common.h"
#include "../leave/leave.h"
#include "../error/error.h"
#endif

#ifdef CCC
#include "../common/common.h"
#include "../leave/leave.h"
#include "../error/error.h"
#endif

#include "randlibs.h"

/*###############################################*/

$! VMS DCL PROCEDURE
$ clr
$ if (P1.eqs."") then GOTO ALL
$ if (P1.eqs."ALL") then GOTO ALL
$ if (P1.eqs."LINK") then GOTO LINK
$ set verify
$ cc/define=VMS 'P1'
$ goto LINK
$ ALL:
$      set verify
```

```
$ cc/define=VMS test
$ cc/define=VMS randlibs
$ LINK:
$ link/executable=test test,randlibs,[-.leave]leave.obj,
[-.error]error.obj
$ copy test.exe [weisfeld.exe]
$ set noverify
```

```
/*###############################################*/

# makefile for BCC/C++ Compiler

OBJS    = test.obj randlibs.obj
LIBS    = ..\leave\leave.obj ..\error\error.obj
HDRS    = proto.h errdefs.h randlibs.h er.h
FLAGS   = -c -DBCC
COMP    = bcc

test.exe:  $(OBJS)
       $(COMP) $(OBJS) $(LIBS)

test.obj: test.c $(HDRS)
       $(COMP) $(FLAGS) test.c

randlibs.obj: randlibs.c $(HDRS)
       $(COMP) $(FLAGS) randlibs.c

test.c:
randlibs.c:

randlibs.h:


/*###############################################*/

# makefile for MSC/C++ Compiler

OBJS    = test.obj randlibs.obj
LIBS    = ..\leave\leave.obj ..\error\error.obj
HDRS    = proto.h errdefs.h randlibs.h er.h
FLAGS   = /c /DMSC
COMP    = cl
```

```
test.exe:  $(OBJS)
       $(COMP) $(OBJS) $(LIBS)

test.obj: test.c $(HDRS)
       $(COMP) $(FLAGS) test.c

randlibs.obj: randlibs.c $(HDRS)
       $(COMP) $(FLAGS) randlibs.c

test.c:
randlibs.c:

randlibs.h:


/*###########################################*/

# makefile for HPUX C Compiler

OBJS     = test.o randlibs.o
LIBS     = ../leave/leave.o ../error/error.o
HDRS     = proto.h errdefs.h randlibs.h er.h
FLAGS    = -c -DHPUX -Aa
COMP     = cc

test.exe:  $(OBJS)
       $(COMP) -o test $(OBJS) $(LIBS)

test.o: test.c $(HDRS)
       $(COMP) $(FLAGS) test.c

randlibs.o: randlibs.c $(HDRS)
       $(COMP) $(FLAGS) randlibs.c

test.c:
randlibs.c:

randlibs.h:

/*###########################################*/

# makefile for SUN SLC C Compiler
```

```
OBJS      = test.o randlibs.o
LIBS      = ../leave/leave.o ../error/error.o
HDRS      = proto.h errdefs.h randlibs.h er.h
FLAGS     = -c -DSLC
COMP      = cc

test.exe:  $(OBJS)
        $(COMP) -o test $(OBJS) $(LIBS)

test.o: test.c $(HDRS)
        $(COMP) $(FLAGS) test.c

randlibs.o: randlibs.c $(HDRS)
        $(COMP) $(FLAGS) randlibs.c

test.c:
randlibs.c:

randlibs.h:

/*###########################################*/

# makefile for SUN GCC C Compiler

OBJS      = test.o randlibs.o ../leave/leave.o ../error/error.o
HDRS      = proto.h errdefs.h randlibs.h er.h ../leave/leave.h \
            ../error/error.h
FLAGS     = -c -DGCC
COMP      = gcc

test.exe:  $(OBJS)
        $(COMP) -o test $(OBJS)

test.o: test.c
        $(COMP) $(FLAGS) test.c

randlibs.o: randlibs.c
        $(COMP) $(FLAGS) randlibs.c

test.c: $(HDRS)
randlibs.c: $(HDRS)
```

```
randlibs.h:

../leave/leave.h:
../error/error.h:


/*###############################################*/

# makefile for CCC Compiler

OBJS    = test.o randlibs.o
LIBS    = ../leave/leave.o ../error/error.o
HDRS    = proto.h errdefs.h randlibs.h er.h
FLAGS   = -c -DCCC
COMP    = cc

test.exe:  $(OBJS)
       $(COMP) -o test $(OBJS) $(LIBS)

test.o: test.c $(HDRS)
       $(COMP) $(FLAGS) test.c

randlibs.o: randlibs.c $(HDRS)
       $(COMP) $(FLAGS) randlibs.c

test.c:
randlibs.c:

randlibs.h:
```

9

Interfacing with the Operating System

Under normal circumstances, a programmer is only concerned with the environment that is in effect when a particular program is being executed and ceases to exist when the process is terminated. There are times, however, when communication needs to be established between a process and an environment outside of that process. In most cases, that environment is the operating system itself. Information such as operating system version and executable PATH are just a few of the pieces of information available.

This is where environment variables come into play. Environment variables are used by an operating system in a manner similar to variables in programs. All the platforms discussed in this book support environment variables. Fortunately, the C constructs to access these variables are quite consistent. Environment variables are defined by the system itself outside of the scope of an individual program, at either the system level or the user level.

9.1 ACCESSING INFORMATION IN ENVIRONMENT VARIABLES

Most operating systems support some form of environment variables. Even though the method for accessing the environment variables is portable within the C program, the various ways of defining the environment variable are system dependent.

There are several portability issues of note. First, VMS and DOS are not case sensitive. Be aware of this when creating variable names. Second, the convention for VMS environment variables is to use dollar signs ($) in the variable names such as *NODE$NAME* and *OS$VERSION*. These variable names are not portable, as UNIX considers the ($) an escape character.

For example, suppose two environment variables need to be defined: one to represent the node name and the other to represent the operating system version. To define the necessary environment variables in the local environment (i.e., only for the local login session), the following statements are executed.

For UNIX:

```
setenv NODE_NAME "NODE (CASPER)"
setenv OS_VERSION "HP_UX A.B8.05 A 9000/720"
```

This information can be viewed by typing the UNIX command *set*.

For VMS:

```
define NODE_NAME "NODE (CASPER)"
define OS_VERSION "VAX/VMS V5.2" ;
```

This information can be viewed by typing the VMS command *sho sym all*.

For DOS:

```
NODE_NAME="NODE (CASPER)"
OS_VERSION="DOS 5.0"
```

This information can be viewed by typing the DOS command *set*.

The code to access these environment variables is the same in all cases:

```
if ( (node_name = (char *) getenv("NODE_NAME")) == NULL) {
    error();
}
```

9.2 CREATING ENVIRONMENT VARIABLES

While all platforms have a *getenv*( ) command that behaves in a consistent manner at the command line, creating environment variables from a program is not as straightforward.

DOS and UNIX have a command called *putenv*( ) which creates an environment variable. The command is:

```
if ( (putenv(string) ) != 0)
    return(-1);
```

where *string* is of the format:

```
string = "var=val"
```

To define an environment variable called *TEST1* and assign it the value *test1,* the following command is used:

```
if ( (putenv("TEST1=test1") ) != 0)
    return(-1);
```

Unlike DOS and UNIX, VMS has no *putenv*( ) command. To set an environment variable in VMS, one of two approaches can be used. Either the VMS low-level commands can be used from within the program, or the *system*( ) command can be used. The system command is more easily understood, so it is used here.

```
system ("define/job TEST1 test1");
```

The */job* flag is necessary because without it the variable would only exist as long as the process itself. By using the */job* qualifier, the variable remains defined even after the process is terminated. If the variable will not be needed after the process terminates, simply use *define*.

It is obvious that VMS, UNIX, and DOS cannot use the same code. Thus a portable library is created to handle all possibilities. Two issues actually arise here. One is the command itself, since two different commands must be incorporated. The other issue is the string, since VMS uses a different format from that required by DOS and UNIX. The portable function is called *put_env( )*. A sample call is:

```
put_env("TEST1", "test1");
```

The routine is built in this way:

```
int put_env(var, string)
char *var;
char *string;
{

    char buffer[80];

#ifdef VMS

    sprintf (buffer, "define/job \"%s \"%s", var, string);

    system (buffer);

#else

    sprintf (buffer, "%s=%s", var, string);

    printf ("buffer = %s\n", buffer);

    if ( (putenv(string) ) != 0)
        return(-1);

#endif

    return(0);

}
```

Since the formats for VMS are different from the others, the string is built in the *put_env( )* function and is thus transparent to the programmer. The *putenv( )* command for DOS and UNIX returns a nonzero if the command fails. The return value is passed back by *put_env( )*. The VMS system command does not know whether or not the command is successful, so the return code does not provide much information.

A portable function for *get_env( )* is also provided. However, since all three platforms use the same format, this function is mostly redundant. The only value it provides is to utilize the *get_env( )* function in a manner similar to that in which the other functions, which are not consistent, are used. Also, *get_env( )* allows the programmer to process any other information or commands from within the routine.

VMS provides a DCL command called *show logical* to view a specific environment variable. You may call *show logical* in this manner:

```
show logical env_var
```

DOS and UNIX do not have a similar construct. To view an environment variable from these operating systems, the *set* command can be used to list all environment variables. A routine called *show_var( )* takes advantage of the VMS command, but cannot be used for DOS or UNIX.

```
if ( (os_version = (char *) getenv("OS_VERSION")) == NULL) {
    error();
}
```

The function *getenv( )* returns a character pointer to the contents of the environment variable.

Note: In VMS, if the argument to *getenv( )* does not match any string in the user's environment array, *getenv( )* will attempt to translate the argument as if it were a logical name. All four VMS logical tables are searched. If this fails, an attempt is made to translate the string as a CLI interface. If this fails, *getenv( )* returns a NULL. This is an important point, since the search order will have an impact on the value returned by *getenv( )* and may produce unexpected results.

9.3 THE COMMAND LINE AND ENVIRONMENT VARIABLES

Two types of parameters can be passed via the command line: the argument list and the environment variable list. The argument list, which calls the child process, is mandatory. The environment variable list is optional but useful because it allows a child process to be initiated within a different environment. Recall that when accepting arguments from a command line, a program's main procedure looks like:

```
main(argc,argv,envp);
int argc;
char *argv[];
char **envp[];
```

When a C command is executed, the command line itself is placed in an argument list called *argv*. The character pointer *argv* points to an array of pointers that in turn point to the individual parameters within the command list. The list is terminated with a NULL. The arguments that make up the list are separated by white space and also terminated by a NULL, making each of them a valid string. The sample command line

```
command one two three
```

is represented internally in Figure 9.1. The optional environment variables are built in the same way as the command line, utilizing a pointer to pointers.

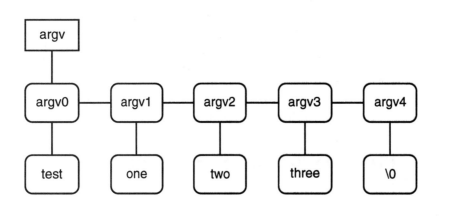

Figure 9.1

Under normal circumstances, a child inherits most of the parent's environment attributes. Using the environment variables when creating child processes allows the child to be initiated within a different environment. The variables that can be changed are HOME, TERM, PATH, and USER. An example is:

```
char *argv[] = {"getenv",NULL};

char *envp[] = { "HOME = /test/home",
            "TERM = vt100",
            "PATH = /test/bin",
            "USER = test"
            NULL                }
```

This command creates an environment for the child without changing the environment of the parent:

```
execve(argv[0], argv, envp);
```

9.4 USING THE ENVIRONMENT LIBRARY

The test program for *envlibs* creates an environment variable called *test6*. To test the *get_env( )* library, the value for the PATH environment variable is extracted. Note that the *show_env( )* function is not supported on all platforms. Make sure that a character pointer is used when the *get_env( )* function is called.

To use operating environment libraries within an application, simply link in the object libraries for *envlibs*. There are no special considerations to take into account.

9.5 CONCLUSION

As application programs become much more sophisticated, users expect to see features that require interaction with the operating system. As an example, consider most DOS software packages purchased today. These programs will most likely offer to alter the *PATH* variable in the *autoexec.bat* file. This communication is facilitated through the use of environment variables.

```
/*******************************************************

   FILE NAME    : test.c
   AUTHOR       : Matt Weisfeld

   DESCRIPTION : test program for environment
                 libraries.

*******************************************************/
#include <stdio.h>
#include <stdlib.h>
#include "proto.h"
#include "errdefs.h"

main()
{

        char *string;
        char path[STRLEN];

        /* test put_env() */

        printf ("PUT TEST6\n");
        if ( (put_env ("TEST6", "test6")) == -1)
              error(ER_BADPUTENV);

        /* test show_env() */

        printf ("SHOW TEST6\n");
        if ( (show_env("TEST6")) == -1)
              error(WR_NOSUPPORT);

        /* test get_env() */

        printf ("GET PATH\n");
        if ( (get_env ("PATH", path)) == -1)
              error(ER_BADPUTENV);

        printf ("PATH = %s\n", path);

        leave(EXIT_NORMAL);
```

```
            return(EXIT_NORMAL);

}


/*#########################################*/


/***************************************************

    FILE NAME    : envlibs.c
    AUTHOR       : Matt Weisfeld

    DESCRIPTION : environment interface routines.

***************************************************/
#include <stdio.h>
#include <stdlib.h>
#include <string.h>
#include "proto.h"


/***************************************************

    ROUTINE NAME : get_env()

    DESCRIPTION  : retrieve environment variable.

    INPUT        : char * (env var name)

    OUTPUT       : char * (env var string)

***************************************************/
int get_env(var, string)
char *var;
char *string;
{

        char *buffer;

        if ( (buffer = getenv(var) ) == NULL) {
                return(-1);
        };
```

```
        strcpy (string, buffer);

        return(0);
}

/**************************************************

  ROUTINE NAME : put_env()

  DESCRIPTION  : create environment variable.

  INPUT        : char * (env var name)
                 char * (env var string)

  OUTPUT       : int (status)

**************************************************/
int put_env(var, string)
char *var;
char *string;
{

        char buffer[80];

#ifdef VMS

        sprintf (buffer, "define/job \"%s\" \"%s\"", var, string);

        system (buffer);

#else

        sprintf (buffer, "%s=%s", var, string);

        if ( (putenv(buffer) ) != 0)
              return(-1);

#endif

        return(0);

}
```

```
/**************************************************

  ROUTINE NAME : show_env()

  DESCRIPTION  : retrieve environment variable.

  INPUT        : char * (env var name)

  OUTPUT       : int (status)

**************************************************/
int show_env(string)
char *string;
{

     int status=0;

#ifdef VMS

     char buffer[80];

     sprintf (buffer, "show logical %s", string);

     system (buffer);

#else

     status = -1;

#endif

     return(status);

}

/*###############################################*/


/**************************************************

  FILE NAME   : envlibs.h
  AUTHOR      : Matt Weisfeld
```

```
   DESCRIPTION : header file for environment
                 libraries.

*****************************************************/
#ifdef ANSI
int show_env(char *);
int put_env(char *, char *);
int get_env(char *, char *);
#else
int show_env();
int put_env();
int get_env();
#endif

/*#############################################*/


/*****************************************************

   FILE NAME   : er.h
   AUTHOR      : Matt Weisfeld

   DESCRIPTION : error definitions for envlibs.

*****************************************************/
#define ER_BADPUTENV0        /* put_env failed */
#define WR_NOSUPPORT1        /* feature not supported */

/*#############################################*/


/*****************************************************

   FILE NAME   : errdefs.h
   AUTHOR      : Matt Weisfeld

   DESCRIPTION : error descriptions for envlibs.

*****************************************************/
#include "er.h"

ERROR_STRUCT error_message[] =
```

```
/* actual error messages */

{

        /* #0 */
        ER_BADPUTENV, EXIT,
        "put_env failed.",
        /* #1 */
        WR_NOSUPPORT, RETURN,
        "This function not supported on this platform.",
        LASTERROR, EXIT,NULL,

};


/*###########################################*/

/***************************************************

  FILE NAME   : proto.h
  AUTHOR      : Matt Weisfeld

  DESCRIPTION : prototype file for the envlibs
                library.

***************************************************/
#ifdef VMS
#include "[-.common]common.h"
#include "[-.leave]leave.h"
#include "[-.error]error.h"
#endif

#ifdef BCC
#include "..\common\common.h"
#include "..\leave\leave.h"
#include "..\error\error.h"
#endif

#ifdef MSC
#include "..\common\common.h"
#include "..\leave\leave.h"
#include "..\error\error.h"
#endif
```

```
#ifdef HPUX
#include "../common/common.h"
#include "../leave/leave.h"
#include "../error/error.h"
#endif

#ifdef SLC
#include "../common/common.h"
#include "../leave/leave.h"
#include "../error/error.h"
#endif

#ifdef GCC
#include "../common/common.h"
#include "../leave/leave.h"
#include "../error/error.h"
#endif

#ifdef CCC
#include "../common/common.h"
#include "../leave/leave.h"
#include "../error/error.h"
#endif

#include "envlibs.h"

/*#############################################*/

$! VMS DCL PROCEDURE
$ clr
$ if (P1.eqs."") then GOTO ALL
$ if (P1.eqs."ALL") then GOTO ALL
$ if (P1.eqs."LINK") then GOTO LINK
$ set verify
$ cc/define=VMS 'P1'
$ goto LINK
$ ALL:
$      set verify
$ cc/define=VMS test
$ cc/define=VMS envlibs
$ LINK:
$ link/executable=test test,envlibs,[-.leave]leave,[-.error]error
```

```
$ copy test.exe [weisfeld.exe]
$ set noverify

/*###############################################*/

# makefile for BCC/C++ Compiler

OBJS    = test.obj envlibs.obj
LIBS    = ..\leave\leave.obj ..\error\error.obj
HDRS    = proto.h errdefs.h envlibs.h er.h
FLAGS   = -c -DBCC
COMP    = bcc

test.exe:  $(OBJS)
       $(COMP) $(OBJS) $(LIBS)

test.obj: test.c $(HDRS)
       $(COMP) $(FLAGS) test.c

envlibs.obj: envlibs.c $(HDRS)
       $(COMP) $(FLAGS) envlibs.c

test.c:
envlibs.c:

envlibs.h:

/*###############################################*/

# makefile for MSC/C++ Compiler

OBJS    = test.obj envlibs.obj
LIBS    = ..\leave\leave.obj ..\error\error.obj
HDRS    = proto.h errdefs.h envlibs.h er.h
FLAGS   = /c /DMSC
COMP    = cl

test.exe:  $(OBJS)
       $(COMP) $(OBJS) $(LIBS)

test.obj: test.c $(HDRS)
       $(COMP) $(FLAGS) test.c
```

```
envlibs.obj: envlibs.c $(HDRS)
        $(COMP) $(FLAGS) envlibs.c

test.c:
envlibs.c:

envlibs.h:

/*#################################################*/

# makefile for HPUX C Compiler

OBJS    = test.o envlibs.o
LIBS    = ../leave/leave.o ../error/error.o
HDRS    = proto.h errdefs.h envlibs.h er.h
FLAGS   = -c -DHPUX -Aa
COMP    = cc

test.exe:  $(OBJS)
        $(COMP) -o test $(OBJS) $(LIBS)

test.o: test.c $(HDRS)
        $(COMP) $(FLAGS) test.c

envlibs.o: envlibs.c $(HDRS)
        $(COMP) $(FLAGS) envlibs.c

test.c:
envlibs.c:

envlibs.h:

/*#################################################*/

# makefile for SUN SLC C Compiler

OBJS    = test.o envlibs.o
LIBS    = ../leave/leave.o ../error/error.o
HDRS    = proto.h errdefs.h envlibs.h er.h
FLAGS   = -c -DSLC
COMP    = cc
```

```
test.exe:  $(OBJS)
       $(COMP) -o test $(OBJS) $(LIBS)

test.o: test.c $(HDRS)
       $(COMP) $(FLAGS) test.c

envlibs.o: envlibs.c $(HDRS)
       $(COMP) $(FLAGS) envlibs.c

test.c:
envlibs.c:

envlibs.h:

/*##############################################*/

# makefile for SUN GCC C Compiler

OBJS      = test.o envlibs.o
LIBS      = ../leave/leave.o ../error/error.o
HDRS      = proto.h errdefs.h envlibs.h er.h
FLAGS     = -c -DGCC
COMP      = gcc

test.exe:  $(OBJS)
       $(COMP) -o test $(OBJS) $(LIBS)

test.o: test.c $(HDRS)
       $(COMP) $(FLAGS) test.c

envlibs.o: envlibs.c $(HDRS)
       $(COMP) $(FLAGS) envlibs.c

test.c:
envlibs.c:

envlibs.h:

/*##############################################*/

# makefile for CCC Compiler
```

```
OBJS      = test.o envlibs.o
LIBS      = ../leave/leave.o ../error/error.o
HDRS      = proto.h errdefs.h envlibs.h er.h
FLAGS     = -c -DCCC
COMP      = cc

test.exe:  $(OBJS)
        $(COMP) -o test $(OBJS) $(LIBS)

test.o: test.c $(HDRS)
        $(COMP) $(FLAGS) test.c

envlibs.o: envlibs.c $(HDRS)
        $(COMP) $(FLAGS) envlibs.c

test.c:
envlibs.c:

envlibs.h:
```

10

Trapping Signals

Program crashes pose a serious problem for any software product. Whether the product is intended solely for internal use or sold externally to customers, it is imperative that the program always maintain control. Program crashes also present a debugging headache since they rarely produce any intelligent information when one does occur.

10.1 TRAPPING SIGNALS

A signal is generated when an unusual event, called an exception, occurs within a program. These events include programming errors, user interrupts (e.g., typing CTRL-C), and signals generated internally by the program itself. Under most conditions, an exception will terminate the process and leave the user at the operating system prompt. However, it is possible to trap certain signals and install a signal handler to determine what action, if any, should be taken. Consider the following C code:

```
int level3()
{
        int i;
```

```
    i = i/0;

    return(3);
}
```

A "divide by zero" exception will obviously occur, leading to a program crash.

The *signal( )* function is used to trap exceptions. Its prototype is as follows:

```
#include <signal.h>

void (*signal(int sig,void (*func)(int,...)))) (int,...);
```

Though the prototype may seem a bit confusing, it can be broken down into two basic parts: the signal type and the signal handler. The integer *sig* is a mnemonic representing a specific signal. For example, the mnemonic for a floating point exception signal is:

```
SIGFPE
```

The value of all mnemonics is listed in *signal.h*. The function pointer *func( )* represents either an action to be taken when a signal is detected, or a function that will act as a handler for that signal. For example, the two actions that can be taken are *SIG_DFL* and *SIG_IGN,* which are called as follows:

```
signal(SIGFPE, SIG_DFL);
signal(SIGFPE, SIG_IGN);
```

In the case of *SIG_DFL,* the default action is taken—usually termination of the receiving process. *SIG_IGN* signifies that the signal should be ignored, since a particular signal may not be critical to a specific process and thus should not cause program termination. However, some signals cannot be ignored and thus will terminate the process in any event.

If neither *SIG_DFL* nor *SIG_IGN* is used, then *func( )* is considered an address to a signal handler. In its basic form, a signal handler will have a structure similar to:

```
void interrupt_handler(int sig)
{

        ...interrupt processing

}
```

When the handler is invoked, *sig* is passed as its argument. When the handler executes a *return( )*, the interrupted process continues at the point where the signal occurred. Note that in some cases the fact that an exception occurred may indicate that the program is in an unstable state. Therefore it may not be advisable or even possible to resume program execution.

A complete, very short program is written to demonstrate how a program can trap a signal using, as before, *SIGFPE:*

```
#include <stdio.h>
#include <signal.h>

void interrupt_handler(int);

main()
{

        int i;

        signal(SIGFPE, interrupt_handler);

        i = i/0;

        return;

}

void interrupt_handler(int sig)
{

        printf ("An interrupt was encountered: %d\n", sig);

        return;
}
```

When this program is executed on VMS, the following output is produced:

```
An interrupt was encountered: 8
```

The number 8 corresponds to the constant *SIGFPE* in VMS. Even though this program may seem trivial, program control is maintained thanks to *signal( )*, whereas without *signal( )* the program crashes. This is a major issue if the program is a product that is being used in a production or customer environment.

All signals can be generated explicitly within the program with a *raise( )* command. For example, to force a floating point exception, add the following code:

```
raise(SIGFPE);
```

Note, however, that VMS does not support *raise( )*.

Three of the signals, *SIGFPE, SIGILL,* and *SIGSEGV,* provide more information than the others. If these signals are generated with a *raise( )* command, when the handler is called an extra parameter specifies that the handler was called from within the program. Calling *raise( )* returns the following values in the second parameter: *FPE_EXPLICITGEN, SEGV_EXPLICITGEN,* and *ILL_EXPLICITGEN.* If *SIGFPE* is generated as a result of a floating point error, the extra parameter contains a constant representing which type of floating point exception occurred. If *SIGILL, SIGSEGV,* or an integer related *SIGFPE* occurs, then the handler is called with a third parameter—an integer pointer to the register list.

As mentioned before, when certain exceptions occur the program is left in an unstable state, and thus continuing program execution is not feasible. In some of these cases, the program state can be made stable by adjusting a register. For example, in DOS, if an integer overflow condition occurs, the AX register can be adjusted as follows to allow the program to continue:

```
*(reglist + 8) = 0;
```

Using the registers in this fashion requires intimate knowledge of what types of problems are likely to occur, and therefore this procedure may not be useful for more general purposes. Register manipulation is not used in the libraries presented in this chapter.

The example program that follows, *level.c,* generates an *FPE_INTDIV0* error. This routine provides a number of different calling sequences to illustrate how the output is presented. Experiment with other errors by using the *raise( )* command and other invalid code. What happens after a signal is trapped is up to the programmer. Some applications, such as editors, must recover and continue in a graceful manner. In other cases, it may be desirable simply to clean up, log the problem, and exit the process. In yet others it is helpful to print pertinent information about how, why, and where the exception occurred. Unfortunately, not all unwanted conditions can be trapped. For example, since DOS does not provide illegal memory protection the following code will cause unexpected results:

```
#include <stdio.h>

main()
{
  int i;
  char array[20];

    for (i=0;;i++)
      array[i] = " ";

  return;
}
```

It is entirely possible, if not probable, that this program will trounce on system memory, hang the system, and require a reboot.

Some bounds checking can be done as a preventative measure. The following simple code illustrates this point:

```
for (i=0;;i++) {
  if (i >= 20) {
  printf ("bounds error\n");
  return(ERROR);
```

```
        }
    array[i] = " ";
}
```

In any event, do not simply assume that all types of abnormal program termination will be trapped by using signals. Verify the specific functionality of signals in the programmer's manual of the individual platform.

10.2 TYPES OF EXCEPTIONS

An operating system produces many types of signals—far too many to discuss individually. For a list of the signals supported in this discussion, check the source code in *siglibs.c.* These signals were chosen for the simple reason that they are documented in the various manuals.

Perhaps the most important pieces of information to present when a signal is trapped are the name of the signal itself and a short description of what the signal is. To facilitate this process, all signals are placed in arrays with a short descriptive message that prints when appropriate. These arrays are defined using the following structures:

```
/* primary signals */

typedef struct signl {
        int   signal;
        char *message;
}SIGS;

/* secondary signal types */

typedef struct fpe {
        int   signal;
        char *message;
}SIGFLOAT;

typedef struct ill {
        int   signal;
        char *message;
}SIGILLEGAL;
```

```
typedef struct seg {
      int   signal;
      char *message;
}SIGSEGMENT;
```

These structures all follow the same format. In fact, they could all share the same structure. However, separate definitions are made for the sake of documentation. For example, the signals for DOS are defined as follows:

```
SIGS sigmess[] = {
    SIGABRT,            "Abnormal termination",
    SIGFPE,             "Arithmetic error",
    SIGILL,             "Illegal operation",
    SIGINT,             "Control-C",
    SIGSEGV,            "Illegal storage access, ",
    SIGTERM,            "Request for program termination",
    NULL,               NULL,
};
```

The expanded signal checking information is contained in the following structures:

```
SIGSEGMENT sigsegment[] = {
    SEGV_BOUND,          "Bound constraint exception",
    SEGV_EXPLICITGEN,    "raise(SIGSEGV) was executed",
    NULL,                NULL,
};

SIGILLEGAL sigillegal[] = {
    ILL_EXECUTION,       "Illegal operation attempted",
    ILL_EXPLICITGEN,     "raise(SIGILL) was executed",
    NULL,                NULL,
};

SIGFLOAT sigfloat[] = {
    FPE_INTOVFLOW,       "FPE_INTOVFLOW",
    FPE_INTDIVO,         "FPE_INTDIVO",
    FPE_INVALID,         "FPE_INVALID",
    FPE_ZERODIVIDE,      "FPE_ZERODIVIDE",
    FPE_OVERFLOW,        "FPE_OVERFLOW",
    FPE_UNDERFLOW,       "FPE_UNDERFLOW",
```

```
    FPE_INEXACT,           "FPE_INEXACT",
    FPE_EXPLICITGEN,       "FPE_EXPLICITGEN",
    NULL,                  NULL,
};
```

Since there are far too many signal variations to print here, it is important to check the code to verify which signals correspond to each platform.

There are a few special cases to note. The HP system generates the following secondary signal types:

```
#define ILLEGAL      8
#define BREAK        9
#define OPERATION   10
#define REGISTER    11

#define OVERFLOW    12
#define CONDITIONAL 13
#define EXCEPTION   14
#define EMULATION   22
```

These signals are not defined in any header file that I could locate. Thus they are explicitly placed in the *siglibs.h* file.

Any application that utilizes these signal libraries must set the signals by calling *set_signals( )*, which simply calls *signal( )* a number of times:

```
/* for DOS */

signal (SIGABRT,interrupt_handler);
signal (SIGFPE,interrupt_handler);
signal (SIGILL,interrupt_handler);
signal (SIGSEGV,interrupt_handler);
signal (SIGABRT,interrupt_handler);
signal (SIGTERM,interrupt_handler);
```

This routine need only be called once; however, if it is not called, the signal handling routines will never be invoked.

10.3 THE INTERRUPT HANDLER

The interrupt handler is designed in such a way that any application can link it in directly. In this application, the file is called *handler.c* and contains the following code:

```
void interrupt_handler(sig, type)
int sig;
int type;
{

  interrupt_message(sig,type);

  leave (EXIT_ERROR);

}
```

Each application that uses this library must have a separate handler routine that follows this convention. This routine calls the signal library routine *interrupt_message( )*, which has a similar prototype:

```
void interrupt_message(sig, type)
int sig;
int type;
```

The first thing that *interrupt_message( )* does is compare *sig* to the signal array to determine if a message is defined. This routine contains all the signal information that is available to print. For example, to print out the message for the signal itself, the following code is used:

```
for (i=0; sigmess[i].signal != NULL; i++) {

    /* if found, executed it */

    if (sigmess[i].signal == sig) {

        printf ("%s", sigmess[i].message);
```

```
            break;

    }

}

if (sigmess[i].signal == NULL) {
      clean_up (ILLSIG);
}
```

This code is very similar to the code used to search for internal functions. The type codes are searched for in the same way. Check the code for more details.

After the primary signal is processed, it is checked to see if it is one of the three signals that allow secondary types. If it is, then the type arrays are checked in a manner similar to the way in which the primary signals were checked.

10.4 USING THE SIGNAL LIBRARY

The test program for *siglibs* simply generates a divide by zero error to produce a signal that is trapped by the signal handler. Depending on the platform, either an integer divide by zero or a floating point divide by zero is executed.

Utilizing the *siglibs* library requires a bit more work than most of the others. For the majority of the libraries presented in this book, the programmer need only call the function just as any other C function and link in the appropriate object library. In the case of *siglibs,* the programmer must: call *set_signals( )* at some point in the code, create a routine called *interrupt_handler( ),* and then call *interrupt_message( )* from within *interrupt_handler( ).* Both the object library for *siglibs* and the interrupt handler must be linked into the code.

Some platforms do not trap the integer divide as defined by the *signal( )* commands in *set_signals( ).* Thus I employed floating point divides, which the nonANSI platforms use. Also, note that the MSC compiler, though it is an ANSI platform, did not trap the integer divide. An interesting point with the MSC compiler is that for floating point arithmetic, it must actually be activated before use with a command such as:

```
volatile double d = 0.0f;
```

Without this command, the floating point signal will not be trapped.

10.5 CONCLUSION

Signal trapping is a powerful program management and debugging tool that gives the programmer much more control of the program environment. Using signals buffers the user against program crashes and protects the program from unwanted user intervention such as entering a CTRL-C. Signals also provide a valuable debugging tool. The *raise*( ) function, employed in tandem with signals, is very useful in tracking down logic problems. By placing a *raise*( ) in an appropriate location, a programmer can track the execution path of a program up to the point where the problem occurred. For all these reasons, signals should be used in any software product that is distributed to users or customers.

```
/***************************************************

   FILE NAME    : test.c
   AUTHOR       : Matt Weisfeld

   DESCRIPTION  : test program for signal handler
                  library.

***************************************************/
#include <stdio.h>
#include <signal.h>
#include <errno.h>
#include "proto.h"
#include "errdefs.h"

int status;

main()
{

     int i;
```

```
#ifdef MSC
       volatile double d = 0.0f;
#else
       double d = 0.0;
#endif

       set_signals();

#ifdef MSC
       d = d/0.0;
#else
       i = i/0;
#endif

       leave (EXIT_NORMAL);

       return(EXIT_NORMAL);

}

/*****************************************************

   ROUTINE NAME : clean_up()

   DESCRIPTION  : clean-up routine for signal
                  handler library

   INPUT        : int (signal code or type)

   OUTPUT       : void

*****************************************************/
void clean_up(code)
int code;
{

       switch (code) {

       case ILLSIG:
             error(ER_ILLSIG, code);
       break;
       case ILLTYPE:
```

```
                error(ER_ILLTYPE, code);
        break;

        default:
                printf ("Cleaning up!\n");
        break;

        }

        leave (EXIT_ERROR);

        return;
}

/*###########################################*/


/***************************************************

  FILE NAME   : siglibs.c
  AUTHOR      : Matt Weisfeld

  DESCRIPTION : signal handling libraries

***************************************************/
#include <stdio.h>
#include <signal.h>
#include "proto.h"

/* used for HPUX */

#ifdef HPUX
#define ILLEGAL 8
#define BREAK 9
#define OPERATION 10
#define REGISTER 11

#define OVERFLOW 12
#define CONDITIONAL 13
#define EXCEPTION 14
#define EMULATION 22
#endif
```

```
#ifdef VMS

SIGS sigmess[] = {
    SIGHUP,   "Hang up, Data set hang up",
    SIGINT,   "Interrupt, VMS CTRL/C interrupt",
    SIGQUIT,  "Quit, CTRL/C if the action for SIGINT is
                SIG_DFL",
    SIGILL,   "Illegal instruction, reserved operand or
                reserved address mode",
    SIGTRAP,  "Trace trap, TBIT trace trap or breakpoint
                fault",
    SIGIOT,   "IOT instruction, Not implemented",
    SIGEMT,   "EMT instruction, Compatibility mode trap or
                op code reserved for customer",
    SIGFPE,   "Floating point overflow",
    SIGKILL,  "Kill, External signal only",
    SIGBUS,   "Bus error, Access violation or change user
                mode",
    SIGSEGV,  "SIGSEGV, Length violation or change mode
                supervisor",
    SIGSYS,   "SIGSYS, Bad argument to system call",
    SIGPIPE,  "Broken pipe, Not implemented",
    SIGALRM,  "Alarm clock, Timer AST",
    SIGTERM,  "Software terminate, External signal only",
    NULL,     NULL,
};

SIGILLEGAL sigillegal[] = {
    ILL_RESAD_FAULT,  "reserved addressing mode fault",
    ILL_PRIVIN_FAULT, "privileged instruction fault",
    ILL_RESOP_FAULT,  "reserved operand fault",
    NULL,             NULL,
};

SIGFLOAT sigfloat[] = {
    FPE_INTOVF_TRAP, "Integer overflow trap",
    FPE_INTDIV_TRAP, "Integer divide trap",
    FPE_FLTOVF_TRAP, "Float overflow trap",
    FPE_FLTDIV_TRAP, "Float divide trap",
    FPE_FLTUND_TRAP, "Float underflow trap",
    FPE_DECOVF_TRAP, "DECOVF trap",
    FPE_SUBRNG_TRAP, "SUBRNG trap",
```

```
        FPE_FLTOVF_FAULT,"FLTIVF fault",
        FPE_FLTDIV_FAULT,"FLTDIV fault",
        FPE_FLTUND_FAULT,"FLTUND fault",
        NULL,           NULL,
};

#endif

#ifdef DOS

SIGS sigmess[] = {
    SIGABRT,          "Abnormal termination",
    SIGFPE,           "Arithmetic error",
    SIGILL,           "Illegal operation",
#ifdef BCC
    ILL_EXPLICITGEN,    "User RASIED sigill exception",
    ILL_EXECUTION,      "Illegal operation attempted",
#endif
    SIGINT,            "Control-C",
    SIGSEGV,           "Illegal storage access, ",
#ifdef BCC
    SEGV_EXPLICITGEN,  "User RASIED segv exception",
    SEGV_BOUND,        "Bound constraint exception",
#endif
    SIGTERM,           "Request for program termination",
    NULL,           NULL,
};

#ifdef BCC

SIGSEGMENT sigsegment[] = {
    SEGV_BOUND,        "Bound constraint exception",
    SEGV_EXPLICITGEN, "raise(SIGSEGV) was executed",
    NULL,           NULL,
};

SIGILLEGAL sigillegal[] = {
    ILL_EXECUTION,   "Illegal operation attempted",
    ILL_EXPLICITGEN, "raise(SIGILL) was executed",
    NULL,           NULL,
};
```

```
SIGFLOAT sigfloat[] = {
    FPE_INTOVFLOW,          "FPE_INTOVFLOW",
    FPE_INTDIVO,            "FPE_INTDIVO",
    FPE_INVALID,            "FPE_INVALID",
    FPE_ZERODIVIDE,         "FPE_ZERODIVIDE",
    FPE_OVERFLOW,           "FPE_OVERFLOW",
    FPE_UNDERFLOW,          "FPE_UNDERFLOW",
    FPE_INEXACT,            "FPE_INEXACT",
    FPE_EXPLICITGEN,        "FPE_EXPLICITGEN",
    NULL,             NULL,
};

#endif

#ifdef MSC

SIGFLOAT sigfloat[] = {
    FPE_INVALID    , "FPE_INVALID",
    FPE_DENORMAL, "FPE_DENORMAL",
    FPE_ZERODIVIDE, "FPE_ZERODIVIDE",
    FPE_OVERFLOW, "FPE_OVERFLOW",
    FPE_UNDERFLOW, "FPE_UNDERFLOW",
    FPE_INEXACT, "FPE_INEXACT",
    FPE_UNEMULATED, "FPE_UNEMULATED",
    FPE_SQRTNEG, "FPE_SQRTNEG",
    FPE_STACKOVERFLOW, "FPE_STACKOVERFLOW",
    FPE_STACKUNDERFLOW, "FPE_STACKUNDERFLOW",
    FPE_EXPLICITGEN , "FPE_EXPLICITGEN",
    NULL,             NULL,
};

#endif

#endif

#ifdef UNIX

SIGS sigmess[] = {
    SIGABRT, "Process abort signal ",
    SIGHUP,  "Hang up, Data set hang up",
    SIGINT,  "Interrupt, VMS CTRL/C interrupt",
    SIGQUIT, "Quit, CTRL/C if the action for SIGINT is
             SIG_DFL",
```

```
        SIGILL,   "Illegal instruction, reserved operand or
                   reserved address mode",
        SIGTRAP,  "Trace trap, TBIT trace trap or breakpoint
                   fault",
        SIGIOT,   "IOT instruction, Not implemented",
        SIGEMT,   "EMT instruction, Compatibility mode trap or
                   op code reserved for customer",
        SIGFPE,   "Floating point overflow",
        SIGKILL,  "Kill, External signal only",
        SIGBUS,   "Bus error, Access violation or change user
                   mode",
        SIGSEGV,   "SIGSEGV, Length violation or change mode
                   supervisor",
        SIGSYS,    "SIGSYS, Bad argument to system call",
        SIGPIPE,   "Broken pipe, Not implemented",
        SIGALRM,   "Alarm clock, Timer AST",
        SIGTERM,   "Software terminate, External signal only",
        NULL,     NULL,

};

#ifdef HPUX

SIGILLEGAL sigillegal[] = {

        ILLEGAL, "Illegal instruction trap",
        BREAK, "Break instruction trap",
        OPERATION, "Privileged operation trap",
        REGISTER, "Privileged register trap",

};

SIGFLOAT sigfloat[] = {

        OVERFLOW, "Overflow trap",
        CONDITIONAL, "Conditional Trap",
        EXCEPTION, "Assist exception trap",
        EMULATION, "Assist emulation trap",

};

#endif
```

```
#ifdef SUN

SIGFLOAT sigfloat[] = {

    FPE_INTDIV_TRAP, "Integer divide by zero",
    FPE_STARTSIG_TRAP, "Trap V",
    FPE_FLTINEX_TRAP, "Inexact result",
    FPE_FLTDIV_TRAP, "Floating point divide by zero",
    FPE_FLTUND_TRAP, "Floating point underflow",
    FPE_FLTOPERR_TRAP, "Operand error",
    FPE_FLTOVF_TRAP, "Floating point overflow",

};

#endif

#endif

/*****************************************************

   ROUTINE NAME : set_signals()

   DESCRIPTION  : set the signals to be trapped

   INPUT        : none

   OUTPUT       : none

*****************************************************/
void set_signals()
{

#ifdef DOS
    signal (SIGABRT,interrupt_handler);
    signal (SIGFPE,interrupt_handler);
    signal (SIGILL,interrupt_handler);
    signal (SIGSEGV,interrupt_handler);
    signal (SIGABRT,interrupt_handler);
    signal (SIGTERM,interrupt_handler);
#else
    signal (SIGHUP,interrupt_handler);
    signal (SIGINT,interrupt_handler);
```

```
        signal (SIGQUIT,interrupt_handler);
        signal (SIGILL,interrupt_handler);
        signal (SIGTRAP,interrupt_handler);
        signal (SIGIOT,interrupt_handler);
        signal (SIGEMT,interrupt_handler);
        signal (SIGFPE,interrupt_handler);
        signal (SIGKILL,interrupt_handler);
        signal (SIGBUS,interrupt_handler);
        signal (SIGSEGV,interrupt_handler);
        signal (SIGSYS,interrupt_handler);
        signal (SIGPIPE,interrupt_handler);
        signal (SIGALRM,interrupt_handler);
        signal (SIGTERM,interrupt_handler);
#endif

}

/****************************************************

   ROUTINE NAME : interrupt_message()

   DESCRIPTION  : print out the signal messages

   INPUT        : int (signal)
                  int (type)

   OUTPUT       : none

****************************************************/
void interrupt_message(sig, type)
int sig;
int type;
{

    int i;
    int status;

    printf ("###################################\n");
    printf ("# An interrupt has been processed #\n");
    printf ("###################################\n\n");

    /* search internal function list for desired function */
```

```c
    for (i=0; sigmess[i].signal != NULL; i++) {

        /* if found, executed it */

        if (sigmess[i].signal == sig) {

            printf ("%s", sigmess[i].message);

            break;

        }

    }

    if (sigmess[i].signal == NULL) {
        clean_up (ILLSIG);
    }

#ifndef CCC

    switch (sig) {

        case SIGFPE:

        for (i=0; sigfloat[i].signal != NULL; i++) {

            /* if found, executed it */

            if (sigfloat[i].signal == type) {

                    printf (": %s", sigfloat[i].message);

                    break;

            }

        }

        if (sigfloat[i].signal == NULL) {
            clean_up (ILLTYPE);
        }
```

```
            break;

#ifndef MSC
#ifdef ANSI
#ifndef SUN
        case SIGILL:

        for (i=0; sigillegal[i].signal != NULL; i++) {

            /* if found, executed it */

            if (sigillegal[i].signal == type) {

                    printf (": %s", sigillegal[i].message);

                    break;

            }

        }

        if (sigillegal[i].signal == NULL) {
            clean_up (ILLTYPE);
        }

        break;

#endif
#endif
#endif

#ifdef BCC

        case SIGSEGV:

        for (i=0; sigsegment[i].signal != NULL; i++) {

            /* if found, executed it */

            if (sigsegment[i].signal == type) {

                    printf (": %s", sigsegment[i].message);
```

```
                    break;

            }

        }

        if (sigsegment[i].signal == NULL) {
            clean_up (ILLTYPE);
        }

        break;

#endif

        default:

        /* do nothing */

        break;

    }

#endif

    printf ("\n\n");

#ifdef VMS
    perror("perror");

#endif

  return;

}

/*#############################################*/
```

```
/****************************************************

    FILE NAME    : handler.c
    AUTHOR       : Matt Weisfeld

    DESCRIPTION  : interrupt handler

****************************************************/
#include <stdio.h>
#include <signal.h>
#include "proto.h"

/****************************************************

    ROUTINE NAME : interrupt_handler()

    DESCRIPTION  : process and handle a program
                   interrupt

    INPUT        : int (signal)
                   int (type)

    OUTPUT       : none

****************************************************/
void interrupt_handler(sig, type)
int sig;
int type;
{

    interrupt_message(sig,type);

    leave (EXIT_ERROR);

}

/*##############################################*/
```

```
/*****************************************************

   FILE NAME   : siglibs.h
   AUTHOR      : Matt Weisfeld

   DESCRIPTION : header file for siglibs

*****************************************************/
#include <signal.h>
#ifndef SLC
#include <float.h>
#endif

typedef struct signl {
    int  signal;
    char *message;
}SIGS;

typedef struct fpe {
    int  signal;
    char *message;
}SIGFLOAT;

typedef struct ill {
    int  signal;
    char *message;
}SIGILLEGAL;

typedef struct seg {
    int  signal;
    char *message;
}SIGSEGMENT;

#define ILLSIG -1
#define ILLTYPE -2

#ifdef ANSI
void interrupt_handler(int sig, int type);
void interrupt_message(int sig, int type);
void set_signals(void);
void clean_up(int);
#else
```

```
void interrupt_handler();
void interrupt_message();
void set_signals();
void clean_up();
#endif


/*##############################################*/


/*************************************************

  FILE NAME    : er.h
  AUTHOR       : Matt Weisfeld

  DESCRIPTION : file defintions for siglibs

*************************************************/
#define ER_ILLSIG    0      /* code not found */
#define ER_ILLTYPE   1      /* type not found */


/*##############################################*/


/*************************************************

  FILE NAME    : errdefs.h
  AUTHOR       : Matt Weisfeld

  DESCRIPTION : error definitions for siglibs

*************************************************/
#include "er.h"

ERROR_STRUCT error_message[] =

/* actual error messages */

{

    /* #0 */
    ER_ILLSIG, EXIT,
    "Illegal signal '%d'.",
```

```
    /* #1 */
    ER_ILLTYPE, EXIT,
    "Illegal type '%d'.",
    /* LAST */
    LASTERROR, EXIT,
};


/*############################################*/


/***************************************************

  FILE NAME   : proto.h
  AUTHOR      : Matt Weisfeld

  DESCRIPTION : prototype file for handler
                libraries.

***************************************************/
#ifdef VMS
#include "[-.common]common.h"
#include "[-.leave]leave.h"
#include "[-.error]error.h"
#endif

#ifdef BCC
#include "..\common\common.h"
#include "..\leave\leave.h"
#include "..\error\error.h"
#endif

#ifdef MSC
#include "..\common\common.h"
#include "..\leave\leave.h"
#include "..\error\error.h"
#endif

#ifdef HPUX
#include "../common/common.h"
#include "../leave/leave.h"
#include "../error/error.h"
#endif
```

```
#ifdef SLC
#include "../common/common.h"
#include "../leave/leave.h"
#include "../error/error.h"
#endif

#ifdef GCC
#include "../common/common.h"
#include "../leave/leave.h"
#include "../error/error.h"
#endif

#ifdef CCC
#include "../common/common.h"
#include "../leave/leave.h"
#include "../error/error.h"
#endif

#include "siglibs.h"

/*##########################################*/

$! VMS DCL PROCEDURE
$ clr
$ if (P1.eqs."") then GOTO ALL
$ if (P1.eqs."ALL") then GOTO ALL
$ if (P1.eqs."LINK") then GOTO LINK
$ set verify
$ cc/define=VMS 'P1'
$ goto LINK
$ ALL:
$    set verify
$ cc/define=VMS test
$ cc/define=VMS siglibs
$ cc/define=VMS handler
$ LINK:
$ link/executable=test test,siglibs,handler,
[-.leave]leave,[-.error]error
$ copy test.exe [weisfeld.exe]
$ set noverify

/*##########################################*/
```

```
# makefile for BCC/C++ Compiler

OBJS     = test.obj siglibs.obj handler.obj
LIBS     = ..\leave\leave.obj ..\error\error.obj
HDRS     = proto.h errdefs.h siglibs.h er.h
FLAGS    = -c -DBCC
COMP     = bcc

test.exe:  $(OBJS)
    $(COMP) $(OBJS) $(LIBS)

test.obj: test.c $(HDRS)
    $(COMP) $(FLAGS) test.c

siglibs.obj: siglibs.c $(HDRS)
    $(COMP) $(FLAGS) siglibs.c

handler.obj: handler.c $(HDRS)
    $(COMP) $(FLAGS) handler.c

test.c:
siglibs.c:
handler.c:

siglibs.h:

/*###########################################*/

# makefile for MSC/C++ Compiler

OBJS     = test.obj siglibs.obj handler.obj
LIBS     = ..\leave\leave.obj ..\error\error.obj
HDRS     = proto.h errdefs.h siglibs.h er.h
FLAGS    = /c /DMSC
COMP     = cl

test.exe:  $(OBJS)
    $(COMP) $(OBJS) $(LIBS)

test.obj: test.c $(HDRS)
    $(COMP) $(FLAGS) test.c
```

```
siglibs.obj: siglibs.c $(HDRS)
    $(COMP) $(FLAGS) siglibs.c

handler.obj: handler.c $(HDRS)
    $(COMP) $(FLAGS) handler.c

test.c:
siglibs.c:
handler.c:

siglibs.h:

/*###########################################*/

# makefile for HPUX C Compiler

OBJS    = test.o siglibs.o handler.o
LIBS    = ../leave/leave.o  ../error/error.o
HDRS    = proto.h errdefs.h siglibs.h er.h
FLAGS   = -c -DHPUX -DSOURCE_HP
COMP    = cc

test:  $(OBJS)
    $(COMP) -o test $(OBJS) $(LIBS)

test.o: test.c $(HDRS)
    $(COMP) $(FLAGS) test.c

siglibs.o: siglibs.c $(HDRS)
    $(COMP) $(FLAGS) siglibs.c

handler.o: handler.c $(HDRS)
    $(COMP) $(FLAGS) handler.c

test.c:
siglibs.c:
handler.c:

siglibs.h:

/*###########################################*/
```

```
# makefile for SUN SLC C Compiler

OBJS     = test.o siglibs.o handler.o
LIBS     = ../leave/leave.o  ../error/error.o
HDRS     = proto.h errdefs.h siglibs.h er.h
FLAGS    = -c -DSLC
COMP     = cc

test:  $(OBJS)
    $(COMP) -o test $(OBJS) $(LIBS)

test.o: test.c $(HDRS)
    $(COMP) $(FLAGS) test.c

siglibs.o: siglibs.c $(HDRS)
    $(COMP) $(FLAGS) siglibs.c

handler.o: handler.c $(HDRS)
    $(COMP) $(FLAGS) handler.c

test.c:
siglibs.c:
handler.c:

siglibs.h:


/*###########################################*/

# makefile for SUN GCC C Compiler

OBJS     = test.o siglibs.o handler.o
LIBS     = ../leave/leave.o  ../error/error.o
HDRS     = proto.h errdefs.h siglibs.h er.h
FLAGS    = -c -DGCC
COMP     = gcc

test:  $(OBJS)
    $(COMP) -o test $(OBJS) $(LIBS)

test.o: test.c $(HDRS)
    $(COMP) $(FLAGS) test.c
```

```
siglibs.o: siglibs.c $(HDRS)
    $(COMP) $(FLAGS) siglibs.c

handler.o: handler.c $(HDRS)
    $(COMP) $(FLAGS) handler.c

test.c:
siglibs.c:
handler.c:

siglibs.h:


/*###########################################*/

# makefile for CCC Compiler

OBJS    = test.o siglibs.o handler.o
LIBS    = ../leave/leave.o  ../error/error.o
HDRS    = proto.h errdefs.h siglibs.h er.h
FLAGS   = -c -DCCC
COMP    = cc

test:  $(OBJS)
    $(COMP) -o test $(OBJS) $(LIBS)

test.o: test.c $(HDRS)
    $(COMP) $(FLAGS) test.c

siglibs.o: siglibs.c $(HDRS)
    $(COMP) $(FLAGS) siglibs.c

handler.o: handler.c $(HDRS)
    $(COMP) $(FLAGS) handler.c

test.c:
siglibs.c:
handler.c:

siglibs.h:
```

## 11

Building a Command Line

A program invoked from another program is referred to as a *child process*. Any invocation of this child process must adhere to the same calling conventions required by a call from the operating environment. When a C program is initiated, the command line itself is placed in an argument list called *argv*. If the program is called directly from the operating system, the local operating system and compiler handle the construction of the *argv*-like structure. However, when a child process is called from within a program, it is up to the programmer to build an appropriate *argv* structure. This chapter presents a library designed to perform that task.

11.1 *argv*-LIKE STRUCTURES

For a program to accept command line input, a program *main( )* function must be declared as follows:

```
main(argc,argv);
int argc;
char **argv;
```

The character pointer *argv* points to an array of pointers that in turn point to the individual parameters within the command list. The list terminates with a NULL. The arguments that make up the list are separated by white space and also terminated by a NULL, making them all valid strings. A sample command line,

```
test one two three
```

is represented internally as shown in Figure 11.1.

This structure is built automatically when a C program is called from the command line. However, assume that a user file contains the following line that represents a complete call to a child process:

```
test file1 file2
```

This line is read as a character string into the variable *command.*

```
char command[STRLEN];
```

Internally, *command* looks like this:

```
command = "test file1 file2\0"
```

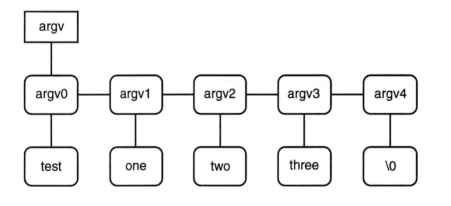

Figure 11.1

In this form, *command* cannot be used to call a child process since it is not in the *argv* structure described previously.

11.2 THE *strargv( )* FUNCTION

What is needed to call a child process from within a program is a function that will take as input a pointer to a character string containing the command, and convert that input into an *argv*-like structure. The function that performs that task, *strargv( )*, is declared as follows:

```
char **strargv(ptr)
char *ptr;
```

The important thing to notice about this function is that it returns a pointer to a pointer—in essence, an *argv*-like structure. The parameter *ptr* is the command line itself.

The main data structures in *strargv( )* are:

```
char **argv;
char buffer[STRLEN];
```

The variable *argv* is used in the same way as the standard *argv* as represented in Figure 11.2. The character string *buffer* holds the value of an individual parameter as it is built. This value is subsequently copied to the appropriate *argv* pointer.

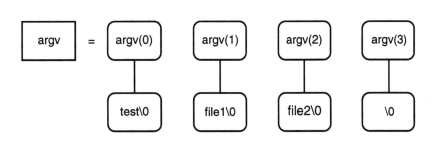

Figure 11.2

Three important counters are used in *strargv( )*:

```
int count;
int index;
int pos;
```

The variable *count* represents the number of parameters contained in the command string, in this case three (*test, file1,* and *file2*). The variable *index* represents the actual location of the parameters within the *argv* structure. For example, the command name *test* is contained in *argv*[0], so in this case *index* is zero. The variable *pos* indicates the current character position in the temporary character string *buffer*.

To identify the number of parameters in the command line, a routine named *strtokens( )* is called. The code for *strtokens( )* resembles the following:

```
#include <stdio.h>
#include "pilot.h"
#ifdef ANSI
#include <stdlib.h>
#endif
#include <ctype.h>

/* determine number of tokens in string, not including the
NULL */

int strtokens(ptr)
char *ptr;
{

    int count =  0;

    char *temp;

    temp = ptr;

    /* bypass white space */

    while (isspace(*temp)) temp++;
```

```
for (count = 0; *temp != '\0'; count++) {

    /* continue until white space of string
    terminator is found */

    while ((!isspace(*temp)) && (*temp != '\0'))
    temp++;

    /* bypass white space */

    while (isspace(*temp)) temp++;
}

return(count);

}
```

This routine accepts a string as input and counts the number of tokens—that is, characters or strings separated by white space. First, all leading white space in the string is bypassed. Then, the routine counts the number of tokens encountered before the NULL is reached. An integer containing the number of parameters is returned to the calling function.

Once *strargv( )* receives the number of parameters from *strtokens( )*, it is necessary to allocate enough space for the *argv* structure. Since *argv* is a pointer to a pointer, space for more than one pointer is required. Thus, the *calloc( )* function is used. The function *calloc( )* requires two parameters: one representing how many elements to return, and one representing the size of each element. In this case, the size of the element is the size necessary to contain a character pointer. The number of elements is already known, since the call to *strtokens( )* placed it in *count*.

```
if ((argv = (char **)calloc(count+1, sizeof(char *))) ==
NULL) {
    printf ("Error: nospace");
    return (NULL);
}
```

Note that at this point only the space for the *argv* pointers is allocated. The space for the individual parameters has not yet been determined.

Once the space for the pointers has been allocated, the *argv* list is built. After *index* is set to 0, to start at *argv*[0], *ptr* increases until the '\0' is encountered. At the outset of each pass through this loop, the variable *pos* must be reset to 0, and the *index* must increase accordingly for *argv*[1], *argv*[2], and so forth. The white space between each parameter—the '\0' terminator—delineates the parameters.

As each parameter is built, it is copied from *ptr* into *buffer,* with a '\0' terminating the resulting string.

```
while ( !isspace(*ptr) && *ptr != '\0'  ) {

    buffer[pos++] = *ptr++;

}

buffer[pos] = '\0';
```

With the parameter now in *buffer,* the space for the appropriate *argv* pointer is obtained by a call to *malloc( )* and the buffer is copied.

```
if ((argv[index] = (char *) malloc(strlen(buffer)+1)) ==
NULL) {
    printf ("Error: nospace\n");
    return (NULL);
}

strcpy (argv[index++], buffer);
```

This process continues until the NULL at the end of *ptr* is encountered. At this point, the final NULL is placed in the final *argv* pointer.

```
argv[count] = NULL;
```

The required *argv* structure is then complete and is returned to the calling program by:

```
return (argv);
```

11.3 RELEASING THE SPACE

Once the pointers are no longer needed, it is necessary to release the memory space obtained by using the *malloc( )* command. This is accomplished by using the *free( )* command. A routine named *freelist( )* is provided to release the space held by all the string pointers, including the pointer to the pointer list. First, the individual pointers obtained by the *malloc( )*s are released. Then the actual *argv,* the pointer to the pointers, is released. Here is the complete *freelist( )* routine.

```
void freelist(ptr)
char **ptr;
{

    for (i=0;ptr[i]!=NULL;i++)
       free(ptr[i]);

    free(ptr);

    return;

}
```

11.4 USING THE COMMAND LINE LIBRARY

The *argvlibs* test program builds a number of character strings in the *buffer* command. These commands are then converted into *argv* structures by calling *strargv( )*. The components of the *argv* list are printed by using a *for* loop that executes until the NULL at the end of the list is identified.

To use the *argvlibs* library, simply link the object library into the appropriate application. Note, however, that there is a major point to consider. Be aware of the space that is consumed by the *argv* lists. On some platforms, such as DOS, this can be a problem if the space is not returned after it is used.

11.5 CONCLUSION

The libraries presented in this chapter provide the tools for converting a character string into an *argv*-like structure. This functionality is necessary whenever you need to call a child process, as you will see when child processes are explained in Chapter 13. To use these library functions, simply compile the file *strargv.c* and link its object file with your application.

```
/**************************************************

  FILE NAME    : test.c
  AUTHOR       : Matt Weisfeld

  DESCRIPTION : test program for strargv

**************************************************/
#include <stdio.h>
#include <stdlib.h>
#include <string.h>
#include "proto.h"
#include "errdefs.h"

main()
{

        int i;
        int status;
        char **argv;

        char command[STRLEN];

        /* build the command */

        strcpy (command, "copy file.lst file.txt file.dat");

        printf ("command = %s\n", command);
```

```
if ( (argv = strargv(command)) == NULL)
      error (ER_ARGVFAIL);

for (i=0; argv[i] != NULL; i++) {
      printf ("argv[%d] = %s\n", i, argv[i]);
}

freelist (argv);

strcpy (command, "list file.txt");

printf ("command = %s\n", command);

argv = strargv(command);

for (i=0; argv[i] != NULL; i++)
      printf ("argv[%d] = %s\n", i, argv[i]);

freelist (argv);

strcpy (command, "remove file.txt");

printf ("command = %s\n", command);

if ( (argv = strargv(command)) == NULL)
      error (ER_ARGVFAIL);

for (i=0; argv[i] != NULL; i++)
      printf ("argv[%d] = %s\n", i, argv[i]);

freelist (argv);

leave(EXIT_NORMAL);

return(EXIT_NORMAL);

}

/*##############################################*/
```

```
/*****************************************************

   FILE NAME    : argvlibs.c
   AUTHOR       : Matt Weisfeld

   DESCRIPTION  : library for command line
                  argument routines

*****************************************************/
#include <stdio.h>
#ifdef ANSI
#include <stdlib.h>
#endif
#include <string.h>
#include <ctype.h>
#include "proto.h"
#ifdef DOS
#include <alloc.h>
#endif
/*****************************************************

   ROUTINE NAME : strargv()

   DESCRIPTION   : convert a string to argv
                   structure

   INPUT         : char *

   OUTPUT        : char **

*****************************************************/
char **strargv(ptr)
char *ptr;
{

        int count = 0, index = 0, pos=0;
        char *temp, **argv;

        char buffer[STRLEN];

        count = strtokens(ptr);
```

```
/* get space for argument */

if ((argv = (char **)calloc(count+1,
sizeof(char *))) == NULL) {
      printf ("Error: nospace");
      return (NULL);
}

while ( isspace(*ptr) )
      ptr++;

index = 0;

while (*ptr != '\0') {

      pos = 0;

      while ( !isspace(*ptr) && *ptr != '\0') {

            buffer[pos++] = *ptr++;

      }

      buffer[pos] = '\0';

      if ((argv[index] =
      (char *)malloc(strlen(buffer)+1)) == NULL) {
            printf ("Error: nospace");
            return (NULL);
      }

      strcpy (argv[index++], buffer);

      while ( isspace(*ptr) )
            ptr++;

}

argv[count] = NULL;

/* return all the arguments */
```

```
        return(argv);

}

/****************************************************

   ROUTINE NAME : freelist()

   DESCRIPTION  : return space help by argv
                  structure

   INPUT        : char **

   OUTPUT       : none

****************************************************/
void freelist(ptr)
char **ptr;
{

        int i;

        for (i=0;ptr[i]!=NULL;i++)
              free (ptr[i]);

        free (ptr);

        return;

}

/****************************************************

   ROUTINE NAME : strtokens()

   DESCRIPTION  : count number of tokens in a
                  string

   INPUT        : char *

   OUTPUT       : int (number of tokens)

****************************************************/
```

```
int strtokens(ptr)
char *ptr;
{

        int count = 0;

        char *temp;

        temp = ptr;

        /* bypass white space */

        while (isspace(*temp)) temp++;

        for (count=0; *temp != '\0'; count++) {

                /* continue until white space of string
                terminator is found */

                while ((!isspace(*temp)) && (*temp != '\0'))
                temp++;

                /* bypass white space */

                while (isspace(*temp)) temp++;

        }

        return(count);

}

/*###########################################*/


/***************************************************

  FILE NAME    : argvlibs.h
  AUTHOR       : Matt Weisfeld

  DESCRIPTION : header file for command line
                argument routines

***************************************************/
```

```
#ifdef ANSI
char **strargv(char *);
void freelist(char **);
int strtokens(char *);
#else
char **strargv();
void freelist();
int strtokens();
#endif

/*###############################################*/


/***************************************************

   FILE NAME    : er.h
   AUTHOR       : Matt Weisfeld

   DESCRIPTION : error definitions for argv library

***************************************************/
#define ER_ARGVFAIL 0      /* strargv failed */

/*###############################################*/


/***************************************************

   FILE NAME    : er.h
   AUTHOR       : Matt Weisfeld

   DESCRIPTION : error strings for argv library

***************************************************/

#include "er.h"

ERROR_STRUCT error_message[] =

/* actual error messages */

{
```

```
        /* #0 */
        ER_ARGVFAIL, EXIT,
        "A call to strargv() failed.",
        /* LAST */
        LASTERROR, EXIT,
};
```

```
/*##############################################*/


/**************************************************

   FILE NAME   : proto.h
   AUTHOR      : Matt Weisfeld

   DESCRIPTION : prototype file for argv
                 libraries.

**************************************************/
#ifdef VMS
#include "[-.common]common.h"
#include "[-.leave]leave.h"
#include "[-.error]error.h"
#endif

#ifdef BCC
#include "..\common\common.h"
#include "..\leave\leave.h"
#include "..\error\error.h"
#endif

#ifdef MSC
#include "..\common\common.h"
#include "..\leave\leave.h"
#include "..\error\error.h"
#endif

#ifdef HPUX
#include "../common/common.h"
#include "../leave/leave.h"
```

```
#include "../error/error.h"
#endif

#ifdef SLC
#include "../common/common.h"
#include "../leave/leave.h"
#include "../error/error.h"
#endif

#ifdef GCC
#include "../common/common.h"
#include "../leave/leave.h"
#include "../error/error.h"
#endif

#ifdef CCC
#include "../common/common.h"
#include "../leave/leave.h"
#include "../error/error.h"
#endif

#include "argvlibs.h"

/*###############################################*/

$! VMS DCL PROCEDURE
$ clr
$ if (P1.eqs."") then GOTO ALL
$ if (P1.eqs."ALL") then GOTO ALL
$ if (P1.eqs."LINK") then GOTO LINK
$ set verify
$ cc/define=VMS 'P1'
$ goto LINK
$ ALL:
$     set verify
$ cc/define=VMS test
$ cc/define=VMS argvlibs
$ LINK:
$ link/executable=test test,argvlibs,[-.leave]leave,
[-.error]error
$ copy test.exe [weisfeld.exe]
$ set noverify
```

```
/*###########################################*/

# makefile for BCC/C++ Compiler

OBJS    = test.obj argvlibs.obj
LIBS    = ..\leave\leave.obj ..\error\error.obj
HDRS    = proto.h errdefs.h argvlibs.h er.h
FLAGS   = -c -DBCC
COMP    = bcc

test.exe:  $(OBJS)
       $(COMP) $(OBJS) $(LIBS)

test.obj: test.c $(HDRS)
       $(COMP) $(FLAGS) test.c

argvlibs.obj: argvlibs.c $(HDRS)
       $(COMP) $(FLAGS) argvlibs.c

test.c:
argvlibs.c:

argvlibs.h:

/*###########################################*/

# makefile for MSC/C++ Compiler

OBJS    = test.obj argvlibs.obj
LIBS    = ..\leave\leave.obj ..\error\error.obj
HDRS    = proto.h errdefs.h argvlibs.h er.h
FLAGS   = /c /DMSC
COMP    = cl

test.exe:  $(OBJS)
      $(COMP) $(OBJS) $(LIBS)

test.obj: test.c $(HDRS)
      $(COMP) $(FLAGS) test.c

argvlibs.obj: argvlibs.c $(HDRS)
      $(COMP) $(FLAGS) argvlibs.c
```

```
test.c:
argvlibs.c:

argvlibs.h:

/*###########################################*/

# makefile for HPUX C Compiler

OBJS    = test.o argvlibs.o
HDRS    = argvlibs.h er.h errdefs.h proto.h
LIBS    = ../leave/leave.o ../error/error.o
FLAGS   = -c -DHPUX -Aa
COMP    = cc

test:   $(OBJS)
        $(COMP) -o test $(OBJS) $(LIBS)

test.o: test.c $(HDRS)
        $(COMP) $(FLAGS) test.c

argvlibs.o: argvlibs.c $(HDRS)
        $(COMP) $(FLAGS) argvlibs.c

test.c: $(HDRS)
argvlibs.c: $(HDRS)

argvlibs.h:
er.h:
errdefs.h:
proto.h:


/*###########################################*/

# makefile for SUN SLC C Compiler

OBJS    = test.o argvlibs.o
LIBS    = ../leave/leave.o ../error/error.o
HDRS    = ../leave/leave.h ../error/error.h
FLAGS   = -c -DSLC
COMP    = cc
```

```
test:    $(OBJS)
         $(COMP) -o test $(OBJS) $(LIBS)

test.o: test.c $(HDRS)
         $(COMP) $(FLAGS) test.c

argvlibs.o: argvlibs.c $(HDRS)
            $(COMP) $(FLAGS) argvlibs.c

test.c:
argvlibs.c:

argvlibs.h:


/*###########################################*/

# makefile for SUN GCC C Compiler

OBJS     = test.o argvlibs.o
LIBS     = ../leave/leave.o ../error/error.o
HDRS     = ../leave/leave.h ../error/error.h
FLAGS    = -c -DGCC
COMP     = gcc

test:    $(OBJS)
         $(COMP) -o test $(OBJS) $(LIBS)

test.o: test.c $(HDRS)
         $(COMP) $(FLAGS) test.c

argvlibs.o: argvlibs.c $(HDRS)
            $(COMP) $(FLAGS) argvlibs.c

test.c:
argvlibs.c:

argvlibs.h:


/*###########################################*/
```

```
# makefile for CCC Compiler

OBJS     = test.o argvlibs.o
LIBS     = ../leave/leave.o ../error/error.o
HDRS     = ../leave/leave.h ../error/error.h
FLAGS    = -c -DSLC
COMP     = cc

test:    $(OBJS)
         $(COMP) -o test $(OBJS) $(LIBS)

test.o: test.c $(HDRS)
         $(COMP) $(FLAGS) test.c

argvlibs.o: argvlibs.c $(HDRS)
         $(COMP) $(FLAGS) argvlibs.c

test.c:
argvlibs.c:

argvlibs.h:
```

12

Function Pointers and Internal Commands

One of the most powerful features of the C programming language is the ability to manipulate pointers. Pointers are used quite extensively with respect to variable structures, files, and so on. However, one type of pointer is rarely used—the pointer to functions.

12.1 FUNCTION CALLING

The program logic required to call a function is fairly straightforward. For example, the following code will invoke a routine called *error:*

```
if (error_encountered)
     error (error_number, parameter_list...);
```

Now assume that there are many functions, and that their execution is dependent on a single variable contained in a case statement:

```
switch (var) {

     case 0:
          func0(vars..);
     break;

     case 1:
          func1(vars..);
     break;

     case 2:
          func2(vars..);
     break;

     default:
          error();
     break;
}
```

This approach may work well with a small case statement, but if the number of possible functions grows large, the case statement can also grow large and cumbersome. Further, as new functions are added to the list, this routine—and any other routine containing a similar structure—must be modified.

To illustrate, consider the following example. Four functions, *list( )*, *comp( )*, *clear( )*, and *pause( )*, are available for a program to call. However, the execution of these functions is not determined by the code, but by user input through a text file or the keyboard. A program called *test* accepts one parameter from the user to determine which of the four routines will be invoked. Possible user responses are:

```
test list
test comp
test clear
test pause
```

A conventional approach to this situation could be coded as follows:

```
#include <stdio.h>

main(argc,argv)
int argc;
char **argv;
{


        if (!strcpy(argv[1], "list)
            list();
        else if (!strcpy(argv[1], "comp")
            comp();
        else if (!strcpy(argv[1], "clear")
            clear();
        else if (!strcpy(argv[1], "pause")
            pause();
        else
            printf ("FUNCTION NOT FOUND\n");

}
```

Again, as with the case statement shown above, this approach will become increasingly unmanageable as the number of possible functions increases.

12.2 INTERNAL FUNCTION STRUCTURE

A more elegant solution to the function calling problem detailed in the previous section is to create a table with pointers to these functions that can be accessed in a simple *for* loop. To do this, you must first build an internal function structure and place it in the header file *intlibs.h* as follows:

```
typedef struct {        /* template for internal commands */
      char *name;        /* name of the internal function */
#ifdef ANSI
      int (*funcptr)(int, char **);
#else
      int (*funcptr)();/* pointer to the internal function */
#endif
}INFUNCS;
```

This structure holds two important pieces of information about the internal functions: the name of the function and the pointer to the function. At this point, the structure is set up so that the functions return an integer, which in this case is a status. However, it is possible to return other data types, as well. The function has an empty parameter list that will be utilized when the function is actually called.

Although the prototypes for the internal functions can be placed in any header file, for reasons of clarity they are located in a separate file called *funcs.h*.

```
int    p_comp ();
int    p_list();
int    p_clear();
int    p_pause();
```

To create and initialize the internal structure, *infuncs,* the following code is included in *funcs.h.*

```
struct infunc infuncs[] = {
      {"comp",  p_comp},
      {"list",     p_list},
      {"clear", p_clear},
      {"pause", p_pause},
      {NULL, NULL},
};
```

This structure defines the name function as a string in quotes and the function pointer as an element to be resolved at link time, and thus contains all the information necessary to replace the potentially lengthy list of *case* and nested *if* statements presented in the previous section.

12.3 INTERNAL FUNCTION CALLS

The actual invocation of the proper function calling routine occurs in the library routine *internal( ).* The header file *intlibs.h* must be included in this routine.

```
#include "internal.h"
```

The function declaration for *internal( )* is:

```
int internal(command)
char *command;
```

A character string structure is passed to the internal command to afford as much flexibility as possible. The string is then turned into an *argv* structure using *strargv( )* and *strtokens( )* as described in Chapter 11.

```
args = strargv(command);

count = strtokens(command);
```

Once the *internal( )* routine has been called with the proper arguments, a search loops through the internal function list until a specified function is matched or NULL is found. All internal functions are called in the same manner as a regular command line.

```
for (i=0; infuncs[i].name != NULL; i++) {

    /* if found, execute it */

    if (!strcmp(infuncs[i].name, args[0])) {

        status = (*(infuncs[i].funcptr))(count, args);

        break;

    }

}

/* if we reach this point, function is not in internal list */

if (infuncs[i].name == NULL)
        status = -1;
return (status);
```

If the specified function is found, it is executed and returns a status. If the function is not found, then the status is set to -1. In any event, the status is returned to the routine that called *internal( )*.

12.4 FUNCTION POINTERS

The most interesting code here is the line that calls the internal function:

```
status = (*(infuncs[i].funcptr))(count, args);
```

First, note that a set of parentheses surrounds the pointer, and an asterisk precedes the left parenthesis. This structure is necessary to differentiate between the address of the routine and the address of the pointer. Similarly, an integer pointer needs to differentiate between the address that it points to and the value that resides at that address. For instance, assume the following *char* pointer:

```
char *ptr;
```

and the following code:

```
char string[10] = "test";
...

ptr = string;
```

In this situation, a *printf( )*,

```
printf ("%s", ptr);
```

will produce the output

```
test
```

However, a *printf( )* used in the following manner:

```
printf ("%c", *ptr);
```

will produce as output

```
t
```

If the pointer is accessed as "ptr," then the address that the pointer is pointing to is accessed. However, if the pointer is referred to as "*ptr," the value that the address contains is accessed. The function pointer behaves in the same manner. For the call

```
status = (*(infuncs[i].funcptr))(count, args);
```

the actual address of the required routine resides at the address of the pointer *infuncs[i].funcptr*.

Note: Compilers treat this pointer to a function as a function call, as might be expected. However, some compilers may not like the fact that the function is declared without a prototype, and will consequently issue a warning.

12.5 INTERNAL FUNCTION ARGUMENTS

In this example, an argument list is passed when the internal function is invoked. The list is the character string contained in the command. Another way is to pass the entire parameter list as one character string (in this example "command") and then break it up after the internal function is called. Turning this character string into an *argv*-like structure is an approach that often works well and can be applied to just about all types of functions. The procedure for transforming a character string into an *argv*-like structure is discussed in Chapter 11.

The test program *test.c* is used to illustrate how *internal( )* works. Note that the parameter list is built inside the program using *strcpy( )* and *strcat( )*. Under normal circumstances, this string comes from a text file or a user-entered command, and the function parameter is contained within the command character string. While the function name alone is needed to search the internal function list, the entire command is required when passing the parameters. This is similar to the way *argv* works when a process is invoked. Again, the manner in which the internal call is made depends on the needs of each programmer. It is possible to call internal with just one parameter, *command,* and then pull out the function name in the internal routine.

The actual internal commands called are found in the file *funcs.c.* One such command is used in the following code for illustration purposes:

```
p_list(count, argv)
int count;
char **argv;
{

    int i;

    printf ("LIST\n");

    for (i=0; i<count; i++)
     printf ("argv[%d] %s\n", i, argv[i]);

    return(EXIT_NORMAL);

}
```

12.6 USING THE INTERNAL LIBRARY

The library for *intlibs* requires that the files *funcs.c* and *funcs.h* be defined. The *funcs.h* file must be included in the application program. A routine called *execute_command( )* is invoked to call the internal function. For example, a possible call is:

```
execute_command("comp one two");
```

The string is then turned into an *argv* structure by calling *strargv( ).* Finally, the resulting *argv* structure is called using the library function *internal( ).* If an invalid internal function is called, an error is reported.

To use the internal library, link the *intlibs* object file with the application. Remember that the files *funcs.c* and *funcs.h* must also be defined and linked to the application.

12.7 CONCLUSION

Internal functions have many applications. In fact, the techniques used in this chapter are the foundation for many other chapters yet to come. Though programmers tend to ignore function pointers, they are actually quite powerful.

```
/**************************************************

  FILE NAME    : test.c
  AUTHOR       : Matt Weisfeld

  DESCRIPTION : test file for internal library

**************************************************/
#include <stdio.h>
#include <string.h>
#include "proto.h"
#include "errdefs.h"
#include "funcs.h"

#ifdef ANSI
void execute_command(char *);
#else
void execute_command();
#endif

main()
{
      int i;

      /* build the command string */

      execute_command("comp one two");
      execute_command("list one two");
      execute_command("clear one two");
      execute_command("pause one two");
```

```
        leave (EXIT_NORMAL);

        return;
}

void execute_command(command)
char *command;
{

        int status;

        /* call the  internal function */

        status = internal(command);

        /* see if the function actually exists */

        if (status == -1)
                error(ER_NOFUNC, command);

        return;

}

/*#######################################################*/


/****************************************************

  FILE NAME    : internal.c
  AUTHOR       : Matt Weisfeld

  DESCRIPTION : library to call internal
                functions.

****************************************************/
#include <stdio.h>
#include <string.h>
#include "proto.h"

extern INFUNCS infuncs[];
```

```
/****************************************************

   ROUTINE NAME : internal()

   DESCRIPTION  : execute internal function.

   INPUT        : char * (function name)

   OUTPUT       : char * (argument to function)

****************************************************/
int internal(command)
char *command;
{
    int i, status;
    char **args;
    int count;

    /* command line information */

    args = strargv(command);
    count = strtokens(command);

    /* Loop through internal function list to
        if command is there. If it is there -
        call it.
    */

    for (i=0; infuncs[i].name != NULL; i++) {
        if (!strcmp(infuncs[i].name, args[0])) {
            status = (*infuncs[i].funcptr)(count, args);
            break;
        }
    }

    freelist(args);

    /* if the end of the list is reached, then
        the function is not in the list */

    if (infuncs[i].name == NULL)
        status = -1;
```

```
      return (status);
}

/*###############################################*/


/****************************************************

  FILE NAME    : func.c
  AUTHOR       : Matt Weisfeld

  DESCRIPTION : test routines for internal
                library.

****************************************************/
#include <stdio.h>
#include "proto.h"

/* internal function p_comp */

int p_comp(count, argv)
int count;
char **argv;
{

      int i;

      printf ("\nCOMP\n");

      for (i=0; i<count; i++)
            printf("argv[%d] %s\n", i, argv[i]);

      return(EXIT_NORMAL);
}

/* internal function p_list */

int p_list(count, argv)
int count;
char **argv;
{
```

```
        int i;

        printf ("\nLIST\n");

        for (i=0; i<count; i++)
                printf("argv[%d] %s\n", i, argv[i]);

        return(EXIT_NORMAL);
}

/* internal function p_clear */

int p_clear(count, argv)
int count;
char **argv;
{

        int i;

        printf ("\nCLEAR\n");

        for (i=0; i<count; i++)
                printf("argv[%d] %s\n", i, argv[i]);

        return(EXIT_NORMAL);
}

/* internal function p_pause */

int p_pause(count ,argv)
int count;
char **argv;
{

        int i;

        printf ("\nPAUSE\n");

        for (i=0; i<count; i++)
                printf("argv[%d] %s\n", i, argv[i]);

        return(EXIT_NORMAL);
}


/*###############################################*/
```

```
/*****************************************************

   FILE NAME   : intlibs.h
   AUTHOR      : Matt Weisfeld

   DESCRIPTION : header for intlibs.c

*****************************************************/

#include <stdio.h>

#ifdef ANSI
int internal(char *);
#else
int internal();
#endif

/* internal function structure */

typedef struct {
   char* name;
#ifdef ANSI
   int  (*funcptr)(int, char **);
#else
   int  (*funcptr)();
#endif
} INFUNCS;

/*###############################################*/


/*****************************************************

   FILE NAME   : funcs.h
   AUTHOR      : Matt Weisfeld

   DESCRIPTION : internal function definitions

*****************************************************/
#include <stdio.h>

/*
   parameter lists must be empty, or a warning
```

```
     will result
*/

int p_comp();
int p_list();
int p_clear();
int p_pause();

/* initialize the internal function list */

INFUNCS infuncs[] = {
      { "comp", p_comp },
      { "list", p_list },
      { "clear", p_clear },
      { "pause", p_pause },
      { NULL, NULL }
};


/*#################################################*/


/***************************************************

   FILE NAME   : er.h
   AUTHOR      : Matt Weisfeld

   DESCRIPTION : error definitions for internal
                 libaries.

***************************************************/
#define ER_INVARGS  0      /* invalid number of arguments
*/
#define ER_NOFUNC   1      /* function not found */

/*#################################################*/


/***************************************************

   FILE NAME   : errdefs.h
   AUTHOR      : Matt Weisfeld
```

```
   DESCRIPTION : error descriptions for internal
                 library.

****************************************************/
#include "er.h"

ERROR_STRUCT error_message[] =

/* actual error messages */

{

      /* #0 */
      ER_INVARGS, EXIT,
      "Invalid number of arguments.",
      /* #1 */
      ER_NOFUNC, EXIT,
      "Function '%s', not defined.",
      LASTERROR, EXIT,NULL,
};


/*#############################################*/


/****************************************************

   FILE NAME   : proto.h
   AUTHOR      : Matt Weisfeld

   DESCRIPTION : prototype file for the internal
                 library.

****************************************************/
#ifdef VMS
#include "[-.common]common.h"
#include "[-.leave]leave.h"
#include "[-.error]error.h"
#include "[-.argvlibs]argvlibs.h"
#endif

#ifdef BCC
#include "..\common\common.h"
```

```
#include "..\leave\leave.h"
#include "..\error\error.h"
#include "..\argvlibs\argvlibs.h"
#endif

#ifdef MSC
#include "..\common\common.h"
#include "..\leave\leave.h"
#include "..\error\error.h"
#include "..\argvlibs\argvlibs.h"
#endif

#ifdef HPUX
#include "../common/common.h"
#include "../leave/leave.h"
#include "../error/error.h"
#include "../argvlibs/argvlibs.h"
#endif

#ifdef SLC
#include "../common/common.h"
#include "../leave/leave.h"
#include "../error/error.h"
#include "../argvlibs/argvlibs.h"
#endif

#ifdef GCC
#include "../common/common.h"
#include "../leave/leave.h"
#include "../error/error.h"
#include "../argvlibs/argvlibs.h"
#endif

#ifdef CCC
#include "../common/common.h"
#include "../leave/leave.h"
#include "../error/error.h"
#include "../argvlibs/argvlibs.h"
#endif

#include "intlibs.h"
```

```
/*###############################################*/

$! VMS DCL PROCEDURE
$ clr
$ if (P1.eqs."") then GOTO ALL
$ if (P1.eqs."ALL") then GOTO ALL
$ if (P1.eqs."LINK") then GOTO LINK
$ set verify
$ cc/define=VMS 'P1'
$ goto LINK
$ ALL:
$     set verify
$ cc/define=VMS test
$ cc/define=VMS intlibs
$ cc/define=VMS funcs
$ LINK:
$ link/executable=test test,intlibs,funcs,[-.leave]leave,
[-.error]error,-
[-.argvlibs]argvlibs
$ copy test.exe [weisfeld.exe]
$ set noverify

/*###############################################*/

# makefile for BCC/C++ Compiler

OBJS    = test.obj intlibs.obj funcs.obj
LIBS    = ..\leave\leave.obj ..\error\error.obj \
          ..\argvlibs\argvlibs.obj
HDRS    = proto.h errdefs.h intlibs.h er.h
FLAGS   = -c -DBCC
COMP    = bcc

test.exe:  $(OBJS)
       $(COMP) $(OBJS) $(LIBS)

test.obj: test.c $(HDRS)
       $(COMP) $(FLAGS) test.c

intlibs.obj: intlibs.c $(HDRS)
       $(COMP) $(FLAGS) intlibs.c
```

```
funcs.obj: funcs.c
        $(COMP) $(FLAGS) funcs.c

test.c:
intlibs.c:
funcs.c:

intlibs.h:

/*#########################################*/

# makefile for MSC/C++ Compiler

OBJS    = test.obj intlibs.obj funcs.obj
LIBS    = ..\leave\leave.obj ..\error\error.obj \
          ..\argvlibs\argvlibs.obj
HDRS    = proto.h errdefs.h intlibs.h er.h
FLAGS   = /c /DMSC
COMP    = cl

test.exe:  $(OBJS)
        $(COMP) $(OBJS) $(LIBS)

test.obj: test.c $(HDRS)
        $(COMP) $(FLAGS) test.c

intlibs.obj: intlibs.c $(HDRS)
        $(COMP) $(FLAGS) intlibs.c

funcs.obj: funcs.c
        $(COMP) $(FLAGS) funcs.c

test.c:
intlibs.c:
funcs.c:

intlibs.h:
```

```
/*###########################################*/

# makefile for HPUX C Compiler

OBJS    = test.o intlibs.o funcs.o
LIBS    = ../leave/leave.o  ../error/error.o \
            ../argvlibs/argvlibs.o
HDRS    = proto.h errdefs.h intlibs.h er.h ../leave/leave.h \
            ../error/error.h
FLAGS   = -c -DHPUX -Aa
COMP    = cc

test:   $(OBJS)
        $(COMP) -o test $(OBJS) $(LIBS)

test.o: test.c $(HDRS)
        $(COMP) $(FLAGS) test.c

intlibs.o: intlibs.c $(HDRS)
        $(COMP) $(FLAGS) intlibs.c

funcs.o: funcs.c $(HDRS)
        $(COMP) $(FLAGS) funcs.c

test.c:
intlibs.c:
funcs.c:

intlibs.h:


/*###########################################*/

# makefile for SUN SLC C Compiler

OBJS    = test.o intlibs.o funcs.o
LIBS    = ../leave/leave.o  ../error/error.o \
            ../argvlibs/argvlibs.o
HDRS    = proto.h errdefs.h intlibs.h er.h
FLAGS   = -c -DSLC
COMP    = cc
```

```
test:   $(OBJS)
        $(COMP) -o test $(OBJS) $(LIBS)

test.o: test.c $(HDRS)
        $(COMP) $(FLAGS) test.c

intlibs.o: intlibs.c $(HDRS)
        $(COMP) $(FLAGS) intlibs.c

funcs.o: funcs.c $(HDRS)
        $(COMP) $(FLAGS) funcs.c

test.c:
intlibs.c:
funcs.c:

intlibs.h:


/*###############################################*/

# makefile for SUN GCC C Compiler

OBJS    = test.o intlibs.o funcs.o
LIBS    = ../leave/leave.o  ../error/error.o
          ../argvlibs/argvlibs.o
HDRS    = proto.h errdefs.h intlibs.h er.h
FLAGS   = -c -DGCC
COMP    = gcc

test:   $(OBJS)
        $(COMP) -o test $(OBJS) $(LIBS)

test.o: test.c $(HDRS)
        $(COMP) $(FLAGS) test.c

intlibs.o: intlibs.c $(HDRS)
        $(COMP) $(FLAGS) intlibs.c

funcs.o: funcs.c $(HDRS)
        $(COMP) $(FLAGS) funcs.c
```

```
test.c:
intlibs.c:
funcs.c:

intlibs.h:


/*##############################################*/

# makefile for CCC Compiler

OBJS    = test.o intlibs.o funcs.o
LIBS    = ../leave/leave.o ../error/error.o \
          ../argvlibs/argvlibs.o
HDRS    = proto.h errdefs.h intlibs.h er.h
FLAGS   = -c -DCCC
COMP    = cc

test:   $(OBJS)
        $(COMP) -o test $(OBJS) $(LIBS)

test.o: test.c $(HDRS)
        $(COMP) $(FLAGS) test.c

intlibs.o: intlibs.c $(HDRS)
        $(COMP) $(FLAGS) intlibs.c

funcs.o: funcs.c $(HDRS)
        $(COMP) $(FLAGS) funcs.c

test.c:
intlibs.c:
funcs.c:

intlibs.h:
```

13

Creating Child Processes

One primary advantage of the C programming language is the ease with which code is ported among various systems. The ANSI standard goes a long way in providing the vehicle for this portability. However, many useful system calls that are specific to certain platforms reduce portability. One such group of system calls that are not bound to a standard involves the creation and execution of child processes. Despite their nonstandard, nonportable nature, these system calls provide a powerful tool for managing child processes. This chapter presents a library of functions that makes the creation and execution of child processes portable across many different computer platforms.

13.1 PORTABILITY ISSUES

No matter how uniform a language design attempts to be, some functions simply cannot be performed on certain systems. This discussion will focus on three operating systems: VMS, UNIX, and DOS. Limitations due to system incompatibility can be the result of either hardware or software constraints. For example, both VMS and UNIX are multitasking systems; thus a parent process can continue to execute even while one of its children is executing. DOS, on the other hand, is not a multitasking system, so a parent process and its child cannot execute simultaneously.

In this discussion, the objective is to produce a routine in which the parent creates the child process, waits for a return code from the child, and then, based on the result of the return code, continues execution. These capabilities are shared by VMS, UNIX, and DOS. My intent is thus to make the function call *look* portable to the application program.

13.2 CHILD PROCESS CONCEPTS

All three operating systems, VMS, UNIX, and DOS, require that sufficient memory be available before a child process can be created. If this is not the case, the system commands will fail. Memory is handled differently depending on which system call is invoked. For VMS and UNIX, the process of creating a child process begins with the system call *fork( )*. This command copies the parent's memory space exactly into newly acquired memory space. To initiate a brand new, totally distinct child, the *exec( )* command is used. An *exec( )* command actually overlays the process space of the duplicated parent with a new process, thus maintaining two distinct processes. There are many flavors of the *exec( )* command and all will be investigated later in this section and in the one that follows.

If the parent has no concern over the child's fate, it can proceed as if the child does not exist. However, if the parent needs a return code from the child, it must execute a *wait( )* command. The *wait( )* command will suspend the parent until the child completes and passes back a return value.

Note: If a parent does not execute a *wait( )*, it may still communicate with a child via pipes and mailboxes. However, these data structures have no bearing on the *fork( )* and *exec( )* commands and are beyond the scope of this discussion.

The basic format of the *fork( )*, *exec( )*, and *wait( )* syntax is:

```
if ( (status = fork()) != 0) {

    /* parent code */
```

```
        if (status < 0)
            error (fork() failed);

        if (wait(&child_status) == -1)
            error (wait failed);

} else {

        /* exec the child */

        if (exec() == -1)
            error(exec failed);

}
```

This format is a bit confusing. The call to *fork( )* actually returns values at two different times. When *fork( )* is initially called, it returns a 0 and enters the *else* part of the example, where the *exec( )* is invoked. If the *exec( )* is successful, control is passed back to the point of the *fork( )*, which now appears to return a second value, this time a 1. At this point the parent can either ignore the child and continue on its way, or execute a *wait( )* command and suspend until the child completes.

The DOS *exec( )* command behaves differently than its VMS and UNIX counterparts. Since DOS does not support multitasking, it is impossible for both the parent and the child to run simultaneously. The parent may choose either to terminate itself or to wait for the child to return a status. The DOS *exec( )* command designates that the parent be terminated. When the *exec( )* command is called, DOS actually overlays the parent process with that of the child. So, the only way that the parent can regain control is if the *exec( )* on the child fails. Once the child is running, the parent process cannot be recovered.

DOS also provides a facility allowing the parent to suspend itself while the child initiates and then re-awaken when the child process completes. The commands to accomplish this are *spawn( )* commands. The *spawn( )* commands have the same functionality as a *fork( )*, *exec( )*, and *wait( )* sequence. DOS must find enough space for the child to occupy or else the *spawn( )* will fail. A sample *spawn( )* format is:

```
if ((status = spawn ()) == -1 )
        error (spawn failed);
```

The DOS version appears to require a lot less code to perform the same function. However, the *fork( )*, *exec( )*, and *wait( )* sequence affords much more flexibility.

13.3 THE DIFFERENT FLAVORS OF *exec( )* AND *spawn( )*

There are many different flavors of the *exec( )* and *spawn( )* commands. The two primary categories are differentiated by the way the argument list is passed. The *execv( )* command has the format:

```
execv(argv[0], argv);
```

In this case the argument list (*argv*) must be built and its pointer passed. In all *exec( )* flavors, the command (*argv*[0]) is the first parameter. Note also that the command is actually passed twice, once as a standalone parameter and then as the first member of the argument list.

The argument list can also be passed explicitly, that is, as hard-coded strings. The command for doing so, *execl( )*, has the format:

```
execl(command, command, arg 1, ..., arg N, NULL);
```

Again, note that the command name is passed twice, and the list is terminated by a NULL. For example, to use *execl( )* to invoke the command line

```
command -x -c -v
```

the required *execl( )* function call is

```
execl ("command", "command", "-x", "-c", "-v", NULL);
```

While there are uses for the *execl( )* family of commands, the hard coding aspects of the command make it less flexible than the *execv( )* commands. In fact, a programmer intent on hard coding the command line can still use *execv( )*. For example:

```
char *argv[] = {"command", "-x", "-c", "-v", NULL}

execv(argv[0], argv);
```

Due to this fact, only the *execv( )* functions will be discussed further.

When the *execv( )* command is called, the current directory is searched for the executable specified by *argv*[0]. If the executable is not found, an error results. If the called executable resides in another directory, the entire path must be explicitly provided. To illustrate, a program called *getenv,* which prints out the current value of the environment variables, is called by *execv( )* as follows:

```
char *argv[] = {"getenv",NULL};

execv(argv[0], argv);
```

The *getenv* executable must reside in the current directory or the command will fail. However, assume that all program executables are kept in a directory called [test.exe] (for VMS), /test/bin (for UNIX), or C:\bin (for DOS). Then the argument lists would look like:

```
char *argv[] = {"[test.exe]getenv",NULL};    /* for VMS */
char *argv[] = {"/test/bin/getenv",NULL};    /* for UNIX */
char *argv[] = {"C:\\bin\\getenv",NULL};     /* for DOS */
```

Explicitly providing the path information is not always the most elegant solution. There is a way to take advantage of the execution paths that UNIX and DOS provide. VMS does not provide a path, but a path variable called VAXC$PATH can be set. The command to utilize the path information is called *execvp( )*, which looks similar to the regular *execv( )*:

```
execvp(argv[0], argv);
```

The only difference is that, if the executable is not found in the current directory, the PATH environment variable is searched. In VMS, the VAXC$PATH variable can be set either at the command line or in the *login.com* file as follows:

```
define VAXC$PATH [test.exe]
```

The last version of *execv( )* that we will consider here is *execve( )*. This command allows the parent to change the environment variables of the child. An example follows:

```
char *argv[] = {"getenv",NULL};

char *envp[] = { "HOME = /test/home",
                 "TERM = vt100",
                 "PATH = /test/bin",
                 "USER = test"
                  NULL          }

execve(argv[0], argv, envp);
```

This command creates an environment for the child without changing the environment of the parent.

All of these *execv( )* commands have an *execl( )* counterpart.

The statement was made earlier that for the sake of brevity, the *execv( )* and *spawnv( )* commands would become synonymous. There is one caveat to this allowance. The DOS command *spawnv( )* has one more parameter than *execv( )*. The DOS reference guides state that the first parameter passed with *spawnv( )* specifies whether or not the parent should wait for the child to return, using either P_WAIT or P_NOWAIT. Then a later note explains that P_NOWAIT is not supported, since DOS cannot support two concurrent processes. This parameter is thus provided for future use. However, it still needs to be included.

13.4 BUILDING A PORTABLE *execv( )*

Since the *execv( )* command is the basis for all of the other extensions, this command will be used as an illustration. The code is in the file *execlibs.c*. My intent is to create a library command, *execv_lib( )*, that will handle all of the overhead involved in creating and executing a child process. In essence, the only code required in an application program should be:

```
status = execv_lib(argv);
```

This one line of code will *fork( )* and *exec( )* in UNIX and VMS, or *spawn( )* in DOS), execute the command, and then return the proper status.

The first order of business is to determine what platform the program is running on. This is defined in the header file *execlibs.h*. Portability issues, such as whether or not the platform is ANSI standard, can be addressed here. Once this information is known, whether it is defined on the compilation line or in the *exec.h* file, the *ifdefs* in the code can handle the portability issues.

Once *execv_lib( )* is called, the first *ifdef* determines whether the platform is DOS. If it is, then only the *spawnv( )* command is executed. If the platform is not DOS, the *fork( )*, *execv( )* and *wait( )* calls are made. In any event, the status, whether the actual child return status or an error code, is passed back to the calling program.

13.5 SPECIAL PORTABILITY ISSUES

Besides the fact that *execv( )* and *spawnv( )* are different commands, there are other portability issues to consider. One is the way that VMS uses VAXC$PATH, as has already been mentioned. Further portability concerns pertain to compiler and operating system bugs, return codes, and word alignment. As of this writing, a bug is registered against the VMS command *execvp( )*. The problem is that the proper value of VAXC$PATH is not returned. One way to get around this is to use the *getenv( )* command to obtain the information. Then the path can be included in advance in the command. The interesting thing to note here is that the VMS command *execlp( )* does work with VAXC$PATH set.

Architecture also plays a role in the lack of portability. The program return codes for VMS and DOS differ from those for some UNIX platforms, at least the ones already ported to. These UNIX systems place the return code in the high-order byte, so the UNIX system contents need to be shifted to conform with the other platforms as follows:

```
child_status = child_status >> 8;
```

The intent of the return codes pose a problem. VMS, UNIX, and DOS all have different ways of interpreting returned information. This portability issue is dealt with in the next section.

13.6 ERROR HANDLING

To make error reporting as portable as possible, error handling is the responsibility of the calling routine, not the *execv* library, which returns only status information. This status information can be either an error code or the status of a successfully invoked child process. The error codes are defined in the include file, *execlibs.h*. It is up to the calling program to process the return status and report any anomalies because the error codes can be tailored to a specific application.

13.7 USING THE CHILD PROCESS LIBRARY

To illustrate how the *exec* library works, a short example is presented. The data structure *envp* holds information that will be used to alter the environment variables when the *execv_lib* commands are invoked. In this example, the command *getenv* is converted into *argv*, with a NULL terminator. Then *argv* is passed to the appropriate *execv_lib( )* routine, which executes the proper sequence of commands. A status is passed back and is checked by the routine *check_status( )*. Then the space used by the *argv* structure is released.

The code presented in this library is easily ported to other platforms. For example, to create a child process on an OS-9 platform, code

```
if (status = os9exec(os9fork()c, argv[0], argv,
environ,0,0,3)) > 0)
      wait(&child_status);
else
      return(BADEXEC);
```

The parameters used in this example are explained in the OS-9 language manual.

13.8 CONCLUSION

Despite the fact that C is a very portable language, some areas still exist where portability is a problem. System calls such as *exec( )* and *spawnv( )* may be specific to an individual platform and, when used, may obstruct portability. These problems can be overcome with code libraries that, when linked into application programs, free the programmer from dealing with such system concerns. With the vast number of platforms and compilers now on the market, it is quite helpful to have these libraries of reusable code available.

```
/**************************************************

  FILE NAME    : test.c
  AUTHOR       : Matt Weisfeld

  DESCRIPTION : test file for libraries to
                create child processes.

**************************************************/
#include <stdio.h>
#ifndef SLC
#include <stdarg.h>
#endif
#include "proto.h"
#include "errdefs.h"

char envp1[50] = "HOME=sys$sysdevice:[weisfeld]";
char envp2[50] = "TERM=vt100";
char envp3[50] = "PATH=sys$sysdevice:[weisfeld.exe]";
char envp4[50] = "USER=test";
```

```
char arg1[50] = "getenv";

#ifdef ANSI
void check_status(int);
#else
void check_status();
#endif

int main()
{

        int status, child_status;

        char **argv;
        char *envp[6];
        char *arg[3];

        envp[0] = envp1;
        envp[1] = envp2;
        envp[2] = envp3;
        envp[3] = envp4;
        envp[4] = 0;

        arg[0] = arg1;
        arg[1] = 0;

        printf ("CALL EXECV\n");
        status = execv_lib(arg);
        check_status(status);

        printf ("CALL EXECVE\n");
        status = execve_lib(arg, envp);
        check_status(status);


        /* do only for VMS */

#ifdef VMS
        if ( (put_env ("CHILD$PATH", "[weisfeld.exe]")) == -1)
                error(ER_BADPUTENV);
#endif
```

```
        printf ("CALL EXECVP\n");
        status = execvp_lib(arg);
        check_status(status);

        leave(EXIT_NORMAL);

        return(EXIT_NORMAL);

}

/****************************************************

  ROUTINE NAME : check_status()

  DESCRIPTION  : check status variable from
                 execv() libraries.

  INPUT        : int (status)

  OUTPUT       : none

****************************************************/

void check_status(status)
int status;
{

      switch(status) {

            case BADFORK:
                  error(ER_BADFORK);
            break;

            case BADEXEC:
                  error(ER_BADEXEC);
            break;

            case BADWAIT:
                  error(ER_BADWAIT);
            break;
```

```
                case BADPATH:
                        error(ER_BADPATH);
                break;

                case BADMALLOC:
                        error(ER_BADMALLOC);
                break;

                default:
                        printf ("Child status = %d\n", status);
                break;

        }

        return;

}

/*##############################################*/


/****************************************************

  FILE NAME   : execlibs.c
  AUTHOR      : Matt Weisfeld

  DESCRIPTION : libraries to create child
                processes.

****************************************************/
#include <stdio.h>
#include <string.h>
#include "proto.h"
#ifdef VMS
#include climsgdef
#include processes
#endif
#ifdef DOS
#include <process.h>
#include <stdlib.h>
#ifdef BCC
#include <alloc.h>
```

```
#endif
#endif

/**************************************************

   ROUTINE NAME : execv_lib()

   DESCRIPTION  : call execv to create a child
                    process.

   INPUT        : char ** (argv structure)

   OUTPUT       : int (status)

**************************************************/
int execv_lib(argv)
char **argv;
{

     int status, child_status;

     /* fork off the child process */

     /*
          vfork returns values on two different occasions :

          1) It returns a 0 the first time it is called,
             before the exec function is called.

          2) After the exec call is made, control is passed
             back to the parent at the point of the vfork.

     */

#ifdef DOS

     if ((child_status = spawnv(P_WAIT,argv[0],argv)) == -1) {
             return (BADEXEC);
     }

#else
```

```
#ifndef CCC
    if ((status = vfork()) != 0) {
#else
    if ((status = fork()) != 0) {
#endif

        /* after the exec, control is returned here */

        if (status < 0) {
            printf ("Parent: child failed\n");
            return (BADFORK);

        } else {

#ifdef DBG
            printf ("Parent - Waiting for child\n");
#endif

            if ((status=wait(&child_status)) == -1) {
                printf ("Parent: wait failed\n");
                return (BADWAIT);
            }

#ifdef VMS
            if (child_status == CLI$_IMAGEFNF)
                return (BADWAIT);
#endif

        }

    } else {      /* if vfork returns a 0 */


        /* execute command after the initial vfork */

#ifdef DBG
        printf ("Parent - Starting Child\n");
#endif

        if ((status=execv(argv[0], argv)) == -1) {
            printf ("Parent: execv on child failed\n");
            return (BADEXEC);
        }
```

```
        }

#endif

/* if the machine is a big-endian */
#ifdef BENDIAN
        child_status = child_status >> 8;
#endif

        return (child_status);

}

/****************************************************

   ROUTINE NAME : execvp_lib()

   DESCRIPTION  : call execvp to create a child
                  process.

   INPUT        : char ** (argv structure)

   OUTPUT       : int (status)

****************************************************/
int execvp_lib(argv)
char **argv;
{

        /* fork off the child process */

        /*
            vfork returns values on two different occasions :

            1) It returns a 0 the first time it is called,
               before the exec function is called.

            2) After the exec call is made, control is passed
               back to the parent at the point of the vfork.

        */
```

```
    int status, child_status;
    int pathlen,comlen;

    char *path;
    char *command;


    /*
        This code has to be here, if it is within the vfork
        domain, then any error return code will be
        interpreted as an error from the child.
    */

#ifdef VMS

    if ( (path = getenv("CHILD$PATH")) == NULL) {;
        printf ("Error: CHILD$PATH not defined\n");
        return(BADPATH);
    }

    pathlen = strlen (path);
    comlen  = strlen (argv[0]);

    if ( (command = malloc(pathlen+comlen+1)) == NULL) {
        printf ("Error: malloc failed\n");
        return(BADMALLOC);
    }

    strcpy (command, path);
    strcat (command, argv[0]);

    argv[0] = command;

#ifdef DBG
    printf ("command = %s\n", command);
#endif

#endif


#ifdef DOS
```

```
        if ((child_status = spawnvp(P_WAIT,argv[0],argv)) == -1) {
                return (BADEXEC);
        }

#else

#ifndef CCC
    if ((status = vfork()) != 0) {
#else
    if ((status = fork()) != 0) {
#endif

        /* after the exec, control is returned here */

        if (status < 0) {
            printf ("Parent: child failed\n");
            return (BADFORK);

        } else {

#ifdef DBG
            printf ("Parent - Waiting for child\n");
#endif

            if ((status=wait(&child_status)) == -1) {
                printf ("Parent: wait failed\n");
                return (BADWAIT);

            }

#ifdef VMS
            if (child_status == CLI$_IMAGEFNF)
                return (BADWAIT);
#endif

        }

    } else {        /* if vfork returns a 0 */


        /* execute command after the initial vfork */
```

```
#ifdef DBG
        printf ("Parent - Starting Child\n");
#endif

#ifdef VMS
        if ((status=execv(argv[0], argv)) == -1) {
#else
        if ((status=execvp(argv[0], argv)) == -1) {
#endif
                printf ("Parent: execv on child failed\n");
                return (BADEXEC);
        }

    }

#endif

/* if the machine is a big-endian */
#ifdef BENDIAN
    child_status = child_status >> 8;
#endif

    return (child_status);

}

/****************************************************

  ROUTINE NAME : execve_lib()

  DESCRIPTION  : call execv to create a child
                 process.

  INPUT        : char ** (argv structure)
               : char ** (environment structure)

  OUTPUT       : int (status)

****************************************************/
int execve_lib(argv, envp)
char **argv;
char **envp;
{
```

```
        int status, child_status;

        /* fork off the child process */

        /*
             vfork returns values on two different occasions :

             1) It returns a 0 the first time it is called,
                before the exec function is called.

             2) After the exec call is made, control is passed
                back to the parent at the point of the vfork.

        */


#ifdef DOS

        if ((child_status = spawnve(P_WAIT,argv[0],argv,envp))
        == -1) {
                return (BADEXEC);
        }

#else

#ifndef CCC
        if ((status = vfork()) != 0) {
#else
        if ((status = fork()) != 0) {
#endif

             /* after the exec, control is returned here */

             if (status < 0) {
                 printf ("Parent: child failed\n");
                 return (BADFORK);

             } else {

#ifdef DBG
                 printf ("Parent - Waiting for child\n");
#endif
```

```
            if ((status=wait(&child_status)) == -1) {
                printf ("Parent: wait failed\n");
                return (BADWAIT);

            }

#ifdef VMS
            if (child_status == CLI$_IMAGEFNF)
                return (BADWAIT);
#endif

        }

    } else {      /* if vfork returns a 0 */


        /* execute command after the initial vfork */

#ifdef DBG
        printf ("Parent - Starting Child\n");
#endif

        if ((status=execve(argv[0], argv, envp)) == -1) {
            printf ("Parent: execve on child failed\n");
            return (BADEXEC);
        }

    }

#endif

/* if the machine is a big-endian */
#ifdef BENDIAN
    child_status = child_status >> 8;
#endif

    return (child_status);

}


/*#####################################################*/
```

```
/****************************************************

  FILE NAME   : getenv.c
  AUTHOR      : Matt Weisfeld

  DESCRIPTION : program called by execlibs test.

****************************************************/
#include <stdio.h>
#include <stdlib.h>

main()
{

    char  *logical;

    logical = getenv("HOME");
    printf ("HOME = %s\n", logical);
    logical = getenv("TERM");
    printf ("TERM = %s\n", logical);
    logical = getenv("PATH");
    printf ("PATH = %s\n", logical);
    logical = getenv("USER");
    printf ("USER = %s\n", logical);

    exit(1);

}

/*##############################################*/


/****************************************************

  FILE NAME   : execlibs.h
  AUTHOR      : Matt Weisfeld

  DESCRIPTION : header file for execlibs.c

****************************************************/
#define BADFORK   -1
#define BADEXEC   -2
```

```
#define BADWAIT   -3
#define BADPATH   -4
#define BADMALLOC -5

#ifdef ANSI
int execv_lib(char **);
int execvp_lib(char **);
int execve_lib(char **, char **);
#else
int execv_lib();
int execvp_lib();
int execve_lib();
#endif

/*###############################################*/


/****************************************************

   FILE NAME   : er.h
   AUTHOR      : Matt Weisfeld

   DESCRIPTION : error definitions for execlibs.

****************************************************/

#define ER_BADFORK    0    /* fork failed */
#define ER_BADEXEC    1    /* execv failed */
#define ER_BADWAIT    2    /* wait failed */
#define ER_BADPATH    3    /* calling path is invalid */
#define ER_BADMALLOC  4    /* malloc failed */
#define ER_BADPUTENV  5    /* put_env failed */

/*###############################################*/
```

```
/*****************************************************

   FILE NAME   : errdefs.h
   AUTHOR      : Matt Weisfeld

   DESCRIPTION : error descriptions for internal
                 library.

*****************************************************/
#include "er.h"

ERROR_STRUCT error_message[] =

/* actual error messages */

{

    /* #0 */
    ER_BADFORK, RETURN,
    "An attempt to fork() failed.",
    /* #1 */
    ER_BADEXEC, RETURN,
    "An attempt to execv() failed.",
    /* #2 */
    ER_BADWAIT, RETURN,
    "A wait() operation failed.",
    /* #3 */
    ER_BADPATH, EXIT,
    "A calling path is invalid.",
    /* #4 */
    ER_BADMALLOC, EXIT,
    "An attempt to obtain space failed.",
    /* #5 */
    ER_BADPUTENV, EXIT,
    "A put_env() failed.",
    LASTERROR, EXIT,NULL,
};


/*##################################################*/
```

```
/*******************************************************

   FILE NAME    : proto.h
   AUTHOR       : Matt Weisfeld

   DESCRIPTION : prototype file for the execv
                 library.

********************************************************/
#ifdef VMS
#include "[-.common]common.h"
#include "[-.leave]leave.h"
#include "[-.error]error.h"
#endif

#ifdef BCC
#include "..\common\common.h"
#include "..\leave\leave.h"
#include "..\error\error.h"
#endif

#ifdef MSC
#include "..\common\common.h"
#include "..\leave\leave.h"
#include "..\error\error.h"
#endif

#ifdef SLC
#include "../common/common.h"
#include "../leave/leave.h"
#include "../error/error.h"
#endif

#ifdef GCC
#include "../common/common.h"
#include "../leave/leave.h"
#include "../error/error.h"
#endif

#ifdef CCC
#include "../common/common.h"
#include "../leave/leave.h"
```

```
#include "../error/error.h"
#endif

#ifdef HPUX
#include "../common/common.h"
#include "../leave/leave.h"
#include "../error/error.h"
#endif

#include "execlibs.h"

/*###########################################*/

$! VMS DCL PROCEDURE
$ clr
$ if (P1.eqs."") then GOTO ALL
$ if (P1.eqs."ALL") then GOTO ALL
$ if (P1.eqs."LINK") then GOTO LINK
$ if (P1.eqs."GETENV") then GOTO GETENV
$ set verify
$ cc/define=VMS 'P1'
$ goto LINK
$ ALL:
$      set verify
$ cc/define=VMS test
$ cc/define=VMS execlibs
$ goto LINK
$ GETENV:
$ set verify
$ cc/define=VMS getenv
$ link/executable=getenv getenv
$ goto END
$ LINK:
$ set verify
$ link/executable=test test,execlibs,[-.leave]leave,
[-.error]error,-
[-.envlibs]envlibs
$ copy test.exe [weisfeld.exe]
$ END:
$ set noverify

/*###########################################*/
```

```
# makefile for BCC/C++ Compiler

OBJS      = test.obj execlibs.obj
LIBS      = ..\leave\leave.obj ..\error\error.obj
HDRS      = proto.h errdefs.h execlibs.h er.h
FLAGS     = -c -DBCC
COMP      = bcc

test.exe:  $(OBJS)
       $(COMP) $(OBJS) $(LIBS)

       $(COMP) $(FLAGS) getenv.c
       $(COMP) getenv.obj

test.obj: test.c $(HDRS)
       $(COMP) $(FLAGS) test.c

execlibs.obj: execlibs.c $(HDRS)
       $(COMP) $(FLAGS) execlibs.c

test.c:
execlibs.c:

getenv.c:

execlibs.h:

/*#############################################*/

# makefile for MSC/C++ Compiler

OBJS      = test.obj execlibs.obj
LIBS      = ..\leave\leave.obj ..\error\error.obj
HDRS      = proto.h errdefs.h execlibs.h er.h
FLAGS     = /c /DMSC
COMP      = cl

test.exe:  $(OBJS)
       $(COMP) $(OBJS) $(LIBS)

       $(COMP) $(FLAGS) getenv.c
       $(COMP) getenv.obj
```

```
test.obj: test.c $(HDRS)
      $(COMP) $(FLAGS) test.c

execlibs.obj: execlibs.c $(HDRS)
      $(COMP) $(FLAGS) execlibs.c

test.c:
execlibs.c:

getenv.c:

execlibs.h:

/*###########################################*/

# makefile for HPUX C Compiler

OBJS     = test.o execlibs.o
LIBS     = ../leave/leave.o ../error/error.o
HDRS     = proto.h errdefs.h execlibs.h er.h
           ../leave/leave.h \
           ../error/error.h
FLAGS    = -c -DHPUX -Aa
COMP     = cc

test:   $(OBJS)
      $(COMP) -o test $(OBJS) $(LIBS)

      $(COMP) $(FLAGS) getenv.c
      $(COMP) -o getenv getenv.o

test.o: test.c $(HDRS)
      $(COMP) $(FLAGS) test.c

execlibs.o: execlibs.c $(HDRS)
      $(COMP) $(FLAGS) execlibs.c

test.c:
execlibs.c:

getenv.c:

execlibs.h:
```

```
/*##############################################*/

# makefile for SUN SLC C Compiler

OBJS      = test.o execlibs.o
LIBS      = ../leave/leave.o ../error/error.o
HDRS      = proto.h errdefs.h execlibs.h er.h
            ../leave/leave.h \
            ../error/error.h
FLAGS     = -c -DSLC
COMP      = cc

test:   $(OBJS)
        $(COMP) -o test $(OBJS) $(LIBS)

        $(COMP) $(FLAGS) getenv.c
        $(COMP) -o getenv getenv.o

test.o: test.c $(HDRS)
        $(COMP) $(FLAGS) test.c

execlibs.o: execlibs.c $(HDRS)
        $(COMP) $(FLAGS) execlibs.c

test.c:
execlibs.c:

getenv.c:

execlibs.h:


/*##############################################*/

# makefile for SUN GCC C Compiler

OBJS      = test.o execlibs.o
LIBS      = ../leave/leave.o ../error/error.o
HDRS      = proto.h errdefs.h execlibs.h er.h
            ../leave/leave.h \
            ../error/error.h
FLAGS     = -c -DGCC
COMP      = gcc
```

```
test:   $(OBJS)
        $(COMP) -o test $(OBJS) $(LIBS)

        $(COMP) $(FLAGS) getenv.c
        $(COMP) -o getenv getenv.o

test.o: test.c $(HDRS)
        $(COMP) $(FLAGS) test.c

execlibs.o: execlibs.c $(HDRS)
        $(COMP) $(FLAGS) execlibs.c

test.c:
execlibs.c:

getenv.c:

execlibs.h:


/*#############################################*/

# makefile for CCC Compiler

OBJS    = test.o execlibs.o
LIBS    = ../leave/leave.o ../error/error.o
HDRS    = proto.h errdefs.h execlibs.h er.h
          ../leave/leave.h \
          ../error/error.h
FLAGS   = -c -DCCC
COMP    = cc

test:   $(OBJS)
        $(COMP) -o test $(OBJS) $(LIBS)

        $(COMP) $(FLAGS) getenv.c
        $(COMP) -o getenv getenv.o

test.o: test.c $(HDRS)
        $(COMP) $(FLAGS) test.c

execlibs.o: execlibs.c $(HDRS)
        $(COMP) $(FLAGS) execlibs.c
```

```
test.c:
execlibs.c:

getenv.c:

execlibs.h:
```

13.9 SELECTED REFERENCE

Material in this chapter appeared in "A Portable Library for Creating Child Processes." *Dr. Dobb's Journal,* vol. #200, p. 46.

14

Creating Portable System Commands

Up to this point, portability issues have focused on the hardware and compilers of the various host systems. Indeed, these two components do account for the majority of porting headaches. However, other areas also pose portability problems. One of these areas is the operating system interface.

It is obvious that one command, issued to several different operating systems, will not illicit the same response. Simply listing a file can tax the memory of a programmer working with several operating systems. The commands to list a file range from *type* (DOS, VMS) to *cat* (UNIX) to *list* (OS9). There are also variations on the theme such as the UNIX command *more*, plus a myriad of options such as the VMS commands *type* and *page*. In actuality, it is almost impossible to memorize all possible available commands and variations. To overcome this dilemma, it is possible to create portable libraries that will keep track of the commands for the programmer, making actual program code more portable and more readable.

14.1 PORTABLE SYSTEM COMMANDS

To illustrate the usefulness of such libraries, assume that an application creates multiple temporary files which consume a lot of disk space. In short, it is necessary to delete the files while the application is still running. It is easy to call the C function *system( )* with the proper, local command such as:

- DOS

```
system("del file.txt");
```

- UNIX

```
system("rm file.txt");
```

- VMS

```
system("delete file.txt");
```

- OS9

```
system("del  file.txt");
```

A portable library for performing a file delete allows all of the different calls to be replaced by one call:

```
remove file.txt
```

which covers all possible variations of the command for each system. Of course, each variation must be accounted for in the library itself. However, once the library is written, this work is transparent to the programmer.

14.2 IMPLEMENTATION

There are actually two ways to use portable libraries such as these. One is in the manner of the internal functions described in Chapter 12. In this case, the command was most likely issued by a user by means of some sort of programming language. The key is that the command came from outside the program, thus requiring a search for valid internal functions. The second way is to call these portable libraries from inside the program as with any other function call. In essence, the call to the library simply replaces the operating system call or the set of *#ifdefs*.

This chapter concentrates on the first method—implementation of internal commands. As outlined above, the example used will create a portable library for file removal. First, a function name must be chosen to represent all possible file removal calls. This may seem trivial, but actually, the name must be chosen with some care. In VMS, for example, choosing a name that conflicts with one of the DCL commands will cause problems at link time. It is thus good practice to avoid names that duplicate any operating system calls. Unfortunately, after eliminating all the operating calls for a particular command, there may be no inherently logical names left. For example, excluding operating system commands for listing a file eliminates the following possibilities: *cat, more, type,* and *list*—and who knows what other operating system commands may be added in the future. In the case of file removal, *remove* and *delete* are also taken. Actually, there are ways around this command name duplication problem that allow the chosen command name to be anything that makes sense to the programmer. One method for overcoming this problem will be explained shortly. For this discussion, the name "remove" will be used for the portable command.

Since the creation of this portable command in effect creates an internal command, it is helpful to review the internal command structures. The structures included in the file *intlibs.h* are:

```
typedef struct {        /* template for internal commands */
      char *name;       /* name of the internal function */
#ifdef ANSI
      int (*funcptr)(int, char**);
#else
      int (*funcptr)(); /* pointer to the internal function
                          */
#endif
}INFUNCS;

int   p_copy ();
int   p_list();
int   p_remove();
```

```
struct infunc infuncs[] = {
     {"copy",   p_copy},
     {"list",   p_list},
     {"remove", p_remove},
     {NULL, NULL},     /* two PNULL's must always be last
                        */
};
```

Note that the internal commands used in Chapter 14 are included, as well as the new command, *remove,* used in this example. Also, note that the actual function names have a "p_" in front of them. This prefix is one method for avoiding the operating system name conflict described above. (This method assumes, of course, that no operating system begins its commands with the same prefix.) The actual prefix is up to the programmer. The issue here is that by using prefixes, conflicts at link time are avoided.

As an alternative to using the prefixes, the programmer can use the more obvious names that are contained as strings in the structure definition of *infuncs*. These names will be utilized by the internal command search function.

14.3 BUILDING THE LIBRARY

The construction of the library begins with the prototype definition. In fact, even before this can be designed, the syntax of the call must be determined. For the file removal example, one possible syntax is:

```
remove file1.txt
```

This works well, but suppose that there is more than one file to remove. For this function, multiple file removals will be part of the specification:

```
remove file1.txt file2.txt ...
```

For a user calling *remove( )* from a programming language, this syntax is fine, since the parsing routine can read it in as a string. However, if the programmer wants to call this function from inside a C program, the following additional syntax is necessary:

```
p_remove ("remove file1.txt file2.txt file3.txt");
```

More likely, the call will look like

```
p_remove (char **);    /* an argv list */
```

where the string is built based on program logic and need. Again, as in most of the libraries in this book, the actual implementation can be based upon the specific needs of the programmer. The implementation presented here is geared more towards the use of internal commands extracted from a user programming language. The concepts of the portable library function are the most important issue in this chapter. The actual implementation is up to the programmer.

Since the *remove* function accepts a command string as a parameter, the prototypes, as previously defined, have the form

```
int   p_remove();
```

The actual function definition is

```
int p_remove(count, args)
int count
char **args;
```

At this point, the command line is treated like any other *argv*-like structure. Since *count* contains the number of arguments, it is possible to ensure that the function itself was called properly. For example, in the case of *p_remove( )*, even though the number of files to delete may vary, there must be at least two arguments: the function name and one file name. It is also possible to echo the command line to a stream, in this case, *stderr:*

```
fprintf (stderr, "REMOVE ");

for (i=1; args != NULL; i++) {
     fprintf (stderr, "%s ", args[i]);
}

fprintf (stderr, "\n");
```

To perform the actual file removal, a simple loop is entered with *argc* as the limiting variable. The following code presents the mechanisms for deleting a file for each supported operating system. One file is removed at a time.

```
for (i=1; i<argc; i++) {

     /* call host removal function */

#ifdef VMS
     status = delete(argv[i]);
#endif

#ifdef UNIX
     strcpy (buffer, "rm ");
     strcat (buffer, argv[i]);

     system (buffer);
#endif

#ifdef OS9
     strcpy (buffer, "del ");
     strcat (buffer, argv[i]);

     system (buffer);
#endif
}
```

If the operating system returns a status, the variable can be checked.

```
     if (status) {
          error(ER_NOTOPEN, argv[i]);
     }
```

However, the system command does not return any status from the invoked command. The only status the system command returns is whether or not the command was initiated. For example, in UNIX, the following command would most likely succeed:

```
status = system("ls");
```

A value of 0 is returned once the operating system determines that *ls* is a valid system command. However, if *ls* were to fail after starting successfully, the calling program would never know, since the 0 had already been returned. If a call to an invalid system command were made, as in

```
status = system("lsxxx");
```

the operating system, unable to start the command, would return a status of 1. Thus, the status in this case has very little use, other than confirming that the command exists. There is no way to obtain information about the command. Note that in VMS an actual call to the *delete* function can be invoked. For the other operating systems, a buffer is built and then used in a system call.

Other system-dependent calls can be placed in portable libraries just like this one created for file removal. There are many advantages to this approach. The most obvious benefit is that lines of code are saved. However, the true value lies in the fact that these libraries can be used by many people for a variety of purposes. In fact, these libraries can even be linked into code for other programming languages.

14.4 USING THE SYSTEM COMMAND LIBRARY

The *syslib* library functions are basically internal functions and thus are handled in the same manner, using the *execute_command*( ) function). The programer is responsible for determining the specific needs for each application. In fact, the routines for the portable system commands are actual libraries themselves, and can thus be shared across programs. To use these libraries, define the files *funcs.c* and *funcs.h,* and link them in the *intlibs* library.

14.5 CONCLUSION

Building portable system libraries is one of the most obvious
ways to make the differences in operating system calls transparent. The number of system command libraries is limited only
by the imagination of the programmer.

```
/*****************************************************

   FILE NAME   : test.c
   AUTHOR      : Matt Weisfeld

   DESCRIPTION : test file for internal library

*****************************************************/
#include <stdio.h>
#include <string.h>
#include "proto.h"
#include "errdefs.h"
#include "funcs.h"

#ifdef ANSI
void execute_command(char *);
#else
void execute_command();
#endif

main()
{

     /* build the command string */

     execute_command("copy file.lst file.txt");
     execute_command("list file.txt");
     execute_command("remove file.txt");

     leave (EXIT_NORMAL);

     return;
}
```

```
void execute_command(command)
char *command;
{

      int status;

      printf ("command = %s\n", command);

      /* call the  internal function */

      status = internal(command);

      /* see if the function actually exists */

      if (status == -1)
            error(ER_NOFUNC, command);

      return;

}

/*############################################*/


/***************************************************

  FILE NAME    : func.c
  AUTHOR       : Matt Weisfeld

  DESCRIPTION : test routines for internal
                library.

***************************************************/
#include <stdio.h>
#include "proto.h"
#include "er.h"
```

```
/*****************************************************

   ROUTINE NAME : p_copy()

   DESCRIPTION  : system function to copy a file

   INPUT        : char *

   OUTPUT       : int (status)

*****************************************************/
int p_copy(count, args)
int count;
char **args;
{
      FILE *fpa, *fpb;
      int c;

      printf ("COPY %s TO %s\n", args[1], args[2]);
      /* open file for reading */

      if ( (fpa = fopen(args[1], "r")) == NULL)
            error(ER_NOFILE, args[1]);

      /* open file for writing */

      if ( (fpb = fopen(args[2], "w")) == NULL)
            error(ER_NOFILE, args[2]);

      /* put file to 'stdout' */

      while((c = getc(fpa)) != EOF) {
            putc(c,fpb);
      }

      fclose(fpa);
      fclose(fpb);

      return(EXIT_NORMAL);
}
```

```
/*****************************************************

  ROUTINE NAME : p_list()

  DESCRIPTION  : system function to list a file

  INPUT        : char *

  OUTPUT       : int (status)

*****************************************************/
int p_list(count, args)
int count;
char **args;
{
      FILE *fpa;
      int c;

      printf ("LIST %s\n", args[1]);
      /* open file */

      fpa = fopen(args[1], "r");

      /* put file to 'stdout' */

      while((c = getc(fpa)) != EOF)
            putchar(c);

      fclose(fpa);

      return(EXIT_NORMAL);
}

/*****************************************************

  ROUTINE NAME : p_remove

  DESCRIPTION  : system function to remove a file

  INPUT        : char *

  OUTPUT       : int (status)

*****************************************************/
```

```c
int p_remove(count, args)
int count;
char **args;
{
#ifndef VMS
      char buffer[80];
#endif
      int status = 0;
      int arguments;
      int i;

      printf ("REMOVE %s\n", args[1]);

      for (i=1; i<count; i++) {

            /* call host removal function */

#ifdef VMS
            status = delete(args[i]);
#endif

#ifdef DOS
            if (remove(args[i]) != 0)
                  perror("remove");
#endif

#ifdef UNIX
            strcpy (buffer, "rm ");
            strcat (buffer, args[i]);
            system (buffer);
#endif

#ifdef OS9
            strcpy (buffer, "del ");
            strcat (buffer, args[i]);

            system (buffer);

#endif
```

```
                      if (status) {
                            printf ("Error: bad status for remove\n");
                            return (EXIT_ERROR);
                      }

            }

      return(EXIT_NORMAL);
}

/*##############################################*/


/***************************************************

  FILE NAME    : funcs.h
  AUTHOR       : Matt Weisfeld

  DESCRIPTION : internal function definitions

***************************************************/
#include <stdio.h>

/*
   parameter lists must be empty, or a warning
   will result
*/

int p_copy();
int p_list();
int p_remove();

/* initialize the internal function list */

INFUNCS infuncs[] = {
      { "copy", p_copy},
      { "list", p_list},
      { "remove", p_remove},
      { NULL, NULL } };


/*##############################################*/
```

```
/****************************************************

   FILE NAME   : er.h
   AUTHOR      : Matt Weisfeld

   DESCRIPTION : error definitions for internal
                 libaries.

****************************************************/


#define ER_INVARGS   0     /* invalid number of arguments */
#define ER_NOFUNC    1     /* function not found */
#define ER_NOFILE    2     /* could not open file */
#define ER_BADREM    3     /* file could not be removed */

/*##########################################*/


/****************************************************

   FILE NAME   : errdefs.h
   AUTHOR      : Matt Weisfeld

   DESCRIPTION : error descriptions for internal
                 library.

****************************************************/
#include "er.h"

ERROR_STRUCT error_message[] =

/* actual error messages */

{

        /* #0 */
        ER_INVARGS, EXIT,
        "Invalid number of arguments.",
        /* #1 */
        ER_NOFUNC, EXIT,
        "Function '%s', not defined.",
```

```
        /* #2 */
        ER_NOFILE, EXIT,
        "File '%s', not found.",
        /* #3 */
        ER_BADREM, EXIT,
        "File '%s'could not be removed.",
        LASTERROR, EXIT,NULL,
};


/*###########################################*/


/****************************************************

  FILE NAME    : proto.h
  AUTHOR       : Matt Weisfeld

  DESCRIPTION : prototype file for the system
                library.

****************************************************/
#ifdef VMS
#include "[-.common]common.h"
#include "[-.leave]leave.h"
#include "[-.error]error.h"
#include "[-.intlibs]intlibs.h"
#include "[-.argvlibs]argvlibs.h"
#include "[-.statlibs]statlibs.h"
#include "[-.timelibs]timelibs.h"
#endif

#ifdef BCC
#include "..\common\common.h"
#include "..\leave\leave.h"
#include "..\error\error.h"
#include "..\intlibs\intlibs.h"
#include "..\argvlibs\argvlibs.h"
#include "..\statlibs\statlibs.h"
#include "..\timelibs\timelibs.h"
#endif
```

```
#ifdef MSC
#include "..\common\common.h"
#include "..\leave\leave.h"
#include "..\error\error.h"
#include "..\intlibs\intlibs.h"
#include "..\argvlibs\argvlibs.h"
#include "..\statlibs\statlibs.h"
#include "..\timelibs\timelibs.h"
#endif

#ifdef HPUX
#include "../common/common.h"
#include "../leave/leave.h"
#include "../error/error.h"
#include "../intlibs/intlibs.h"
#include "../argvlibs/argvlibs.h"
#include "../statlibs/statlibs.h"
#include "../timelibs/timelibs.h"
#endif

#ifdef SLC
#include "../common/common.h"
#include "../leave/leave.h"
#include "../error/error.h"
#include "../intlibs/intlibs.h"
#include "../argvlibs/argvlibs.h"
#include "../statlibs/statlibs.h"
#include "../timelibs/timelibs.h"
#endif

#ifdef GCC
#include "../common/common.h"
#include "../leave/leave.h"
#include "../error/error.h"
#include "../intlibs/intlibs.h"
#include "../argvlibs/argvlibs.h"
#include "../statlibs/statlibs.h"
#include "../timelibs/timelibs.h"
#endif

#ifdef CCC
#include "../common/common.h"
```

```
#include "../leave/leave.h"
#include "../error/error.h"
#include "../intlibs/intlibs.h"
#include "../argvlibs/argvlibs.h"
#include "../statlibs/statlibs.h"
#include "../timelibs/timelibs.h"
#endif


/*#############################################*/

$! VMS DCL PROCEDURE
$ clr
$ if (P1.eqs."") then GOTO ALL
$ if (P1.eqs."ALL") then GOTO ALL
$ if (P1.eqs."LINK") then GOTO LINK
$ set verify
$ cc/define=VMS 'P1'
$ goto LINK
$ ALL:
$     set verify
$ cc/define=VMS test
$ cc/define=VMS funcs
$ LINK:
$ link/executable=test test,funcs,[-.leave]leave,
[-.error]error,-
[-.statlibs]statlibs.obj,[-.intlibs]intlibs.obj,
[-.argvlibs]argvlibs.obj,-
[-.timelibs]timelibs.obj
$ copy test.exe [weisfeld.exe]
$ set noverify

/*#############################################*/

# makefile for BCC/C++ Compiler

OBJS    = test.obj funcs.obj
LIBS    = ..\leave\leave.obj ..\error\error.obj \
          ..\argvlibs\argvlibs.obj ..\intlibs\intlibs.obj \
          ..\statlibs\statlibs.obj
HDRS    = proto.h errdefs.h funcs.h er.h
FLAGS   = -c -DBCC
COMP    = bcc
```

```
test.exe:  $(OBJS)
       $(COMP) @listobjs

test.obj: test.c $(HDRS)
       $(COMP) $(FLAGS) test.c

funcs.obj: funcs.c $(HDRS)
       $(COMP) $(FLAGS) funcs.c

test.c:
funcs.c:

funcs.h:

/*###########################################*/

# makefile for MSC/C++ Compiler

OBJS      = test.obj funcs.obj
LIBS      = ..\leave\leave.obj ..\error\error.obj \
            ..\argvlibs\argvlibs.obj ..\intlibs\intlibs.obj \
            ..\statlibs\statlibs.obj
HDRS      = proto.h errdefs.h funcs.h er.h
FLAGS     = /c /DMSC
COMP      = cl

test.exe:  $(OBJS)
       $(COMP) @listobjs

test.obj: test.c $(HDRS)
       $(COMP) $(FLAGS) test.c

funcs.obj: funcs.c $(HDRS)
       $(COMP) $(FLAGS) funcs.c

test.c: $(HDRS)
funcs.c: $(HDRS)

funcs.h:

/*###########################################*/
```

```
/*
LISTOBJS
*/

test.obj
funcs.obj
..\leave\leave.obj
..\error\error.obj
..\argvlibs\argvlibs.obj
..\intlibs\intlibs.obj
..\statlibs\statlibs.obj
..\timelibs\timelibs.obj

/*###############################################*/

# makefile for HP C Compiler

OBJS     = test.o funcs.o ../timelibs/timelibs.o
           ../leave/leave.o \
             ../error/error.o ../statlibs/statlibs.o \
             ../argvlibs/argvlibs.o ../intlibs/intlibs.o
HDRS     = syslibs.h proto.h ../common/common.h
FLAGS    = -DHPUX -Aa

test.exe:  $(OBJS)
      cc -o test $(OBJS)

test.o: test.c $(HDRS) errdefs.h er.h
../timelibs/timelibs.h \
            ../leave/leave.h ../error/error.h
      cc $(FLAGS) -c test.c

funcs.o: funcs.c $(HDRS)
      cc $(FLAGS) -c funcs.c

test.c:
syslibs.c:

errdefs.h:
er.h:
syslibs.h:
```

```
/*###############################################*/

# makefile for SUN SLC C Compiler

OBJS     = test.o funcs.o
LIBS     = ../leave/leave.o ../error/error.o
           ../argvlibs/argvlibs.o \
           ../intlibs/intlibs.o ../statlibs/statlibs.o
           ../timelibs/timelibs.o
HDRS     = proto.h errdefs.h funcs.h er.h
FLAGS    = -c -DSLC
COMP     = cc

test.exe:  $(OBJS)
       $(COMP) -o test $(OBJS) $(LIBS)

test.o: test.c $(HDRS)
       $(COMP) $(FLAGS) test.c

funcs.o: funcs.c $(HDRS)
       $(COMP) $(FLAGS) funcs.c

test.c:
funcs.c:

funcs.h:


/*###############################################*/

# makefile for SUN GCC C Compiler

OBJS     = test.o funcs.o
LIBS     = ../leave/leave.o ../error/error.o
           ../argvlibs/argvlibs.o \
           ../intlibs/intlibs.o ../statlibs/statlibs.o
           ../timelibs/timelibs.o
HDRS     = proto.h errdefs.h funcs.h er.h
FLAGS    = -c -DGCC
COMP     = gcc

test.exe:  $(OBJS)
       $(COMP) -o test $(OBJS) $(LIBS)
```

```
test.o: test.c $(HDRS)
      $(COMP) $(FLAGS) test.c

funcs.o: funcs.c $(HDRS)
      $(COMP) $(FLAGS) funcs.c

test.c:
funcs.c:

funcs.h:



/*############################################*/

# makefile for CCC Compiler

OBJS    = test.o funcs.o
LIBS    = ../leave/leave.o ../error/error.o
          ../argvlibs/argvlibs.o \
          ../intlibs/intlibs.o ../statlibs/statlibs.o
          ../timelibs/timelibs.o
HDRS    = proto.h errdefs.h funcs.h er.h
FLAGS   = -c -DSLC
COMP    = cc

test.exe:  $(OBJS)
      $(COMP) -o test $(OBJS) $(LIBS)

test.o: test.c $(HDRS)
      $(COMP) $(FLAGS) test.c

funcs.o: funcs.c $(HDRS)
      $(COMP) $(FLAGS) funcs.c

test.c:
funcs.c:

funcs.h:
```

## 15

An Options Engine

There are many ways to process options—far too many to explore here. Regardless of which method is used, it is important to keep the process consistent. Software projects, as well as related software products, should keep the command line interface standard, just as graphical user interfaces attempt to do. Decisions such as which options flag to use, if any, or whether to allow multiple options to a single options flag need to be made early, so everyone involved in the project is working from the same page.

15.1 THE COMMAND LINE

Before going any further, it is important to illustrate how the command line is actually presented to the options parser. Consider the following command line:

```
test -d 5 -l -re -f file.txt -n 7.7
```

These options represent:

Option	Definition
d(ebug)	indicate the integer debugging level (eg: 1–5)
f(ile)	specify a filename to be used for output
l(ist)	list informational messages
n(umber)	specify a floating point number
re(direct)	redirect *stdout* to a file

Note that all the options in the command line begin with a hyphen (-). This flag is required before each option. If it is not present, the option will be ignored, and the parser will look for the next valid option. The flag is defined as such by:

```
#define OPTIONS_FLAG '-'
```

The important point in this design is that only one option is represented by a single option flag. This is simply a design choice. There are many implementations where a flag indicates one or more options. For example, the option '-re' may indicate either one option, "re", or it may actually define two separate options, "r" and "e". The multiple option situation causes many conflicts to arise. If an option has an identifier, such as the debug option in this example, then the user is forced to use a separate flag for other options, as illustrated by:

```
test -d 5 e        /* this is invalid */
```

Because some options, such as the redirect option, are composed of more than one character, it is a programming headache to differentiate options such as:

```
test -re
```

Is this meant to be the single option "re," or two options "r" and "e"? Since using a flag for each option is not that much of a nuisance, the decision here is to require that each option have its own flag. The flag itself is required to differentiate between an actual option and an identifier. It is true that in most cases the parsing can be accomplished by context, without the option flags; however, the use of the flags is so helpful in error checking and recovery that the flag is a desired construct.

The test command line is passed from the operating system to the C program via the arguments *argc* and *argv*. These arguments are required by the options parsing routine. Thus, the prototype for the parser is:

```
int parse_options (argc,argv);
int argc;
char **argv;
```

In most cases, the call to *parse_options( )* should be one of the first actions of the program.

15.2 THE OPTIONS STRUCTURE

The options processor presented here is driven by an options engine which is linked in by any process that requires option processing. This engine is totally generic. Only the header files need to be changed from one application to the next. The logic behind this approach is based on the same technique used in the calling of internal functions. In fact, processing the options is actually accomplished by using internal function calls. A structure called *OPTIONS* is created and made available to all necessary functions by defining it as external.

To begin, it is helpful to look at the options structure itself:

```
#define STRING_LENGTH 80

typedef struct opnode {
        int     debug_level;
        float   number;
        int     list;
        int     redirect;
} OPTIONS;
```

The actual instance of the structure is declared in the main module:

```
OPTIONS options;
```

In this example, there are four options in the options structure. The first two options represent actual number values. The last two are boolean values used as flags. By keeping all these fields in a single structure, all the options are readily available to any module with an *extern* declaration such as:

```
extern OPTIONS options;
```

Thus any of the options is easily accessed. For example, to check the list flag, the following code is used:

```
if (options.list) {

        ...do something

}
```

15.3 OPTION PARSER DEFINITIONS

The code for *parse_options( )* is compact and totally portable to any application without change. The information specific to each application is contained in the header files and a file that contains the code for each option. A file called *opt.c* is actually a collection of routines that handles the option processing. For example, when the option list is identified, the following routine is called:

```
extern OPTIONS options;

int p_list(argv,loop)
char **argv;
int loop;
{
        options.list = ON;
```

```
        return(0);

}
```

The use of the arguments is explained in the next section. The main point here is that the routine *p_list*( ) simply turns the list flag on. The other options are handled in a similar manner, though of course some are more complex.

As indicated before, the option routines are actually internal commands. The internal command structure, called *optfunc,* is defined as:

```
typedef struct optfunc {    /* template for internal
                               commands */
        char *string;       /* option string */
        int (*funcptr)();   /* pointer to the internal
                               function */
} OPTFUNC;
```

The field *string* is the actual options string (e.g., "re" for *redirect*), and the pointer *funcptr* addresses the function that corresponds to the string. The functions used in this example are defined as:

```
int    p_list( );       /* option list */
int    p_debug( );      /* option debug */
int    p_echo( );       /* option echo */
int    p_redirect( );   /* option redirect */
```

At this point we can define the actual instance of the OPTFUNC structure:

```
struct OPTFUNC optfuncs[] = {
        {"l", p_list},
        {"d", p_debug},
        {"e", p_echo},
        {"re",p_redirect},
        {NULL, NULL},
};
```

This definition may be placed anywhere in the code. However, it makes more sense and is more consistent if the structure is created at the start of the program.

15.4 THE OPTIONS PARSER

With all the preliminary work completed, the actual options parser is presented. The logic is to identify an option flag and call the appropriate option routine. The code located in the file *optlibs.c*, illustrates this process.

The main things to note are the variables *loop, skip,* and *opt*. The variable *loop* is used to keep track of which parameter the parser is currently processing. Each option and identifier increments *loop* by one. Thus *loop* is compared with *argc* to determine when the parser reaches the end of the command line. If *loop* were only incremented for each option, then it would become out of sync with *argc* as soon as an identifier was encountered. To correct this situation, the variable *skip* is used. Since the actual number of identifiers is unknown to the options engine—being known only to the actual routines in *opt.c*—the information is passed back as the return value from these routines to the variable *skip:*

```
skip = (*(optfuncs[i].funcptr))(argv,loop);
```

Then *loop* is incremented by the value of *skip:*

```
loop = loop + skip;
```

The actual call to the internal option functions involved the two parameters, *argv* and the value of *loop*. The reasons why these parameters need to be passed are obvious, since the actual command line and the current parsing position are required. Since all option parsing routines require the same parameters and return the same information, using internal function calls is a logical choice for this application.

The options flag must always be in the first character of the parameter string. Thus the comparison looks like

```
if (argv[loop][0] != OPTIONS_FLAG)
```

If this comparison fails, the parameter is ignored, a message is printed, and the parser looks for the next valid option (a "-"). If the option flag is found, the actual option is copied to the string *opt:*

```
strcpy (opt, ++argv[loop]);
```

The ++ operator is used to advance the pointer past the options flag, since it is no longer needed. The next issue determined is whether the option is legal. This determination is made by comparing the option to each option defined in the option structure. If the option is not defined, it is ignored, and the parser again looks for the next valid option.

15.5 THE OPTION ROUTINES

The number of possible options is infinite as is the number of possible applications. The option parser for *list* was already used as an example, and we will now explore a few more options that seem useful in most types of situations. The option definition contains five options. One of these, the debug option, processes an integer value:

```
int p_debug(argv,loop)
char **argv;
int loop;
{

    if (argv[loop+1] == NULL) {
        printf ("Error: parameter expected\n");
        return (-1);
    }

    if ( !(strinteger(argv[loop+1])) ) {
        printf ("Error: valid number expected\n");
        return (-1);
    }
```

```
        options.debug_level = atoi(argv[loop+1]);

        return(1);

}
```

The debug option expects an integer identifier to follow. For example:

```
test -d 5
```

Since all command line parameters are strings, each must be converted to an integer. This is acomplished with the *atoi( )* function.

```
options.debug_level = atoi(argv[loop+1]);
```

Before this function is performed, the routine looks to see if a parameter is available. If none is, an error occurs and an error code is returned. The library function *strinteger( )* is used to verify that the string is indeed an integer. A float value is processed in the same manner, while a string involves a simple *strcpy( )*.

One useful function is to redirect *stdout* to a file. This function is performed in the option routine *p_redirect( )* that uses the C function *freopen( )*:

```
freopen(argv[loop+1],"w", stdout);
```

In this context, the argument *loop*+1 represents a filename passed on the command line:

```
test -re file.txt
```

The *freopen( )* command actually reassigns the file pointer of *stdout* to the file *file.txt*. Thus, all output such as *printf( )s* will no longer go to the screen, but will instead be placed in *file.txt*. This technique is very useful when logging tests or other information that normally goes to the screen.

15.6 USING THE OPTIONS LIBRARY

The *optlibs* test program tests several option types. The *debug* flag supports debugging levels from 0 to 5. The *redirect* flag will create a file and send all screen output to it. The other library flags are simply boolean flags.

The options engine is portable to any application. The only files that need to change are *opt.c* and *opt.h*. If more than one application uses the same options, then none of the files need to change—simply link them into the application and call the options parser from the necessary routine. However, if the option requirements vary from one application to the next, simply add or delete the option of concern from the structures in the header files and then add the appropriate logic to the *opts.c* and *opt.h* files. In all cases, the files *optlibs.c* and *opts.c* must be linked with the application.

15.7 CONCLUSION

The need for options parsing is so common that a standard and efficient method of dealing with options is almost a necessity. Since most applications today require a consistent look and feel, it is important to develop a strategy early and stick to it. The library presented in this chapter is just one example of a valid options parsing scheme.

```
/***************************************************

  FILE NAME    : test.c
  AUTHOR       : Matt Weisfeld

  DESCRIPTION : test file for options library.

***************************************************/
#include <stdio.h>
#include "proto.h"
#include "opts.h"
#include "errdefs.h"

/* this is the array structure to hold the internal
commands */
```

```
OPTFUNCS optfuncs[] = {
    {"l",  p_list},
    {"d",  p_debug},
    {"e",  p_echo},
    {"re", p_redirect},
    {NULL,   NULL}
};

OPTIONS options = {0,OFF,OFF,OFF};

main(argc,argv)
int argc;
char **argv;
{

    printf ("\nThis to stdout\n");

    parse_options(argc,argv);

    printf ("LIST OPTIONS:\n");

    if (options.debug_level)
        printf ("DEBUG ON: level = %d\n", options.debug_level);

    if (options.echo)
        printf ("ECHO ON\n");

    if (options.list)
        printf ("LIST ON\n");

    if (options.redirect)
        printf ("REDIRECT ON\n");

    leave (EXIT_NORMAL);

    return (EXIT_NORMAL);

}

/*############################################*/
```

```
/*****************************************************

   FILE NAME    : optlibs.c
   AUTHOR       : Matt Weisfeld

   DESCRIPTION : options driver

*****************************************************/
#include <stdio.h>
#include <string.h>
#ifdef DOS
#include <stdlib.h>
#endif
#include "proto.h"

extern OPTFUNCS optfuncs[];

/*****************************************************

   ROUTINE NAME : parse_options

   DESCRIPTION   : parse options comming from the
                   command line.

   INPUT         : argc, argv

   OUTPUT        : none

*****************************************************/
void parse_options(argc, argv)
int argc;
char **argv;
{
    int i;         /* internal loop control */
    int loop=0;

    int skip;

    char opt[STRLEN];

    /*
        Begin the search for parameters. All options must
        begin with a minus sign(-). The value string and
```

```
        location string are positional. They may exist
        anywhere in the parameter list as long as the
        value string preceeds the location string. Both
        must be present!
*/

while (++loop < argc) {

    skip = 0;

    /* check for option */

    if (argv[loop][0] != OPTIONS_FLAG) {

        printf ("Warning: no option flag for '%s' -
        ignored\n",
            argv[loop]);

    } else {

        strcpy (opt, ++argv[loop]);

        /* search internal function list for desired
        function */

        for (i=0; optfuncs[i].string != NULL; i++) {

            /* if found, executed it */

            if (!strcmp(optfuncs[i].string, opt)) {

                skip = (*(optfuncs[i].funcptr))
                (argv,loop);

                break;

            }

        }

        /* if we reach this point, function is not in
        internal list */
```

```
                    if (optfuncs[i].string == NULL)
                        printf ("Warning: invalid option '%s' -
                        ignored\n",
                            argv[loop]);

            }

        loop = loop + skip;

    }

    return;

}

/*###########################################*/


/***************************************************

  FILE NAME   : opts.c
  AUTHOR      : Matt Weisfeld

  DESCRIPTION : option routines

***************************************************/
#include <stdio.h>
#include <stdlib.h>
#include "proto.h"
#include "opts.h"
#include "er.h"

extern OPTIONS options;

int p_list(argv,loop)
char **argv;
int loop;
{

    options.list = ON;

    return(0);
```

```
}

int p_debug(argv,loop)
char **argv;
int loop;
{

    /* there must be a parameter */

    if (argv[loop+1] == NULL) {
        error (ER_PARAMEXP, "debug");
    }

    /* the parameter must be an integer */

    if ( !(strinteger(argv[loop+1])) ) {
        error (ER_VALIDNUM, argv[loop+1]);
        return(1);
    }

    options.debug_level = atoi(argv[loop+1]);

    return(1);

}

int p_echo(argv,loop)
char **argv;
int loop;
{

    options.echo = ON;

    return(0);

}

int p_redirect(argv,loop)
char **argv;
int loop;
{
```

```
    /* redirect, redirect output into */
    /*          specified log */

    options.redirect = ON;

    /* redirect stdout */
    if (freopen(argv[loop+1],"w", stdout)==NULL) {
        error(ER_NOREDIRECT, argv[loop+1]);
    } else {
        fprintf (stderr, "Output redirected to %s\n",
        argv[loop+1]);
    }

    return(1);

}

/*################################################*/


/****************************************************

  FILE NAME   : optlibs.h
  AUTHOR      : Matt Weisfeld

  DESCRIPTION : header file for options library.

****************************************************/
#ifdef ANSI
void parse_options(int, char**);
void check_error(int, char **, int, int);
int check_args(int,char **,int,int);
#else
void parse_options();
void check_error();
int check_args();
#endif

#define OPTIONS_FLAG '-'

#define LEVEL0 0
#define LEVEL1 1
#define LEVEL2 2
```

```
#define NOFLAG -1
#define INVOPT -2

/* this structure is used to hold an internal command
definition */

typedef struct {        /* template for internal commands */
    char *string;       /* option string */
#ifdef ANSI
    int (*funcptr)(char **, int);        /* pointer to the
                                            internal function */
#else
    int (*funcptr)(); /* pointer to the internal function */
#endif
} OPTFUNCS;


/*###########################################*/


/***************************************************

  FILE NAME   : opts.h
  AUTHOR      : Matt Weisfeld

  DESCRIPTION : prototypes for options routines

***************************************************/

/* current internal commands */

typedef struct opnode {
    int debug_level;
    int echo;
    int list;
    int redirect;
} OPTIONS;

int p_list();
int p_debug();        /* option debug */
int p_echo();         /* option echo */
int p_redirect();     /* option redirect */

/*###########################################*/
```

```
/****************************************************

    FILE NAME    : er.h
    AUTHOR       : Matt Weisfeld

    DESCRIPTION : error definitions for options.

*****************************************************/
#define ER_PARAMEXP    0    /* parameter expected */
#define ER_NOREDIRECT  1 /* attempt to redirect failed */
#define ER_VALIDNUM    2 /* attempt to redirect failed */

/*###########################################*/


/****************************************************

    FILE NAME    : errdefs.h
    AUTHOR       : Matt Weisfeld

    DESCRIPTION : error descriptions for options.

*****************************************************/
#include "er.h"

ERROR_STRUCT error_message[] =

/* actual error messages */

{

    /* #0 */
    ER_PARAMEXP, EXIT,
    "Parameter expected for '%s' option.",
    /* #1 */
    ER_NOREDIRECT, EXIT,
    "Redirection failed for file '%s'.",
    /* #2 */
    ER_VALIDNUM, EXIT,
    "'%s' not a valid number.",
    LASTERROR, EXIT,NULL,

};
```

```
/*###############################################*/


/***************************************************

   FILE NAME   : proto.h
   AUTHOR      : Matt Weisfeld

   DESCRIPTION : prototype file for the options
                 library.

***************************************************/
#ifdef VMS
#include "[-.common]common.h"
#include "[-.leave]leave.h"
#include "[-.error]error.h"
#include "[-.strlibs]strlibs.h"
#endif

#ifdef BCC
#include "..\common\common.h"
#include "..\leave\leave.h"
#include "..\error\error.h"
#include "..\strlibs\strlibs.h"
#endif

#ifdef MSC
#include "..\common\common.h"
#include "..\leave\leave.h"
#include "..\error\error.h"
#include "..\strlibs\strlibs.h"
#endif

#ifdef HPUX
#include "../common/common.h"
#include "../leave/leave.h"
#include "../error/error.h"
#include "../strlibs/strlibs.h"
#endif

#ifdef SLC
#include "../common/common.h"
```

```
#include "../leave/leave.h"
#include "../error/error.h"
#include "../strlibs/strlibs.h"
#endif

#ifdef GCC
#include "../common/common.h"
#include "../leave/leave.h"
#include "../error/error.h"
#include "../strlibs/strlibs.h"
#endif

#include "optlibs.h"

/*###############################################*/

$! VMS DCL PROCEDURE
$ clr
$ if (P1.eqs."") then GOTO ALL
$ if (P1.eqs."ALL") then GOTO ALL
$ if (P1.eqs."LINK") then GOTO LINK
$ set verify
$ cc/define=VMS 'P1'
$ goto LINK
$ ALL:
$    set verify
$ cc/define=VMS test
$ cc/define=VMS optlibs
$ cc/define=VMS opts
$ LINK:
$ link/executable=test test,optlibs,opts,[-.leave]leave,
[-.error]error,[-.strlibs]strlibs
$ copy test.exe [weisfeld.exe]
$ set noverify

/*###############################################*/

# makefile for BCC/C++ Compiler

OBJS    = test.obj optlibs.obj opts.obj
LIBS    = ..\leave\leave.obj ..\error\error.obj
          ..\strlibs\strlibs.obj
```

```
HDRS     = proto.h errdefs.h optlibs.h er.h
FLAGS    = -c -DBCC
COMP     = bcc

test.exe:  $(OBJS)
    $(COMP) $(OBJS) $(LIBS)

test.obj: test.c $(HDRS)
    $(COMP) $(FLAGS) test.c

optlibs.obj: optlibs.c $(HDRS)
    $(COMP) $(FLAGS) optlibs.c

opts.obj: opts.c $(HDRS)
    $(COMP) $(FLAGS) opts.c

test.c:
optlibs.c:
opts.c:

optlibs.h:


/*###########################################*/

# makefile for MSC/C++ Compiler

OBJS     = test.obj optlibs.obj opts.obj
LIBS     = ..\leave\leave.obj ..\error\error.obj
           ..\strlibs\strlibs.obj
HDRS     = proto.h errdefs.h optlibs.h er.h
FLAGS    = /c /DMSC
COMP     = cl

test.exe:  $(OBJS)
    $(COMP) $(OBJS) $(LIBS)

test.obj: test.c $(HDRS)
    $(COMP) $(FLAGS) test.c

optlibs.obj: optlibs.c $(HDRS)
    $(COMP) $(FLAGS) optlibs.c
```

```
opts.obj: opts.c $(HDRS)
    $(COMP) $(FLAGS) opts.c

test.c:
optlibs.c:
opts.c:

optlibs.h:


/*##############################################*/

# makefile for HP C Compiler

OBJS     = test.o optlibs.o opts.o
LIBS     = ../leave/leave.o ../error/error.o \
            ../strlibs/strlibs.o
HDRS     = optlibs.h opts.h proto.h ../common/common.h
FLAGS    = -DHPUX -Aa

test.exe:  $(OBJS)
    cc -o test $(OBJS) $(LIBS)

test.o: test.c $(HDRS) errdefs.h er.h
    cc $(FLAGS) -c test.c

optlibs.o: optlibs.c $(HDRS)
    cc $(FLAGS) -c optlibs.c

opts.o: opts.c $(HDRS)
    cc $(FLAGS) -c opts.c

test.c:
optlibs.c:
opts.c:

errdefs.h:
er.h:
internal.h:

/*##############################################*/
```

```
# makefile for SUN SLC C Compiler

OBJS      = test.o optlibs.o opts.o
LIBS      = ../leave/leave.o ../error/error.o
            ../strlibs/strlibs.o
HDRS      = proto.h errdefs.h optlibs.h er.h
FLAGS     = -c -DSLC
COMP      = cc

test.exe:  $(OBJS)
    $(COMP) -o test $(OBJS) $(LIBS)

test.o: test.c $(HDRS)
    $(COMP) $(FLAGS) test.c

optlibs.o: optlibs.c $(HDRS)
    $(COMP) $(FLAGS) optlibs.c

opts.o: opts.c $(HDRS)
    $(COMP) $(FLAGS) opts.c

test.c:
optlibs.c:
opts.c:

optlibs.h:



/*###########################################*/

# makefile for SUN GCC C Compiler

OBJS      = test.o optlibs.o opts.o
LIBS      = ../leave/leave.o ../error/error.o
            ../strlibs/strlibs.o
HDRS      = proto.h errdefs.h optlibs.h er.h
FLAGS     = -c -DGCC
COMP      = gcc

test.exe:  $(OBJS)
    $(COMP) -o test $(OBJS) $(LIBS)
```

```
test.o: test.c $(HDRS)
    $(COMP) $(FLAGS) test.c

optlibs.o: optlibs.c $(HDRS)
    $(COMP) $(FLAGS) optlibs.c

opts.o: opts.c $(HDRS)
    $(COMP) $(FLAGS) opts.c

test.c:
optlibs.c:
opts.c:

optlibs.h:


/*###########################################*/

# makefile for CCC Compiler

OBJS    = test.o optlibs.o opts.o
LIBS    = ../leave/leave.o ../error/error.o
          ../strlibs/strlibs.o
HDRS    = proto.h errdefs.h optlibs.h er.h
FLAGS   = -c -DCCC
COMP    = cc

test.exe:  $(OBJS)
    $(COMP) -o test $(OBJS) $(LIBS)

test.o: test.c $(HDRS)
    $(COMP) $(FLAGS) test.c

optlibs.o: optlibs.c $(HDRS)
    $(COMP) $(FLAGS) optlibs.c

opts.o: opts.c $(HDRS)
    $(COMP) $(FLAGS) opts.c

test.c:
optlibs.c:
opts.c:

optlibs.h:
```

16

Controlling the Screen

Screen handling is another area that is very nonportable across systems. Again, we must deal with the fact that some platforms (DOS) map directly to the terminal, while others (VMS and UNIX) can drive many terminals at the same time. Thus, one way to build portable screen handlers is to take into account each platform's system calls.

Given the vast number of combinations of platforms and terminals available, I concentrated on the ANSI standard for screen control, using a VT100 terminal for the VMS and SUN platforms. Portability is not such a clearcut situation when so many variables are present, so some code modification may be needed for certain hardware combinations.

16.1 SCREEN ADDRESSING

Since the objective is to control the screen, it is necessary to understand how to maneuver around the screen. The text screen is composed of characters in a two-dimensional window addressed by coordinates x and y. The size of the screen depends on the platform and the device that is being used. For example, to address the upper left-hand corner of the screen, the coordinates are (0,0)—some coordinate systems may start at (1,1).

The two types of addressing that are of concern are absolute and relative. *Absolute addressing* refers to a specific location on the screen, regardless of the current cursor position. The points (0,0) and (1,1) are absolute addresses. *Relative addressing* is referenced from a specific position, usually the current cursor position. Thus, if the current position is (10,10), moving 10 positions right on the x axis would put the new location at (20,10). Absolute and relative addressing produce very different results, so it is important to know the context of the application where they are used.

16.2 ESCAPE SEQUENCES

Each platform has it own way of controlling the screen. Again, the fact that DOS can map directly into memory to control the screen sets it apart from other platforms—most nonDOS platforms are device-independent. One way to deal with device independence is to send out escape sequences which must be interpreted by the terminal itself.

ANSI has provided a set of escape sequences that all ANSI-compliant platforms conform to. In the example library in this chapter, the VT100s use these ANSI sequences, while the HP-UX machine does not. DOS also supports ANSI escape sequences if ANSI.SYS has been loaded. To send an escape sequence, a simple *printf* is executed, as in the examples given here.

Escape sequences are basically strings that begin with an escape code. For all escape sequences used here, that code is "\033[". When this code is recognized, the system knows that an escape sequence follows. Escape sequences are quite cryptic. They are, in effect, simply codes. The ANSI code for absolute cursor addressing is:

```
"\033[x;yH"
```

To move the cursor to address (10,15), the following code is used:

```
printf ("\033[10;15H");
```

Of course, this one line of code is not that useful unless the location (10,15) is the only one of interest on the screen. To make the string more generic, conventional *printf( )* escape sequences are added:

```
printf ("\033[%d;%dH",x,y);
```

Even with this more flexible version, it is still necessary to remember what the exact escape sequence is. To make this process more mnemonic, the following approach is used:

```
static char curabs[] = {"\033[%d;%dH"};
```

Thus any need for absolute addressing is executed as:

```
printf (curabs,x,y);
```

For nonANSI-compliant platforms, simply substitute the necessary code:

```
"\033&a%dc%dY"        (for the HP-UX)
```

Relative addressing requires more escape sequences, since the cursor can move in any of four directions (up, down, right, and left). For ANSI, the code for moving the cursor up is

```
static char curseup[] = {"\033[1A"};
```

For HP, it is

```
static char curseup[] = {"\033&a-%dR"};
```

For relative cursor movement, the ANSI codes have an added feature. Note that there is a "1" to the right of the bracket in each of the ANSI codes. This signifies that the cursor is to move only one position. If the cursor must move up 3 positions, the code will be

```
static char curseup[] = {"\033[3A"};
```

Or, more generally,

```
static char curseup[] = {"\033[%dA"};
```

Other categories of escape sequences include screen control, line control, character control, page control, and attribute control. All escape sequences are provided in the file *scrlibs.h*. The specific categories are discussed as the actual libraries are presented.

16.3 ABSOLUTE ADDRESSING

Since most screen functions involve cursor movement, building a portable function to handle this task is a good place to start. This discussion focuses on the ANSI escape sequences for doing so, though other ways exist to move the cursor.

Thus a portable function for absolute addressing has the form:

```
void cursor_abs(x,y)
int x,y;
{

#ifdef HPUX
        printf (curabs, y,x);
#else
        printf (curabs, x,y);
#endif
        fflush(stdout);

        return;

}
```

The *fflush(stdout)* is also necessary, at least for VMS and UNIX. I have found that, as in other cases with buffered output, the actual prints do not always occur when expected. Thus, to ensure that the escape sequences are executed after the *printf( )* is executed, use a *fflush( )*.

16.4 RELATIVE ADDRESSING

Moving the cursor in relative terms may take more than one operation. Whereas an absolute movement goes directly to one location, a relative move must move a specific number of positions along the x and y axis. Remember that the ANSI code can move more than one position at a time:

```
void cursor_up(move)
int move;
{

        int i;

        printf (curseup, move);

        fflush(stdout);
        return;


}
```

Other cursor movement routines and screen handling routines are found in *scrlibs.c.* So far, movement in relative terms has only been in one direction at a time. It is possible to construct a function that will move the cursor relative to both the x and the y axis at the same time, as follows:

```
void cursor_rel(x,y)
int x,y;
{

        if (x<0)
                cursor_left(abs(x));
        else
                cursor_right(x);

        if (y<0)
                cursor_down(abs(y));
        else
                cursor_up(y);
```

```
fflush(stdout);

return;
}
```

16.5 CLEARING THE SCREEN

While the *clrscr*( ) function in BORLAND C++ clears the entire physical screen regardless of the cursor position, the ANSI escape sequence for clearing the screen clears only from the current cursor position on some systems. Thus before the *clear* is executed, the cursor must be positioned at coordinates (0,0).

To clear the screen a library called *clear_screen*( ) is constructed:

```
void clear_screen()
{

        cursor_abs(0,0);
        printf (clear);
        fflush(stdout);

        return;

}
```

16.6 LINE OPERATIONS

The screen line functions are fairly straightforward. One thing to be aware of is how the line controls ('/n', '/r', and so on) are used. For example, using the statement

```
printf ("Line 1\n");
```

followed immediately by a line insert will put the inserted line after "Line 1". To insert the line before line 1, do not use the new line sequence.

The line clearing sequence works in the same way as that for clearing the screen—it clears all characters to the right of the cursor. Thus to clear the entire line, move the cursor to the beginning of the line.

16.7 CHARACTER OPERATIONS

Both ANSI and HP provide the means for character manipulation such as inserting and deleting characters from the screen. DOS does not provide this capability, but it can be built. The delete sequence will remove the character where the cursor resides. The insert sequence is a bit different.

For the platforms that use escape sequences, there are two modes that dictate whether the mode is insertion or overstrike. If the mode is insertion, a blank is inserted at the cursor position, and all characters to the right are moved right one position. If the mode is overstrike, a character simply replaces the one at the cursor position. The overstrike mode is the default. When insertions are necessary, change the mode to insert, then enter the needed characters. Make sure that insert mode is turned off when the insertion is completed. The routine for character deletion is as follows:

```
void delete_char()
{

#ifdef BCC
        char buffer[4096];
        int savex,savey;

        gettext(wherex()+1,wherey(),80,wherey(),buffer);

        puttext(wherex(),wherey(),79,wherey(),buffer);
        savex = wherex();
        savey = wherey();
        gotoxy(80,savey);
        printf ("%c", ' ');
        gotoxy(savex,savey);
#else
        printf (delchar);
#endif
        fflush(stdout);
```

```
      return;


}
```

As was mentioned previously, delete character and insert character routines can be built for BORLAND C++. To do this you need the *gettext( )* and *puttext( )* commands. To delete the character at the cursor, perform a *gettext( )* on the line to the right of the cursor and then use a *puttext( )* to move all the characters one position to the left. In this case the last position on the line is updated with a blank, just to ensure that no garbage emerges, though this is not always the best approach for an application such as an editor.

The insert line routine follows the same strategy, except that the line to the right of the cursor is moved one character to the right. Note that if the last position is occupied, then the line will move off the screen.

16.8 SPECIAL SCREEN ATTRIBUTES

It is also possible to change the attributes of characters to utilize features such as bolding, reverse video, and so on. For example, the routine to use bold video is:

```
void do_bold()
{

      printf (bold);

      fflush(stdout);

      return;

}
```

Other attributes include underlining and reverse video. Note that the HP system does not support bolding, so the half-bright attribute is used. Some HP platforms do not support blinking.

To return to normal mode use the following:

```
void do_normal()
{

        printf (normal);
        fflush(stdout);
        return;

}
```

Some escape sequences, such as the double height and width attributes in VMS, are specific to one platform. In addition, note that though the double height and width attributes may only be intended for one character, using these attributes will affect the entire line, even those characters that have already been written.

16.9 USING THE SCREEN LIBRARIES

The test program for *scrlibs* tests all the functions developed in this chapter, including cursor movement and screen atributes. Make sure that when these libraries are used the curent terminal device is taken into consideration. To use the screen libraries, simply link the *scrlibs* object library with the appropriate application. When using the ANSI escape sequences on a DOS machine, make sure that the ANSI.SYS driver is loaded.

Despite the ANSI escape sequences, there are still some areas that are not as standard as a programmer would like. In addition to the functions explained in this chapter, several other screen functions reside in the screen handling library just to give a flavor of what else is possible. The header files explain their behavior. Many of them may need to be tailored for specific platforms and applications.

16.10 CONCLUSION

Screen operations are not very portable. However, if an attempt is made to stick to the ANSI escape sequences, then a certain level of portability is attainable. Due to the vast number of platforms and terminals available, it is very difficult to create libraries that are portable to each variation. The programmer must thus make some decisions as to what coverage is appropriate.

```
/*****************************************************

   FILE NAME    : test.c
   AUTHOR       : Matt Weisfeld

   DESCRIPTION : test file for screen libraries

*****************************************************/
#include <stdio.h>
#include "proto.h"

#ifdef DOS
#include <dos.h>
#endif

#define SLEEP 2
#define PAUSE 10000000

main()
{

        clear_screen();

        printf ("here we go again");
        printf ("\n");

        do_reverse();

        printf ("reverse video");
        printf ("\n");

        do_normal();

        do_bold();

        printf ("bold video");
        printf ("\n");
```

```
do_normal();
do_blink();

printf ("blink video");
printf ("\n");

do_normal();

printf ("normal video");
printf ("\n");

printf ("double width video");
printf ("\n");

do_width("hello");
printf ("\n");

printf ("double height video");
printf ("\n");

do_double("hello");
printf ("\n");

do_normal();

printf ("normal video");
printf ("\n");

do_sleep();

clear_screen();

printf ("cursor movement\n");

inform("CURSOR DOWN 10");
cursor_down(10);
do_sleep();

inform("CURSOR RIGHT 10");
cursor_right(10);
do_sleep();
```

```
        inform("CURSOR UP 5");
        cursor_up(5);
        do_sleep();

        inform("CURSOR LEFT 5");
        cursor_left(5);
        do_sleep();

        inform("CURSOR RELATIVE 5,5");
        cursor_rel(5,5);
        do_sleep();

        inform("CURSOR RELATIVE -5,-5");
        cursor_rel(-5,-5);
        do_sleep();

        inform("CURSOR RELATIVE -5,5");
        cursor_rel(-5,5);
        do_sleep();

        inform("CURSOR RELATIVE 5,-5");
        cursor_rel(5,-5);
        do_sleep();

        inform("CURSOR ABSOLUTE 0,0");
        cursor_abs(0,0);
        do_sleep();

        clear_screen();

#ifndef MSC

        inform("DELETE LINE");
        printf ("\nI am to be deleted");
        do_sleep();
        delete_line();
#ifndef HPUX
        save_cursor();
        cursor_abs(22,0);
        delete_line();
        restore_cursor();
#endif
        do_sleep();
```

```
#endif

        inform("REMOVE LAST WORD");
        printf ("\rThe last word will be removed");
        do_sleep();
        cursor_left(7);
        do_sleep();
        clear_line();
        do_sleep();

#ifndef MSC

        inform("INSERT A LINE");
        printf ("\nInsert a line");
        do_sleep();
        insert_line();
        do_sleep();

#endif

        printf("\rBye\n\n");
        do_sleep();

        printf ("\n");

        clear_screen();

        leave (EXIT_NORMAL);

        return(EXIT_NORMAL);

}

/***************************************************
*                                                 *
*   ROUTINE NAME : inform()                       *
*                                                 *
*   DESCRIPTION  : write out message to screen    *
*                                                 *
*   INPUT        : char * (message string)        *
*                                                 *
*   OUTPUT       : none                           *
*                                                 *
***************************************************/
```

```c
void inform(message)
char *message;
{

#ifndef HPUX
       save_cursor();
       cursor_abs(23,0);
       delete_line();
       cursor_abs(23,0);
       do_bold();
       printf (message);
       do_normal();
       restore_cursor();
#endif

       return;
}


/****************************************************

   ROUTINE NAME : do_sleep()

   DESCRIPTION  : pause the program

   INPUT        : none

   OUTPUT       : none

****************************************************/
void do_sleep()
{
#ifdef MSC
       unsigned long i;

       for (i=1;i<=PAUSE;i++);
#else
       sleep(SLEEP);
#endif
}
```

```
/****************************************************

  FILE NAME   : scrlibs.c
  AUTHOR      : Matt Weisfeld

  DESCRIPTION : screen handling libraries

****************************************************/
#include <stdio.h>
#include "proto.h"
#ifdef DOS
#include <math.h>
#include <conio.h>
#endif

void home()
{
#ifdef DOS
      printf (curhome);
#endif
#ifdef VMS
      printf (curhome);
#endif
#ifdef HPUX
      cursor_abs(0,0);
#endif
}

/****************************************************

  ROUTINE NAME : clear_screen()

  DESCRIPTION  : clears the physical screen

  INPUT        : none

  OUTPUT       : none

****************************************************/
```

```
void clear_screen()
{

        cursor_abs(0,0);
        printf (clear);
        fflush(stdout);

        return;

}

/**************************************************

   ROUTINE NAME : do_reverse()

   DESCRIPTION  : write text out in reverse mode

   INPUT        : none

   OUTPUT       : none

**************************************************/
void do_reverse()
{

        printf (reverse);
        fflush(stdout);
        return;
}

/**************************************************

   ROUTINE NAME : do_normal()

   DESCRIPTION  : write text out in normal mode

   INPUT        : none

   OUTPUT       : none

**************************************************/
```

```
void do_normal()
{

      printf (normal);
      fflush(stdout);
      return;

}
/****************************************************

  ROUTINE NAME : do_bold()

  DESCRIPTION  : write text out in bold mode

  INPUT        : none

  OUTPUT       : none

****************************************************/
void do_bold()
{

      printf (bold);

      fflush(stdout);

      return;

}

/****************************************************

  ROUTINE NAME : do_blink()

  DESCRIPTION  : write text out in blink mode

  INPUT        : none

  OUTPUT       : none

****************************************************/
```

```c
void do_blink()
{

       printf (blink);
       fflush(stdout);

       return;

}

/*****************************************************

   ROUTINE NAME : do_double()

   DESCRIPTION  : write string out in double
                  height

   INPUT        : char *

   OUTPUT       : none

*****************************************************/
void do_double(string)
char *string;
{

#ifdef VMS
       printf ("%s%s\n\r%s%s%s", dht, string, dhb, string,
       normal);
#else
       printf ("NOT SUPPORTED\n");
#endif
       return;

}
/*****************************************************

   ROUTINE NAME : do_width  ()

   DESCRIPTION  : write string out in double width
```

```
  INPUT        : char *

  OUTPUT       : none

****************************************************/
void do_width(string)
char *string;
{

#ifdef VMS
      printf ("%s%s", dw, string);
#else
      printf ("NOT SUPPORTED\n");
#endif
      return;

}

/***************************************************

  ROUTINE NAME : cursor_abs()

  DESCRIPTION  : move cursor to absolute position
                 on screen

  INPUT        : int, int (coords x,y)

  OUTPUT       : none

****************************************************/
void cursor_abs(x,y)
int x,y;
{

#ifdef HPUX
      printf (curabs, y,x);
#else
      printf (curabs, x,y);
#endif
      fflush(stdout);
```

```
        return;

}
/***************************************************

  ROUTINE NAME : cursor_rel()

  DESCRIPTION  : move cursor to relative position
                 on screen

  INPUT        : int, int (coords x,y)

  OUTPUT       : none

***************************************************/
void cursor_rel(x,y)
int x,y;
{

        if (x<0)
                cursor_left(abs(x));
        else
                cursor_right(x);

        if (y<0)
                cursor_down(abs(y));
        else
                cursor_up(y);

        fflush(stdout);

        return;
}
/***************************************************

  ROUTINE NAME : cursor_up()

  DESCRIPTION  : move cursor up
```

```
   INPUT        : int, (position up)

   OUTPUT       : none

**************************************************/
void cursor_up(move)
int move;
{

      int i;

      printf (curseup, move);

      fflush(stdout);
      return;

}
/**************************************************

   ROUTINE NAME : cursor_down()

   DESCRIPTION  : move cursor down

   INPUT        : int, (position down)

   OUTPUT       : none

**************************************************/
void cursor_down(move)
int move;
{

      int i;

      printf (cursedown, move);
      fflush(stdout);
      return;

}
```

```
/******************************************************

   ROUTINE NAME : cursor_right()

   DESCRIPTION  : move cursor right

   INPUT        : int, (position right)

   OUTPUT       : none

******************************************************/
void cursor_right(move)
int move;
{

        int i;

        printf (curseright, move);
        fflush(stdout);
        return;

}
/******************************************************

   ROUTINE NAME : cursor_left()

   DESCRIPTION  : move cursor left

   INPUT        : int, (position left)

   OUTPUT       : none

******************************************************/
void cursor_left(move)
int move;
{

        int i;

        printf (curseleft, move);
        fflush(stdout);
```

```
        return;
}

/**************************************************

  ROUTINE NAME : clear_line()

  DESCRIPTION  : clear entire line

  INPUT        : none

  OUTPUT       : none

**************************************************/
void clear_line()
{

      printf (clrline);
      fflush(stdout);
      return;

}
/**************************************************

  ROUTINE NAME : delete_line()

  DESCRIPTION  : delete entire line

  INPUT        : none

  OUTPUT       : none

**************************************************/
void delete_line()
{
#ifndef MSC

#ifdef BCC
      delline();
#else
      printf (delline);
```

```
#endif
        fflush(stdout);
#endif
        return;

}

/****************************************************

  ROUTINE NAME : insert_line()

  DESCRIPTION  : insert line before

  INPUT        : none

  OUTPUT       : none

****************************************************/
void insert_line()
{

#ifndef MSC
#ifdef BCC
        insline();
#else
        printf (insline);
#endif
        fflush(stdout);
#endif
        return;

}
/****************************************************

  ROUTINE NAME : save_cursor

  DESCRIPTION  : save cursor position

  INPUT        : none

  OUTPUT       : none

****************************************************/
```

```
void save_cursor()
{

        printf (savecur);
        fflush(stdout);
        return;

}
/****************************************************

   ROUTINE NAME : restore_cursor()

   DESCRIPTION  : restore cursor position

   INPUT        : none

   OUTPUT       : none

****************************************************/
void restore_cursor()
{

        printf (restcur);
        fflush(stdout);
        return;

}
/****************************************************

   FILE NAME    : scrlibs.h
   AUTHOR       : Matt Weisfeld

   DESCRIPTION  : header file for scrlibs.c

****************************************************/
#ifdef ANSI
void do_sleep(void);
void inform(char *);
void clear_screen(void);
void get_initial(void);
void do_reverse(void);
void do_normal(void);
```

```
void do_bold(void);
void do_blink(void);
void do_double(char *string);
void do_width(char *string);
void save_cursor(void);
void restore_cursor(void);
void cursor_up(int move);
void cursor_down(int move);
void cursor_right(int move);
void cursor_left(int move);
void cursor_abs(int,int);
void cursor_rel(int,int);
void home(void);
void delete_line(void);
void clear_line(void);
void insert_line(void);
#else
void inform();
void do_sleep();
void clear_screen();
void get_initial();
void do_reverse();
void do_normal();
void do_bold();
void do_blink();
void do_double();
void do_width();
void save_cursor();
void restore_cursor();
void cursor_up();
void cursor_down();
void cursor_right();
void cursor_left();
void cursor_abs();
void cursor_rel();
void home();
void delete_line();
void clear_line();
void insert_line();
#endif
```

```
#ifdef VT100
#ifdef DOS
static char bold[] = {"\033[36;1m"};
#else
static char delline[] = {"\033[M"};
static char insline[] = {"\033[L"};
static char bold[] = {"\033[1m"};
#endif
static char savecur[] = {"\033[s"};
static char restcur[] = {"\033[0u"};
static char normal[] = {"\033[0m"};
static char blink[] = {"\033[5m"};
static char reverse[] = {"\033[7m"};
static char curseup[] = {"\033[%dA"};
static char cursedown[] = {"\033[%dB"};
static char curseright[] = {"\033[%dC"};
static char curseleft[] = {"\033[%dD"};
static char curhome[] = {"\033[2H"};
static char curabs[] =   {"\033[%d;%dH"};
static char dht[] = {"\033#3"};
static char dhb[] = {"\033#4"};
static char sw[] = {"\033#5"};
static char dw[] = {"\033#6"};
static char cr[] = {"\033G"};
static char clear[] = {"\033[J"};
static char clrline[] = {"\033[K"};
static char delchar[] = {"\033[P"};
static char inschar[] = {"\033[4h"};
static char leaveins[] = {"\033[4l"};
static char scrollup[] = {"\033[S"};
static char scrolldown[] = {"\033[T"};
static char pageup[] = {"\033[U"};
static char pagedown[] = {"\033[V"};

#endif
#ifdef HPUX
static char savecur[] = {"\033s"};
static char restcur[] = {"\0330u"};
static char bold[] = {"\033&dH"};
static char reverse[] = {"\033&dK"};
static char underline[] = {"\033&dD"};
```

```
static char blink[] = {"\033&dA"};
static char normal[] = {"\033&d@"};
static char curseup[] = {"\033&a-%dR"};
static char cursedown[] = {"\033&a+%dR"};
static char curseright[] = {"\033&a+%dC"};
static char curseleft[] = {"\033&a-%dC"};
static char curabs[] = {"\033&a%dx%dY"};
static char currel[] = {"\033&a+%dc-%dR"};

static char cr[] = {"\033G"};
static char clear[] = {"\033J"};
static char clrline[] = {"\033K"};
static char delline[] = {"\033M"};
static char insline[] = {"\033L"};
static char delchar[] = {"\033P"};
static char inschar[] = {"\033Q"};
static char leaveins[] = {"\033R"};
static char scrollup[] = {"\033S"};
static char scrolldown[] = {"\033T"};
static char pageup[] = {"\033U"};
static char pagedown[] = {"\033V"};
#endif


/****************************************************

   FILE NAME   : proto.h
   AUTHOR      : Matt Weisfeld

   DESCRIPTION : prototype file for screen
                 libraries.

****************************************************/
#ifdef VMS
#include "[-.common]common.h"
#include "[-.leave]leave.h"
#endif

#ifdef BCC
#include "..\common\common.h"
#include "..\leave\leave.h"
#endif
```

```
#ifdef MSC
#include "..\common\common.h"
#include "..\leave\leave.h"
#endif

#ifdef HPUX
#include "../common/common.h"
#include "../leave/leave.h"
#endif

#ifdef SLC
#include "../common/common.h"
#include "../leave/leave.h"
#endif

#ifdef GCC
#include "../common/common.h"
#include "../leave/leave.h"
#endif

#ifdef CCC
#include "../common/common.h"
#include "../leave/leave.h"
#endif

#include "scrlibs.h"

$! VMS DCL PROCEDURE
$ clr
$ if (P1.eqs."") then GOTO ALL
$ if (P1.eqs."ALL") then GOTO ALL
$ if (P1.eqs."LINK") then GOTO LINK
$ set verify
$ cc/define=VMS 'P1'
$ goto LINK
$ ALL:
$     set verify
$ cc/define=VMS test
$ cc/define=VMS scrlibs
$ LINK:
$ link/executable=test test,scrlibs,[-.leave]leave
```

```
$ copy test.exe [weisfeld.exe]
$ set noverify

# makefile for BCC/C++ Compiler

OBJS    = test.obj scrlibs.obj
LIBS    = ..\leave\leave.obj
HDRS    = proto.h scrlibs.h
FLAGS   = -c -DBCC -DVT100
COMP    = bcc

test:   $(OBJS)
        $(COMP) $(OBJS) $(LIBS)

test.obj: test.c $(HDRS)
        $(COMP) $(FLAGS) test.c

scrlibs.obj: scrlibs.c $(HDRS)
        $(COMP) $(FLAGS) scrlibs.c

test.c:
scrlibs.c:

scrlibs.h:

# makefile for MSC/C++ Compiler

OBJS    = test.obj scrlibs.obj
LIBS    = ..\leave\leave.obj
HDRS    = proto.h scrlibs.h
FLAGS   = /c /DMSC /DVT100
COMP    = cl

test:   $(OBJS)
        $(COMP) $(OBJS) $(LIBS)

test.obj: test.c $(HDRS)
        $(COMP) $(FLAGS) test.c

scrlibs.obj: scrlibs.c $(HDRS)
        $(COMP) $(FLAGS) scrlibs.c
```

```
test.c:
scrlibs.c:

scrlibs.h:

# makefile for HPUX C Compiler

OBJS      = test.o scrlibs.o
LIBS      = ../leave/leave.o
HDRS      = proto.h scrlibs.h
FLAGS     = -c -DHPUX
COMP      = cc

test.exe:  $(OBJS)
       $(COMP) -o test $(OBJS) $(LIBS)

test.o: test.c $(HDRS)
       $(COMP) $(FLAGS) test.c

scrlibs.o: scrlibs.c $(HDRS)
       $(COMP) $(FLAGS) scrlibs.c

test.c:
scrlibs.c:

scrlibs.h:

# makefile for SUN SLC C Compiler

OBJS      = test.o scrlibs.o
LIBS      = ../leave/leave.o
HDRS      = proto.h scrlibs.h
FLAGS     = -c -DSLC
COMP      = cc

test.exe:  $(OBJS)
       $(COMP) -o test $(OBJS) $(LIBS)

test.o: test.c $(HDRS)
       $(COMP) $(FLAGS) test.c
```

```
scrlibs.o: scrlibs.c $(HDRS)
        $(COMP) $(FLAGS) scrlibs.c

test.c:
scrlibs.c:

scrlibs.h:

# makefile for SUN GCC C Compiler

OBJS     = test.o scrlibs.o
LIBS     = ../leave/leave.o
HDRS     = proto.h scrlibs.h
FLAGS    = -c -DGCC
COMP     = gcc

test.exe:  $(OBJS)
        $(COMP) -o test $(OBJS) $(LIBS)

test.o: test.c $(HDRS)
        $(COMP) $(FLAGS) test.c

scrlibs.o: scrlibs.c $(HDRS)
        $(COMP) $(FLAGS) scrlibs.c

test.c:
scrlibs.c:

scrlibs.h:

# makefile for CCC Compiler

OBJS     = test.o scrlibs.o
LIBS     = ../leave/leave.o
HDRS     = proto.h scrlibs.h
FLAGS    = -c -DCCC -DVT100
COMP     = cc

test.exe:  $(OBJS)
        $(COMP) -o test $(OBJS) $(LIBS)
```

```
test.o: test.c $(HDRS)
        $(COMP) $(FLAGS) test.c

scrlibs.o: scrlibs.c $(HDRS)
        $(COMP) $(FLAGS) scrlibs.c

test.c:
scrlibs.c:

scrlibs.h:
```

17

Keyboard Input

One of the curious features of C is the great difficulty simply retrieving one character causes. The reason for this, of course, is the fact that all I/O is buffered for greater efficiency, and this strategy dictates that a program cannot receive a single character until the buffer is full or flushed. For the user, this means that a program will not recognize a single character until a return is entered. This behavior is not always desirable. In fact, this behavior make some applications, such as screen editors, unworkable.

Some C environments, among them DOS, do provide a means to capture one character at a time, based on the fact that the keyboard is mapped directly into memory and is not a device. To provide the same functionality on VMS and UNIX, platform-dependent code must be introduced. Thus returning a single input character, including nonprintable characters, is a good application for a portable library.

17.1 GETTING A KEY FROM DOS

As indicated above, DOS provides the most straightforward method of capturing a single character. BORLAND C's *getch( )* command also provides this functionality as follows:

```
char c;

c = getch();
```

The only tricky part with this command involves receiving non-printable characters such as the arrow keys and the function keys (F1, F2, and so on). All printable characters such as letters, numbers, and others are returned directly. However, some non-printable characters are identified by a two-character sequence. When a *getch*( ) is executed, a nonprintable character returns as a 0. When this 0 is recognized by the program, a second *getch*( ) must be executed immediately to retrieve the second character of the sequence, which holds the desired code.

For example, for BORLAND C to recognize when the F1 key is depressed, the following code is required:

```
char c,c1;

if ( (c=getch()) != 0) {
        printf ("code = %d\n", c); /* printable char */
} else {
        c1=getch();
        if (c1 == 59)
                printf ("F1 key depressed.\n");
}
```

To begin constructing a library that returns only a single character, I present the following code:

```
#include <stdio.h>
#include <conio.h>

char c;

/* this has a bug */
char getkey(void)
{
        if ( (c=getch()) == 0)
                c=getch();
```

```
    return(c);

}
```

This does indeed return one character, though unfortunately, not necessarily the proper one. The problem lies with the second *getch*( ), which returns 59 when the F1 key is pressed. In the context of the second *getch*( ), this erroneous result is perfectly correct. However, when the 59 is passed back to the calling routine, it is unclear whether the 59 represents the F1 key or the key that 59 really represents in this case, a semi-colon. To overcome this problem, the values for the nonprintables can be redefined for use by a specific application.

In the following example, the nonprintable keys used are the arrow keys and F1 through F4. The codes representing these keys, after the NULL is recognized, are:

Key	Code
F1	59
F2	60
F3	61
F4	62
LEFT_ARROW	75
RIGHT_ARROW	77
UP_ARROW	72
DOWN_ARROW	80

A simple way of redefining these codes is to subtract a constant from the values for all nonprintable characters to make them fall into a range of numbers that is of no concern to the application. For example, since these numbers are all under 100, subtracting 100 from them will make them all negative— and the resulting numbers do not conflict with the remaining codes needed for this example and summarized in the following list:

Key	Codes
F1	-41
F2	-40
F3	-39
F4	-38
LEFT_ARROW	-25
RIGHT_ARROW	-23
UP_ARROW	-28
DOWN_ARROW	-20
ESCAPE	27
RETURN	13 } Original values
TAB	0

These definitions are placed in a header file, so the following code is used:

```
#include <stdio.h>
#include <conio.h>

char c;

char getkey(void)
{

        if ( (c=getch()) == 0)
            c= (getch())-100;

        return(c);

}
```

Expanding this example to include other nonprintable keys is trivial. In this way, one call to *getkey*( ) will return a one-character code that represents any possible keys entered from the keyboard.

17.2 GETTING A KEY FROM VMS

VMS does not provide the ability within C to obtain just one character. To accomplish this task, certain VMS system commands called SCREEN MANAGEMENT (SMG) must be used. Two are needed to perform character input: SMG$CREATE_VIRTUAL_KEYBOARD and SMG$READ_KEYSTROKE.

The SMG concepts and commands are not covered here, except where directly applicable to this discussion. For full coverage of the SMG commands, see the VMS RTL *Screen Management Manual*. The following sample program illustrates how to use SMG commands:

```
#include <stdio.h>

char getkey(void)
{

    int keyboard;
    char c;

    if ( ((status=SMG$CREATE_VIRTUAL_KEYBOARD
    (&keyboard))&1)!=1)
        return(-1);
    if ( ((status=SMG$READ_KEYSTROKE
    (&keyboard,c))&1)!=1)
        return(-1);
    if ( ((status=SMG$DELETE_VIRTUAL_KEYBOARD
    (&keyboard))&1)!=1)
        return(-1);
    printf ("c = %d\n", c);

    return;

}
```

The SMG$CREATE_VIRTUAL_KEYBOARD command must be called before any character input is attempted. This command assigns the program a virtual keyboard and maps it directly to a physical keyboard, usually the one associated with SYS$INPUT, which is assigned to *stdin*. This id is stored in the variable keyboard, which is used by other SMG commands. The command has many parameters; however, only the first affects this application. A corresponding command, SMG$DELETE_VIRTUAL_KEYBOARD, deletes the virtual keyboard.

To get a character, the SMG$READ_KEYSTROKE command is used. Again, even though this command has many parameters, as you will discover in the SMG manual, only the first two are needed here. The first parameter is the virtual keyboard id defined with the SMG$CREATE_VIRTUAL_KEYBOARD command. The second is the character where the code will be placed.

Unlike the situation involving DOS, no character conversions need be done in this case. The key codes are as follows:

Key	Code
F1	0
F2	1
F3	2
F4	3
ESCAPE	35
RETURN	13
TAB	9
LEFT_ARROW	20
RIGHT_ARROW	21
UP_ARROW	18
DOWN_ARROW	19

17.3 GETTING A KEY FROM UNIX

UNIX poses a special problem. There is really no easy way to capture just one keystroke with UNIX since all keyboard input is in buffered mode. To get out of this buffered mode and into raw mode, many system-level actions must be taken. Getting raw mode to work reliably requires a very low-level understanding of how the UNIX I/O system works. These constraints simply do not constitute a good foundation for a portable library.

Due to the problems mentioned above, this chapter required much more investigation than the others. In all my queries about specific UNIX platforms with regard to capturing a single keystroke, one overriding question arose: why not use Curses? Curses is a graphics package available on most systems as part of the C package or as shareware. In trying to force the issue with the UNIX systems, I finally came to the conclusion that in the best interests of portability and ease of use, the Curses approach is indeed the best solution to portable keyboard input across systems.

17.4 THE BASICS OF CURSES

Just as the C language defines *stdout, stdin,* and *stderr* for input and output, Curses defines *stdscr* to represent the entire screen. This definition of *stdscr* is present in all Curses programs by default—you need not create it. Other Curses constructs must be explicitly created. In most cases, *stdscr* is treated separately from other windows. For example, to clear a window, the *wclear(win)* command is performed, whereas to clear *stdscr,* the *clear( )* command, with no parameters, is used.

All Curses applications, regardless of the platform, must include the file *curses.h,* which is part of the Curses package. One of the data structures contained in *curses.h* is WINDOW. Each window created must correspond to a pointer of this structure type, which contains information such as window location and size. When a window is created, space is reserved in memory. All window operations affect only the memory representation. The screen itself is not updated until a refresh is executed—even when a window is deleted.

17.5 ACCEPTING KEYBOARD INPUT

Keyboard input in Curses is achieved by calling *wgetch( )*. However, this command does not have the proper functionality to perform the tasks required. These tasks include recognizing when a nonprintable character is typed because this application requires the use of the arrow keys.

To get a Curses program to accept input one keystroke at a time, the *cbreak( )* command must be executed. Unless this command is used, input is buffered, and a carriage return is necessary. The *noecho( )* command is also called to prevent keystrokes from being echoed to the screen.

Using the arrow keys from the keypad on MS-DOS is very straightforward. Either the *getch( )* or the *wgetch( )* commands will return the necessary key codes.

Obtaining non-printable characters with VMS requires the use of the low-level Screen Management(SMG) commands described earlier in the chapter. Note that VMS returns a short.

UNIX presents two different cases. Both the HP and SUN systems return keystrokes from the keypad with escape sequences. Some systems, among them HP, include a function called *keypad( )*. This function activates the keypad and returns the proper key code directly, saving the programmer from having to interpret the escape sequences. When the keypad function is not available, the method for dealing with the escape sequences is system-dependent. For example, on the SUN system entering a keypad character will return an escape sequence in three parts. When the first *getch( )* is recognized as an escape, two more *getch( )* commands must be called in succession. The third character contains the code needed. For example:

```
#ifdef HPUX
    term_code = getch();
#endif
#ifdef SUN
    term_code = getch();
    if (term_code == ESCAPE) {
      c=getch();
      term_code = getch();
    }
#endif
```

The characters codes used in these libraries are defined in the file *menu.h* as: UP_ARROW, DOWN_ARROW, LEFT_ARROW, RIGHT_ARROW, ESCAPE, and RETURN.

17.6 USING THE KEYBOARD LIBRARY

The *keylibs* library is a simple case statment that accepts keyboard input. When a recognizable key is entered, its name is displayed on the screen. All other keys will simply echo the single character to the screen. To use the *keylibs* library, the object library must be linked with the application as well as with the platform's *curses* library.

17.7 CONCLUSION

Despite the fact that capturing a single keystroke is a straightforward concept, it is not so simple in practice. Each platform has its own specific way of handling I/O. To overcome the platform differences, Curses is used to make keyboard input quite portable.

```c
/*****************************************************

   FILE NAME   : test.c
   AUTHOR      : Matt Weisfeld

   DESCRIPTION : test file for key libraries

*****************************************************/
#include <stdio.h>
#include "proto.h"
#include "errdefs.h"

main()
{

    int i;
    char c;
    char buffer[STRLEN];

    initscr();
```

```
#ifdef VMS
    crmode();
#else
    cbreak();
#endif

#ifdef HPUX
    keypad(stdscr, TRUE);
#endif

    noecho();

    wclear(stdscr);

#ifdef DOS

    wattrset(stdscr, F_RED | B_BLUE);
    for (i=0;i<24;i++)
        mvinsertln(i,0);

    refresh();

#endif

    move (0,0);

    addstr("GET KEYSTROKE\n");

    refresh();

    while ( (c = getkey()) != ESCAPE ) {

        switch (c) {
            case KEYERR:
                error(ER_BADKEY);
            break;
            case ENTER:
                addstr ("ENTER\n");
            break;
            case LEFT_ARROW:
                addstr ("LEFT_ARROW\n");
            break;
```

```
                    case RIGHT_ARROW:
                        addstr ("RIGHT_ARROW\n");
                    break;
                    case UP_ARROW:
                        addstr ("UP_ARROW\n");
                    break;
                    case DOWN_ARROW:
                        addstr ("DOWN_ARROW\n");
                    break;
                    case TAB:
                        addstr ("TAB\n");
                    break;
                    case DEL:
                        addstr ("DEL\n");
                    break;
                    case INS:
                        addstr ("INS\n");
                    break;
                    default:
                        sprintf (buffer, "default: c = %c : %d\n",
                        c, c);
                        addstr (buffer);
                    break;


            }

        refresh();

    }


    endwin();

    leave(EXIT_NORMAL);

    return;

}

/*##############################################*/
```

```c
/****************************************************

   FILE NAME   : keylibs.c
   AUTHOR      : Matt Weisfeld

   DESCRIPTION : libraries for keyboard input

****************************************************/
#include <stdio.h>
#include "proto.h"

char getkey()
{

  int status;
  char c;
  char buffer[20];

#ifdef VMS
  int keyboard;
  short term_code;
#else
  char term_code;
#endif

#ifdef VMS
  if ( ((  status =
      SMG$CREATE_VIRTUAL_KEYBOARD(&keyboard))&1)!=1) {
       return(KEYERR);
  }
#endif

  term_code = 0;

  /* get a single keystroke */

#ifdef VMS
    if ( ((  status = SMG$READ_KEYSTROKE
        (&keyboard,&term_code))&1)!=1) {
      return(KEYERR);
    }
#endif
#ifdef DOS
```

```
        term_code = getch();
#endif
#ifdef HPUX
        term_code = getch();
#endif
#ifdef SUN
        term_code = getch();
        if (term_code == ESCAPE) {
          c=getch();
          refresh();
          term_code = getch();
        }
#endif

    return(term_code);

}

/*################################################*/


/****************************************************

  FILE NAME   : keylibs.h
  AUTHOR      : Matt Weisfeld

  DESCRIPTION : header file for key libraries

****************************************************/

#include <stdio.h>

/* screen dimensions*/
#define MAX_ROWS 24
#define MAX_COLUMNS 80

/* keystroke codes and color */
#ifdef HPUX
#define UP_ARROW       3
#define DOWN_ARROW     2
#define LEFT_ARROW     4
#define RIGHT_ARROW    5
#define ENTER          10
```

```
#define ESCAPE          27
#define TAB             9
#define INS             75
#define DEL             74
#endif
#ifdef SUN
#define UP_ARROW        65
#define DOWN_ARROW      66
#define LEFT_ARROW      68
#define RIGHT_ARROW     67
#define ENTER           10
#define ESCAPE          27
#define TAB             9
#define INS             75
#define DEL             127
#endif
#ifdef VMS
#define UP_ARROW        18
#define DOWN_ARROW      19
#define LEFT_ARROW      20
#define RIGHT_ARROW     21
#define ENTER           13
#define ESCAPE          35 /* F11 */
#define TAB             9
#define INS             56
#define DEL             57
#endif
#ifdef BCC
#define MAINCOLOR       (F_RED | B_BLACK)
#define DIALOGCOLOR     (F_CYAN | B_BLACK)
#define UP_ARROW        56
#define DOWN_ARROW      50
#define LEFT_ARROW      52
#define RIGHT_ARROW     54
#define  ENTER          10
#define ESCAPE          27
#define TAB             9
#define INS             48
#define DEL             46
#endif

/* macros for portability */
#ifndef VMS
```

```
#define BEGX _begx
#define BEGY _begy
#define MAXX _maxx
#else
#define BEGX _beg_x
#define BEGY _beg_y
#define MAXX _max_x
#endif

/* box characters */

#ifdef BCC
#define SINGLE_SIDE   -77 /* single bar */
#define SINGLE_ACROSS -60
#define DOUBLE_SIDE   -70 /* double bar */
#define DOUBLE_ACROSS -51
#else
#define SINGLE_SIDE   '|'
#define SINGLE_ACROSS '-'
#define DOUBLE_SIDE   '"'
#define DOUBLE_ACROSS '='
#endif

#define KEYERR    -1

#ifdef ANSI
char getkey(void);
#else
char getkey();
#endif

/*###############################################*/


/**************************************************

  FILE NAME   : er.h
  AUTHOR      : Matt Weisfeld

  DESCRIPTION : error descriptions for key
                libraries.

**************************************************/
```

```c
#define ER_BADKEY 0    /* keyboard input failed */


/*###############################################*/


/****************************************************

   FILE NAME   : errdefs.h
   AUTHOR      : Matt Weisfeld

   DESCRIPTION : error strings for key
                 libraries.

****************************************************/
#include "er.h"

ERROR_STRUCT error_message[] =

/* actual error messages */

{

     /* #0 */
     ER_BADKEY, EXIT,
     "An attempt to get keyboard input failed.",
     /* LAST */
     LASTERROR, EXIT,
};


/*###############################################*/


/****************************************************

   FILE NAME   : proto.h
   AUTHOR      : Matt Weisfeld

   DESCRIPTION : prototype file for key
                 libraries.

****************************************************/
```

```
#ifdef VMS
#include "[-.common]common.h"
#include "[-.leave]leave.h"
#include "[-.error]error.h"
#endif

#ifdef BCC
#include "..\common\common.h"
#include "..\leave\leave.h"
#include "..\error\error.h"
#endif

#ifdef MSC
#include "..\common\common.h"
#include "..\leave\leave.h"
#include "..\error\error.h"
#endif

#ifdef HPUX
#include "../common/common.h"
#include "../leave/leave.h"
#include "../error/error.h"
#endif

#ifdef SLC
#include "../common/common.h"
#include "../leave/leave.h"
#include "../error/error.h"
#endif

#ifdef GCC
#include "../common/common.h"
#include "../leave/leave.h"
#include "../error/error.h"
#endif

#ifdef CCC
#include "../common/common.h"
#include "../leave/leave.h"
#include "../error/error.h"
#endif
```

```
#include "keylibs.h"
#include "curses.h"

/*###########################################*/

$! VMS DCL PROCEDURE
$ clr
$ if (P1.eqs."") then GOTO ALL
$ if (P1.eqs."ALL") then GOTO ALL
$ if (P1.eqs."LINK") then GOTO LINK
$ set verify
$ cc/define=VMS 'P1'
$ goto LINK
$ ALL:
$    set verify
$ cc/define=VMS test
$ cc/define=VMS keylibs
$ LINK:
$ link/executable=test test,keylibs,[-.leave]leave,
[-.error]error
$ copy test.exe [weisfeld.exe]
$ set noverify

/*###########################################*/

# makefile for BCC/C++ Compiler

OBJS      = test.obj keylibs.obj
LIBS      = ..\leave\leave.obj ..\error\error.obj
HDRS      = proto.h keylibs.h
FLAGS     = -c -DBCC
COMP      = bcc

test:    $(OBJS)
    $(COMP) $(OBJS) $(LIBS) scurses.lib

test.obj: test.c $(HDRS)
    $(COMP) $(FLAGS) test.c

keylibs.obj: keylibs.c $(HDRS)
    $(COMP) $(FLAGS) keylibs.c
```

```
test.c:
keylibs.c:

keylibs.h:

/*#############################################*/

# makefile for MSC/C++ Compiler

OBJS     = test.obj keylibs.obj
LIBS     = ..\leave\leave.obj
HDRS     = proto.h keylibs.h
FLAGS    = /c /DMSC
COMP     = cl

test:   $(OBJS)
    $(COMP) $(OBJS) $(LIBS) scurses.lib

test.obj: test.c $(HDRS)
    $(COMP) $(FLAGS) test.c

keylibs.obj: keylibs.c $(HDRS)
    $(COMP) $(FLAGS) keylibs.c

test.c:
keylibs.c:

keylibs.h:

/*#############################################*/

# makefile for HPUX C Compiler

OBJS     = test.o keylibs.o
LIBS     = ../leave/leave.o ../error/error.o
HDRS     = proto.h keylibs.h ../leave/leave.h
FLAGS    = -c -DHPUX -Aa
COMP     = cc

test:  $(OBJS)
    $(COMP) -o test $(OBJS) $(LIBS) -lcurses -ltermcap
```

```
test.o: test.c $(HDRS)
    $(COMP) $(FLAGS) test.c

keylibs.o: keylibs.c $(HDRS)
    $(COMP) $(FLAGS) keylibs.c

test.c:
keylibs.c:

keylibs.h:


/*###########################################*/

# makefile for SUN SLC C Compiler

OBJS    = test.o keylibs.o
LIBS    = ../leave/leave.o ../error/error.o
HDRS    = proto.h keylibs.h ../leave/leave.h
FLAGS   = -c -DSLC
COMP    = cc

test:  $(OBJS)
    $(COMP) -o test $(OBJS) $(LIBS) -lcurses -ltermcap

test.o: test.c $(HDRS)
    $(COMP) $(FLAGS) test.c

keylibs.o: keylibs.c $(HDRS)
    $(COMP) $(FLAGS) keylibs.c

test.c:
keylibs.c:

keylibs.h:


/*###########################################*/

# makefile for SUN GCC C Compiler

OBJS    = test.o keylibs.o
LIBS    = ../leave/leave.o ../error/error.o
```

```
HDRS     = proto.h keylibs.h ../leave/leave.h
FLAGS    = -c -DGCC
COMP     = gcc

test:  $(OBJS)
    $(COMP) -o test $(OBJS) $(LIBS) -lcurses -ltermcap

test.o: test.c $(HDRS)
    $(COMP) $(FLAGS) test.c

keylibs.o: keylibs.c $(HDRS)
    $(COMP) $(FLAGS) keylibs.c

test.c:
keylibs.c:

keylibs.h:


/*###########################################*/

# makefile for CCC Compiler

OBJS     = test.o keylibs.o
LIBS     = ../leave/leave.o ../error/error.o
HDRS     = proto.h keylibs.h ../leave/leave.h
FLAGS    = -c -DCCC -DSUN
COMP     = cc

test:  $(OBJS)
    $(COMP) -o test $(OBJS) $(LIBS) -lcurses -ltermcap

test.o: test.c $(HDRS)
    $(COMP) $(FLAGS) test.c

keylibs.o: keylibs.c $(HDRS)
    $(COMP) $(FLAGS) keylibs.c

test.c:
keylibs.c:

keylibs.h:
```

## 18

A Portable User Interface

The topics of portability and user interfaces (UIs) are usually not mentioned in the same conversation. The reason for this is that UIs are notoriously difficult to port, due mainly to the hardware-dependent nature of terminal devices. However, if portability is the overriding concern, there are alternatives to writing a separate UI for each platform. This chapter presents a library of routines that allow a programmer to create portable, text-based, User Interfaces using Curses. Curses is a graphics package available on most systems as part of the C package or as shareware.

18.1 THE USER INTERFACE

The goal of this discussion is to create a UI that looks similar on all platforms, including VMS, DOS, and UNIX. The display consists of a main window, a menu bar and a dialog box (see Figure 18.1).

The main window occupies the entire screen and is the backdrop for all other constructs. At the top of the main window is a single-line menu bar, which presents the user with the available program options. The user chooses an option either by entering the first letter of the option or by using the arrow and return

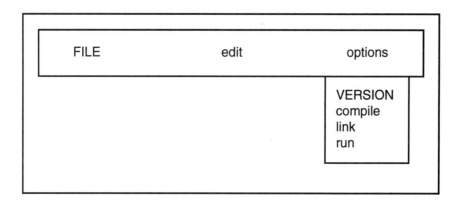

Figure 18.1

keys. Choosing one of these options will activate a pulldown menu which presents further options. Residing at the bottom of the main window is the dialog box, which is used to print informational messages and to accept user input when required.

Library functions to handle these UI constructs and other specific tasks are designed to simplify the process of building screen applications. These libraries are kept in a separate file and are linked into specific user applications. There are three major reasons for using Curses to build such libraries: portability, availability and usability. Even if Curses is inappropriate for a specific application, the methods presented here for creating a menu bar and pulldown menus are applicable to any UI. The libraries can be treated as shells, with the Curses commands replaced by other UI commands. By using appropriate *#ifdefs,* the libraries become portable to multiple platforms.

Note that the input routines used here are the same ones developed in Chapter 17 involving keyboard input. They are not revisited here in the text, but they are present in the code. Despite the advantages of using libraries, there are times when code must be transported as a single entity. For these occasions, it may be more convienient to embed the library code in the actual application or library.

18.2 CREATING A POP-UP WINDOW

Since most operations for any UI involve windows, a library function called *popup( )* is built to create a pop-up window. To create a window that will cover *stdscr,* the following calling convention is used:

```
WINDOW *mainwin;

mainwin = popup(MAX_ROWS, MAX_COLUMNS, 0,0);
```

The constants MAX_ROWS and MAX_COLUMNS represent the standard screen size. All the constants and structures defined for the UI created here are included in the header file *uilibs.h.*

Three windows make up this application: the menubar, the dialog box, and a window used for pulldown purposes. These are global to all functions and thus are declared as *extern* in most of the files.

All libraries of code presented here, including *popup( ),* are listed in the file *uilibs.c.* The logic for creating a pop-up window is self explanatory, with color the only portabililty issue. Since PC Curses has color capabilities, whereas VMS and UNIX do not, *ifdefs* are used to take advantage of this feature. The PC Curses command to introduce color is called *wattrset( ).* The colors representing the foreground and background are ORed together as follows:

```
wattrset(mainwin, F_RED | B_BLACK);
```

PC Curses also has many more box characters from which to choose. Many different effects can be obtained by using colors and box characters on the PC. However, if an effect similar to VMS and UNIX is desired, simply set the background to black and execute the box command on all platforms.

18.3 CREATING A MENU BAR

Producing a menu bar is the first step in creating the display. To ensure that the libraries are of a generic nature, a mechanism must allow the programmer to define what a menu bar looks like without having to make any changes to the code itself. To accomplish this task, a menu bar structure is defined as follows:

```
typedef struct mbar {
        char string[80];
        char letter;
        int pos;
}MENUBAR;
```

The first field in this structure holds the actual string that represents the particular option. For example, if one of the options across the top relates to printing, then the string "print" is a logical choice. The second field is the letter that invokes the option from the keyboard. The final field, *pos,* holds the location within the menu bar where the string is located.

In this example, the following menubar is used:

```
#define TCHOICES 3

MENUBAR menubar[TCHOICES] = {
        "file", 'f', 0,
        "edit", 'e', 0,
        "options", 'o', 0,
};
```

This declaration creates a menu bar with three different options: file, edit, and options, invoked by entering "f," "e," or "o," respectively. The positions are initially set to zero and will be calculated, when needed, by the menu bar routine. The constant TCHOICES is used throughout the libraries to identify the number of options available. Adding or deleting options is quite easy. Simply adjust TCHOICES and add or delete the appropriate number of lines in the menu bar structure.

The routine to generate the menu bar window, excluding its contents, is called *topbar( ).* One new issue to consider for this routine is the concept of a subwindow. In most cases, windows are created as separate entities. However, the menu bar is a permanent part of *stdscr.* Certain efficiency concerns therefore make a subwindow more attractive in this instance. When refreshing the screen, it is more efficient simply to refresh *stdscr* instead of refreshing both *stdscr* and the menu bar. The menu bar is created with the command

```
WINDOW *swin;

if((swin = subwin(win,3,(win->MAXX)-4,(win->BEGY)+1,
                   (win->BEGX)+2)) == NULL)
        clean_up();
```

The parameter list for the *subwin*( ) command includes the window pointer of the parent. This pointer is used to calculate where the menu bar is positioned, with reference to *curses.h*. Be careful not to use a pointer until the actual window is created, for until a *newwin*( ) or *subwin*( ) command is invoked, the pointer is NULL, and passing a NULL pointer to a function may cause unexpected results.

Even though the Curses implementations for all the platforms are highly consistent, the variable names provided are somewhat different. To position the menu bar, the WINDOW structure coordinates of the parent window are needed. VMS uses *_beg_x* and *_beg_y,* while MS-DOS and UNIX use *beg_x* and *beg_y.* To make the code more portable, macros such as BEGX are used.

The function *do_menubar*( ) performs all the tasks associated with selecting an option from a menu bar, the first of which is to print the string in the window. The sample menubar includes three strings: file, edit, and options. It is necessary to space these three strings appropriately so that they fill the top of the screen evenly. To accomplish this, a function called *strmenu*( ) is used. This function takes as parameters the menu bar structure and the width of the parent window. The logic is completed in three stages.

First, the number of spaces allocated to each string is calculated by dividing the width of the parent window by the number of strings in the menu bar, in this case three. Second, a loop is entered to build the menu bar by copying each string and padding it with the proper number of spaces. The choice that is currently active, initially the one on the left, is always highlighted and presented in uppercase characters. Finally, the string pointer is returned to the calling function. The menu bar is printed using the *mvwaddstr( )* function.

Once the menu bar is in place, the user must be able to select one of the options, either by typing the first character of the option or by pressing the return key to activate the highlighted option. The left and right arrow keys are used to select different options. After a keystroke is received, a switch statement controls the action. If it encounters an arrow, it adjusts the cursor position properly by moving the highlight either to the left or right, with allowances for wraparound. An escape terminates the program, while a return breaks out of the loop and invokes the option currently highlighted. The default case is any other sequence, which is sent back to the calling program as a character code.

18.4 CREATING A PULLDOWN MENU

The pulldown menus contain the suboptions under each main option. As with most pulldown menu schemes, each submenu here drops down underneath the spot where the main option resides in the menu bar. A pulldown menu is basically a pop-up window. The tricky part of creating a pulldown menu lies in calculating the size of the window. The pulldown routine must be able to adjust for windows of different dimensions.

To define the choices contained in each pulldown menu, the structure CHOICES is created:

```
typedef struct choices {
        char string[20];
        char letter;
        int (*funcptr)();
} CHOICES;
```

As with the menu bar structure, CHOICES contains the string that represents the option and the letter that invokes it. The third field, a function pointer, represents the function that will be executed when the option is chosen.

For example, suppose that invoking the menu bar option file

produces a pulldown menu with three options: open, close, and exit. The following structure is initialized:

```
CHOICES choices1[3] = {
      "open ", 'o', c_open,
      "close", 'c', c_close,
      "exit ", 'e', c_exit,
};
```

Thus, if *open* is chosen, the function *c_open( )* is called. The reason for using the *c_* prefix is to avoid possible function name conflicts. Simply calling the function *open( )* would conflict with the C language function of the same name.

In this chapter's example application there are three options (see *test.c*), all tied together as follows:

```
typedef struct pmenu {
      int num;
      int maxlength;
      CHOICES *ptr;
} PULLDOWN;
```

The structure PULLDOWN contains three pieces of information. The first field represents the number of options in the pulldown. The second indicates the maximum string length. The *close* option has five letters while the other two have only four, so five is the maximum length. When you create the pulldown menu, bear in mind that its components should have equal proportions. Thus, shorter strings in each field are padded with spaces to match the length of the longest string. The third field is the pointer to the structure that holds the choice information for this particular menu. The initialization of the entire PULLDOWN structure is

```
PULLDOWN pullmenu[3] = {
      3, 5, choices1,
      4, 6, choices2,
      3, 7, choices3,
};
```

To create a pulldown, the function *do_pulldown( )* is called. Choosing an option from the pulldown menu follows the same logic as for the menu bar, the only difference being that the UP_ARROW and DOWN_ARROW are used.

Unlike the menu bar, the pulldown menu is not a permanent structure. Thus when an option has been chosen, the pulldown menu must be erased. This requires that whatever was underneath the pulldown menu be restored, as simply erasing the menu will leave blanks on the screen. The command *touchwin( )* performs this task. In this chapter's example, the pulldown window occludes both the menu bar and *stdscr*. Thus both must be restored.

18.5 USING THE USER INTERFACE LIBRARY

The program *test.c* demonstrates the advantages of building user interface libraries. The actual application requires only a dozen or so lines of code. The program consists of two basic parts: building the screen and implementing the menu logic. The logic is fairly self-explanatory based on the previous discussions.

The functions that the menu choices invoke are simply shells. The programmer must substitute the appropriate functionality. The only functions that perform any tasks are the version function, which displays the current program version, and the exit function, which terminates the application.

To run the application, compile *test.c, uilibs.c,* and *funcs.c* with the appropriate *define*s for the host platform. Then link them together with the Curses library provided by your C package. When the program is invoked, the menu screen will appear.

18.6 CONCLUSION

There are many other Curses functions that have not been introduced in this discussion. An understanding of the material presented here should make any additions including these functions relatively simple. Note, however, that the Curses interface has its limitations. A commercial package written in Curses will most likely not show up on the store shelves. But if a quick, portable, easy to use method of creating User Interfaces is your overriding concern, Curses may be the only available option.

```c
/*****************************************************

   FILE NAME   : test.c
   AUTHOR      : Matt Weisfeld

   DESCRIPTION : test file for portable user
                 interface.

*****************************************************/
#include <stdio.h>
#include <stdlib.h>
#include <signal.h>
#include <time.h>
#include <string.h>
#ifdef BCC
#include <dos.h>
#include <conio.h>
#endif

#include "proto.h"
#include "errdefs.h"

char choice;

/* windows global to all routines */

WINDOW *dialogue;
WINDOW *tbar;

/* define menubar with three options */

MENUBAR menubar[TCHOICES] = {
  "file",    'f',    0,
  "edit",    'e',    0,
  "options", 'o',    0,
};

/* define pulldown menu sub-choices */
```

```
CHOICES choices1[3] = {
  "open ", 'o', c_open,
  "close", 'c', c_close,
  "exit ", 'e', c_exit,
};

CHOICES choices2[4] = {
  "copy  ", 'c', c_copy,
  "paste ", 'p', c_paste,
  "delete", 'd', c_delete,
  "move  ", 'm', c_move,
};

CHOICES choices3[4] = {
  "version", 'v', c_version,
  "compile", 'c', c_compile,
  "link   ", 'l', c_link,
  "run    ", 'r', c_run,
};

/* tie all choices into one struct */

PULLDOWN pullmenu[TCHOICES] = {
  3, 5, choices1,
  4, 6, choices2,
  4, 7, choices3,
};

main()
{


  int i,j,k;


  initscr();

  /* needed to return one keystroke at a time */

#ifndef VMS
  cbreak();
#else
```

```
      crmode();
#endif

   /* activate keypad code */

#ifdef HPUX
   keypad(stdscr, TRUE);
#endif

   noecho();

#ifdef BCC
   cursoff();
#endif

   /* set up screen */

   set_stdscr();

   dialogue = popup(3, MAX_COLUMNS-4, MAX_ROWS-4, 2);

   clear_dialogue();

   tbar = topbar(stdscr);

   /* enter loop to process options */

   for (;;) {

     choice = do_menubar(tbar, menubar);

     for (i=0;i<TCHOICES;i++) {

        if ( choice == menubar[i].letter) {

          choice = do_pulldown(i,pullmenu,menubar);

          execute_command(i, choice, pullmenu);

          break;

        } /* if */
     }    /* for loop */
```

```
  }         /* end main loop (for (;;))*/

}

/****************************************************

  ROUTINE NAME : clean_up()

  DESCRIPTION  : perform housekeeping at program's
                 exit.

  INPUT        : none

  OUTPUT       : none

****************************************************/
/* these commands must be called at exit */
void clean_up()
{

  erase();
  refresh();
  endwin();

#ifdef BCC
  clrscr();
#endif

  return;
}

/*###############################################*/


/****************************************************

  FILE NAME    : uilibs.c
  AUTHOR       : Matt Weisfeld

  DESCRIPTION  : portable user interface
                 function libraries.

****************************************************/
```

```
#include <stdio.h>
#include <stdlib.h>
#include <signal.h>
#include <time.h>
#include <string.h>
#ifdef VMS
#include <smgdef.h>
#endif
#ifdef BCC
#include <dos.h>
#include <conio.h>
#include <ctype.h>
#endif

#include "proto.h"
#include "er.h"

extern WINDOW *dialogue;
extern WINDOW *tbar;

static bar_size;    /* size of menubar */
static int menu_pos;  /* position in menubar */


/***************************************************

  ROUTINE NAME : topbar()

  DESCRIPTION  : display a menubar

  INPUT        : WINDOW * (main window)

  OUTPUT       : WINDOW * (menubar)

****************************************************/
WINDOW *topbar(win)
WINDOW *win;
{

  WINDOW  *swin;

  int string_count, string_size;
```

```
    if((swin = subwin(win,3,(win->MAXX)-4,(win->BEGY)+1,
        (win->BEGX)+2)) == NULL) {
      clean_up();
      error(ER_BADSUBWIN, "topbar");
    }

#ifdef BCC
    wattrset(swin, F_BLUE | B_GRAY);
#endif

    box (swin, SINGLE_SIDE,SINGLE_ACROSS);

    bar_size = (swin->MAXX)-2;
    menu_pos=0;

    return  (swin);
}
/****************************************************

    ROUTINE NAME : do_menubar()

    DESCRIPTION  : determine active option

    INPUT        : WINDOW *  (sub window)
                   MENUBAR * (menubar)

    OUTPUT       : char (option to highlight)

****************************************************/
char do_menubar(swin, menubar)
WINDOW *swin;
MENUBAR *menubar;
{

    char * menu;

    char buffer[80];

    int status;

#ifdef VMS
    int keyboard;
```

```
      short term_code;
#else
  char term_code;
#endif

#ifdef VMS
  if ( (( status =
      SMG$CREATE_VIRTUAL_KEYBOARD(&keyboard))&1)!=1) {
      clean_up();
      error(ER_BADKEY, "do_menubar");
  }
#endif

  term_code = 0;

  while (term_code != ENTER) {

    /* get the new menubar string */
    menu = strmenu(bar_size, menubar, menu_pos);

    mvwaddstr(swin, 1, 1, menu);
    wrefresh(swin);

    /* get a single keystroke */

#ifdef VMS
    if ( (( status = SMG$READ_KEYSTROKE
        (&keyboard,&term_code))&1)!=1) {
     clean_up();
     error(ER_BADKEY, "do_menubar");
    }
#endif
#ifdef BCC
    term_code = wgetch(swin);
#endif
#ifdef HPUX
    term_code = getch();
#endif
#ifdef SUN
    term_code = getch();
    if (term_code == ESCAPE) {
      getch();
      term_code = getch();
```

```
    }
#endif

    /* process keystroke */
    switch (term_code) {

      /* arrows check for wrap-around */
      case LEFT_ARROW:
        if (menu_pos == 0)
          menu_pos = TCHOICES-1;
        else
          menu_pos—;
      break;

      case RIGHT_ARROW:
        if (menu_pos == TCHOICES-1)
          menu_pos = 0;
        else
          menu_pos++;
      break;

      /* do nothing */
      case ENTER:
      break;

      /* exit program */
      case ESCAPE:
        clean_up();
      break;

      /* return keyboard input */
      default :
        return (term_code);
      break;

    }

  }

  /* return highlighted option */
  return (menubar[menu_pos].letter);

}
```

```
/*****************************************************

  ROUTINE NAME : popup()

  DESCRIPTION  : create a popup window

  INPUT        : int (rows)
                 int (columns)
                 int (start x)
                 int (start y)


  OUTPUT       :

*****************************************************/
WINDOW *popup(rows, columns, sy, sx)
int rows;
int columns;
int sy;
int sx;
{
  WINDOW *win;

  win = newwin(rows, columns, sy, sx);

  if(win == NULL) {
    endwin();
    clean_up();
    error(ER_BADWIN, "popup");
  }

#ifdef BCC
  wattrset(win, F_BLACK | B_GRAY);
#endif
  box(win, SINGLE_SIDE, SINGLE_ACROSS);
  wrefresh(win);

  return (win);

}
```

```
/****************************************************

   ROUTINE NAME : erase_window()

   DESCRIPTION  : completely erase a window

   INPUT        : WINDOW * (window to erase)

   OUTPUT       : none

****************************************************/
void erase_window(win)
WINDOW *win;
{


   werase(win);
   box(win, ' ', ' ');
   wrefresh(win);


}

/****************************************************

   ROUTINE NAME : delete_window()

   DESCRIPTION  : delete a window

   INPUT        : WINDOW * (window to delete)

   OUTPUT       : none

****************************************************/
void delete_window(win)
WINDOW *win;
{

   delwin(win);


}
```

```
/**************************************************

  ROUTINE NAME : refresh_window()

  DESCRIPTION  : refresh a window

  INPUT        : WINDOW * (window to refresh)

  OUTPUT       : none

**************************************************/
void refresh_window(win)
WINDOW *win;
{

  wrefresh(win);


}

/**************************************************

  ROUTINE NAME : touch_window()

  DESCRIPTION  : touch a window

  INPUT        : WINDOW * (window to touch)

  OUTPUT       : none

**************************************************/
void touch_window(win)
WINDOW *win;
{

  touchwin(win);
  wrefresh(win);


}
```

```
/*****************************************************

   ROUTINE NAME : do_pulldown()

   DESCRIPTION  : process pulldown menu options

   INPUT        : int (number of options)
                  PULLDOWN * (pulldown menu)
                  MENUBAR *  (menubar)

   OUTPUT       : char (option to highlight)

*****************************************************/
/* process pulldown menu options */
char do_pulldown (i, pullmenu, menubar)
int i;
PULLDOWN *pullmenu;
MENUBAR *menubar;
{

   WINDOW *subwin1;

   int j;
   int position, oldpos;

   char *ptr;

   int status;

#ifdef VMS
   int keyboard;
   short term_code;
#else
   char term_code;
#endif

#ifdef VMS
   if ( ((  status =
       SMG$CREATE_VIRTUAL_KEYBOARD(&keyboard))&1)!=1) {
       clean_up();
       error(ER_BADKEY, "menubar");
   }
#endif
```

```
   subwin1 = popup( (pullmenu[i].num)+2,
     (pullmenu[i].maxlength)+2,stdscr->BEGY+3,
       (menubar[i].pos)+2 );

   /* print pulldown options */

   for (j=0;j<pullmenu[i].num;j++) {

     ptr = pullmenu[i].ptr[j].string;

     mvwaddstr(subwin1, j+1, 1, ptr );

   }

   term_code = 0;

   position=0;
   oldpos = 0;

   while (term_code != ENTER) {

     /* highlight selected option */

     ptr = pullmenu[i].ptr[position].string;

     strcnvtupp(ptr);

     mvwaddstr(subwin1, position+1, 1, ptr );

     wrefresh(subwin1);

     /* get keystroke */

#ifdef VMS
     if ( (( status =SMG$READ_KEYSTROKE
         (&keyboard,&term_code)) & 1)!=1) {
       clean_up();
       error(ER_BADKEY, "do_pulldown");
     }
#endif
#ifdef BCC
     term_code = wgetch(subwin1);
```

```
#endif
#ifdef HPUX
    term_code = getch();
#endif
#ifdef SUN
    term_code = getch();
    if (term_code == ESCAPE) {
      getch();
      term_code = getch();
    }
#endif


    oldpos = position;

    /* process keystroke */

    switch (term_code) {

      case UP_ARROW:

        if (position == 0)
          position = pullmenu[i].num-1;
        else
          position-;

      break;

      case DOWN_ARROW:

        if (position == pullmenu[i].num-1)
          position = 0;
        else
          position++;

      break;

      /* do nothing */
      case ENTER:
      break;

      /* get keyboard input and
         erase menu */
```

```
        default :
          erase_window(subwin1);
          delwin(subwin1);

          touchwin(stdscr);
          wrefresh(stdscr);
          touchwin(dialogue);
          wrefresh(dialogue);

          return (term_code);
        break;

    }

    /* restore to lowercase */

    ptr = pullmenu[i].ptr[oldpos].string;

    strcnvtlow(ptr);

    mvwaddstr(subwin1, oldpos+1, 1, ptr );

    wrefresh(subwin1);

  }

  /* return highlighted option
     and erase menu */
  delwin(subwin1);
  erase_window(subwin1);
  touchwin(stdscr);
  wrefresh(stdscr);
  touchwin(dialogue);
  wrefresh(dialogue);
  return (pullmenu[i].ptr[position].letter);


}
```

```
/*****************************************************

   ROUTINE NAME : strmenu()

   DESCRIPTION  : calculate and produce menubar
                  string

   INPUT        : int (length of string)
                  MENUBAR * (menubar)
                  int (position in string)

   OUTPUT       : none

*****************************************************/
char *strmenu(length, menubar, pos)
int length;
MENUBAR *menubar;
int pos;
{

  int i,j,k;
  int count;
  int string_length;

  static char buffer[100];

  /* determine max length for string */
  string_length = length/TCHOICES;

  k = 0;
  j = 0;

  /* add proper number of options */
  for (i=0;i<TCHOICES;i++) {

    menubar[i].pos = k;

    /* add each option, highlight as necessary */
    for (j=0;menubar[i].string[j]!='\0';j++,k++) {
      if (pos == i)
        buffer[k] = toupper(menubar[i].string[j]);
      else
```

```
      buffer[k] = tolower(menubar[i].string[j]);
    }

    /* pad with spaces to proper length */
    while (k<(string_length*(i+1)+2)) {
      buffer[k] = ' ';
      k++;
    }

  }


  return(buffer);

}

/**************************************************

  ROUTINE NAME : set_stdscr()

  DESCRIPTION  : initialize the screen at start

  INPUT        : none

  OUTPUT       : none

**************************************************/
/* initialize the screen at start */
void set_stdscr()
{

  int i;

  wclear (stdscr);

#ifdef BCC
  wattrset(stdscr, F_RED | B_BLUE);
  /* fill in screen with color */
  for (i=0;i<MAX_ROWS;i++)
    mvinsertln(i,0);
#endif
  box(stdscr, DOUBLE_SIDE, DOUBLE_ACROSS);
```

```
  refresh();

  return;

}

/****************************************************

  ROUTINE NAME : to_dialogue()

  DESCRIPTION  : print string to dialogue box

  INPUT        : char * (string)

  OUTPUT       : none

****************************************************/
void to_dialogue(string)
char *string;
{

  clear_dialogue();
  mvwaddstr(dialogue, 1, 1, string);
  box(dialogue, SINGLE_SIDE, SINGLE_ACROSS);
  wrefresh(dialogue);

  return;

}

/****************************************************

  ROUTINE NAME : clear_dialogue()

  DESCRIPTION  : clear dialogue box

  INPUT        : none

  OUTPUT       : none

****************************************************/
```

```
void clear_dialogue()
{

  werase(dialogue);
  box(dialogue, SINGLE_SIDE, SINGLE_ACROSS);
  wrefresh(dialogue);

  return;

}

/****************************************************

  ROUTINE NAME : execute_command()

  DESCRIPTION  : execute an option command

  INPUT        : int (position)
                 int (optoins choice)
                 PULLDOWN * (pulldown menu)

  OUTPUT       : none

****************************************************/
void execute_command (i, choice, pullmenu)
int i;
int choice;
PULLDOWN *pullmenu;
{

  int j;

  touch_window(tbar);

  for (j=0;j<pullmenu[i].num;j++) {

    /* use function pointer to execute command */
    if ( choice == pullmenu[i].ptr[j].letter) {
      (*(pullmenu[i].ptr[j].funcptr))();
      break;
    };
```

```
    }

    clear_dialogue();

}


/*###############################################*/


/****************************************************

    FILE NAME   : funcs.c
    AUTHOR      : Matt Weisfeld

    DESCRIPTION : internal functions for UI

****************************************************/
#include <stdio.h>
#ifdef BCC
#include <dos.h>
#endif
#include "proto.h"

/*
    all these functions are shells
    except for c_exit & c_version
*/

int c_open()
{

        to_dialogue("open");

        sleep(3);

        return;
}

int c_close()
{
```

```
        to_dialogue("close");
        sleep(3);

        return;
}

int c_exit()
{
        to_dialogue("exit");
        clean_up();
        leave(EXIT_NORMAL);

        return;

}

int c_copy()
{
        to_dialogue("copy");
        sleep(3);

        return;
}

int c_paste()
{
        to_dialogue("paste");
        sleep(3);

        return;
}

int c_delete()
{
        to_dialogue("delete");
        sleep(3);

        return;
}

int c_move()
{
```

```
        to_dialogue("move");
        sleep(3);

        return;

}

int c_compile()
{
        to_dialogue("compile");
        sleep(3);

        return;

}

int c_link()
{
        to_dialogue("link");
        sleep(3);

        return;

}

int c_run()
{
        to_dialogue("run");
        sleep(3);

        return;
}

int c_version()
{

        to_dialogue("Version 3.0");
        sleep(3);

        return;

}
```

```
/*###############################################*/


/***************************************************

   FILE NAME   : uilibs.h
   AUTHOR      : Matt Weisfeld

   DESCRIPTION : header file for user
                 interface.

***************************************************/

#include <stdio.h>
#include "curses.h"

/* screen dimensions*/
#define MAX_ROWS 24
#define MAX_COLUMNS 80

/* keystroke codes and color */
#ifdef HPUX
#define UP_ARROW    3
#define DOWN_ARROW  2
#define LEFT_ARROW  4
#define RIGHT_ARROW 5
#define ENTER       10
#define ESCAPE      27
#endif
#ifdef SUN
#define UP_ARROW    65
#define DOWN_ARROW  66
#define LEFT_ARROW  68
#define RIGHT_ARROW 67
#define ENTER       10
#define ESCAPE      27
#endif
#ifdef VMS
#define UP_ARROW    274
#define DOWN_ARROW  275
#define LEFT_ARROW  276
#define RIGHT_ARROW 277
```

```
#define ENTER       13
#define ESCAPE      291 /* F11 */
#endif
#ifdef BCC
#define MAINCOLOR   (F_RED | B_BLACK)
#define DIALOGCOLOR (F_CYAN | B_BLACK)
#define UP_ARROW    56
#define DOWN_ARROW  50
#define LEFT_ARROW  52
#define RIGHT_ARROW 54
#define         ENTER 10
#define ESCAPE      27
#endif

/* macros for portability */
#ifndef VMS
#define BEGX _begx
#define BEGY _begy
#define MAXX _maxx
#else
#define BEGX _beg_x
#define BEGY _beg_y
#define MAXX _max_x
#endif

/* box characters */

#ifdef BCC
#define SINGLE_SIDE    -77 /* single bar */
#define SINGLE_ACROSS -60
#define DOUBLE_SIDE    -70 /* double bar */
#define DOUBLE_ACROSS -51
#else
#define SINGLE_SIDE    '|'
#define SINGLE_ACROSS '-'
#define DOUBLE_SIDE    '"'
#define DOUBLE_ACROSS '='
#endif

#define TCHOICES 3

/* menubar structure */
typedef struct mbar {
```

```
        char string[80];
        char letter;
        int pos;
}MENUBAR;

/* pulldown menu choices */
typedef struct choices {
        char string[20];
        char letter;
        int (*funcptr)();
} CHOICES;

/* pulldown menu structure */
typedef struct pmenu {
        int num;
        int maxlength;
        CHOICES *ptr;
} PULLDOWN;

/* prototypes */
#ifdef ANSI
WINDOW *topbar(WINDOW *);
WINDOW *pulldown(int,int,int,int);
WINDOW *popup(int,int,int,int);
void move_window(WINDOW *win,int y, int x);
void print_string(WINDOW *,int, int, char *);
void erase_window(WINDOW *);
void delete_window(WINDOW *);
void refresh_window(WINDOW *);
void to_dialogue(char *);
void clear_dialogue(void);
void touch_window(WINDOW *);
char *strmenu(int, MENUBAR *, int);
char menu_choice(char *);
void clean_up(void);
void repaint(void);
char do_pulldown(int,PULLDOWN *, MENUBAR *);
void set_stdscr(void);
void execute_command(int, int, PULLDOWN *);
char do_menubar(WINDOW *, MENUBAR *);
void set_stdscr(void);
char get_keystroke(void);
#else
```

```
WINDOW *topbar();
WINDOW *pulldown();
WINDOW *popup();
void move_window();
void print_string();
void erase_window();
void delete_window();
void refresh_window();
void to_dialogue();
void clear_dialogue();
void touch_window();
char *strmenu();
char menu_choice();
void clean_up();
void repaint();
char do_pulldown();
void set_stdscr();
void execute_command();
char do_menubar();
void set_stdscr();
char get_keystroke();
#endif


/*###############################################*/


/**************************************************

   FILE NAME   : funcs.h
   AUTHOR      : Matt Weisfeld

   DESCRIPTION : prototypes for internal functions

**************************************************/
extern int c_open();
extern int c_close();
extern int c_exit();
extern int c_copy();
extern int c_paste();
extern int c_delete();
extern int c_move();
extern int c_compile();
```

```
extern int c_link();
extern int c_run();
extern int c_version();
extern int c_testchar();

/*###########################################*/


/*****************************************************

   FILE NAME    : er.h
   AUTHOR       : Matt Weisfeld

   DESCRIPTION : error definitions

*****************************************************/
#define ER_BADWIN     0      /* window creation failed  */
#define ER_BADSUBWIN1        /* subwindow creation failed  */
#define ER_BADKEY     2      /* keyboard input failed */


/*###########################################*/


/*****************************************************

   FILE NAME    : errdefs.h
   AUTHOR       : Matt Weisfeld

   DESCRIPTION : error strings

*****************************************************/
#include "er.h"

ERROR_STRUCT error_message[] =

/* actual error messages */

{

     /* #0 */
     ER_BADWIN, EXIT,
     "Window creation failed in '%s'.",
```

```
        /* #1 */
        ER_BADSUBWIN, EXIT,
        "Sub window creation failed in '%s'.",
        /* #2 */
        ER_BADKEY, EXIT,
        "Keyboard input failed in '%s'.",
        /* LAST */
        LASTERROR, EXIT,
};


/*###############################################*/


/****************************************************

   FILE NAME   : proto.h
   AUTHOR      : Matt Weisfeld

   DESCRIPTION : prototype file for user
                 interface.

****************************************************/
#ifdef VMS
#include "[-.common]common.h"
#include "[-.leave]leave.h"
#include "[-.error]error.h"
#include "[-.strlibs]strlibs.h"
#endif

#ifdef BCC
#include "..\common\common.h"
#include "..\leave\leave.h"
#include "..\error\error.h"
#include "..\strlibs\strlibs.h"
#endif

#ifdef HPUX
#include "../common/common.h"
#include "../leave/leave.h"
#include "../error/error.h"
#include "../strlibs/strlibs.h"
#endif
```

```
#ifdef SLC
#include "../common/common.h"
#include "../leave/leave.h"
#include "../error/error.h"
#include "../strlibs/strlibs.h"
#endif

#ifdef GCC
#include "../common/common.h"
#include "../leave/leave.h"
#include "../error/error.h"
#include "../strlibs/strlibs.h"
#endif

#ifdef CCC
#include "../common/common.h"
#include "../leave/leave.h"
#include "../error/error.h"
#include "../strlibs/strlibs.h"
#endif

#include "uilibs.h"
#include "funcs.h"


/*##############################################*/

$ VMS DCL PROCEDURE
$ clr
$ if (P1.eqs."START") then GOTO START
$ if (P1.eqs."") then GOTO ALL
$ if (P1.eqs."ALL") then GOTO ALL
$ if (P1.eqs."LINK") then GOTO LINK
$ set verify
$ cc/DEFINE=VMS 'P1'
$ goto LINK
$ ALL:
$       set verify
$ cc/define=VMS test
$ cc/define=VMS uilibs
$ cc/define=VMS funcs
$ LINK:
```

```
$ link/executable=test test,uilibs,funcs,[-.leave]leave,
[-.error]error,-
[-.strlibs]strlibs,sys$library:vaxccurse/library
$ copy test.exe [weisfeld.exe]
$ set noverify
```

```
/*###########################################*/
```

```
# makefile for BCC\C++ Compiler

OBJS     = test.obj uilibs.obj funcs.obj
LIBS     = ..\leave\leave.obj ..\error\error.obj \
           ..\strlibs\strlibs.obj
HDRS     = proto.h errdefs.h uilibs.h er.h
FLAGS    = -c -DBCC
COMP     = bcc

test:   $(OBJS)
        $(COMP) $(OBJS) $(LIBS) scurses.lib

test.obj: test.c $(HDRS)
        $(COMP) $(FLAGS) test.c

uilibs.obj: uilibs.c $(HDRS)
        $(COMP) $(FLAGS) uilibs.c

funcs.obj: funcs.c $(HDRS)
        $(COMP) $(FLAGS) funcs.c

test.c:
uilibs.c:
funcs.c:

uilibs.h:
```

```
/*###########################################*/
```

```
# makefile for MSC\C++ Compiler

OBJS     = test.obj uilibs.obj funcs.obj
LIBS     = ..\leave\leave.obj ..\error\error.obj \
           ..\strlibs\strlibs.obj scurses.lib
```

```
HDRS    = proto.h errdefs.h uilibs.h er.h
FLAGS   = /c /DMSC
COMP    = cl

test:   $(OBJS)
        $(COMP) $(OBJS) $(LIBS)

test.obj: test.c $(HDRS)
        $(COMP) $(FLAGS) test.c

uilibs.obj: uilibs.c $(HDRS)
        $(COMP) $(FLAGS) uilibs.c

funcs.obj: funcs.c $(HDRS)
        $(COMP) $(FLAGS) funcs.c

test.c:
uilibs.c:
funcs.c:

uilibs.h:

/*###############################################*/

# makefile for HPUX C Compiler

OBJS    = test.o uilibs.o funcs.o
LIBS    = ../leave/leave.o ../error/error.o
          ../strlibs/strlibs.o
HDRS    = proto.h errdefs.h uilibs.h er.h
FLAGS   = -c -DHPUX -Aa
COMP    = cc

test:   $(OBJS)
        $(COMP) -o test $(OBJS) $(LIBS) -lcurses -ltermcap

test.o: test.c $(HDRS)
        $(COMP) $(FLAGS) test.c

uilibs.o: uilibs.c $(HDRS)
        $(COMP) $(FLAGS) uilibs.c
```

```
funcs.o: funcs.c $(HDRS)
        $(COMP) $(FLAGS) funcs.c

test.c:
uilibs.c:
funcs.c:

uilibs.h:


/*###########################################*/

# makefile for SUN SLC C Compiler

OBJS     = test.o uilibs.o funcs.o
LIBS     = ../leave/leave.o ../error/error.o
           ../strlibs/strlibs.o
HDRS     = proto.h errdefs.h uilibs.h er.h
FLAGS    = -c -DSLC
COMP     = cc

test:   $(OBJS)
        $(COMP) -o test $(OBJS) $(LIBS) -lcurses -ltermcap

test.o: test.c $(HDRS)
        $(COMP) $(FLAGS) test.c

uilibs.o: uilibs.c $(HDRS)
        $(COMP) $(FLAGS) uilibs.c

funcs.o: funcs.c $(HDRS)
        $(COMP) $(FLAGS) funcs.c

test.c:
uilibs.c:
funcs.c:

uilibs.h:


/*###########################################*/
```

```
# makefile for SUN GCC C Compiler

OBJS    = test.o uilibs.o funcs.o
LIBS    = ../leave/leave.o ../error/error.o
          ../strlibs/strlibs.o
HDRS    = proto.h errdefs.h uilibs.h er.h
FLAGS   = -c -DGCC
COMP    = gcc

test:   $(OBJS)
        $(COMP) -o test $(OBJS) $(LIBS) -lcurses -ltermcap

test.o: test.c $(HDRS)
        $(COMP) $(FLAGS) test.c

uilibs.o: uilibs.c $(HDRS)
        $(COMP) $(FLAGS) uilibs.c

funcs.o: funcs.c $(HDRS)
        $(COMP) $(FLAGS) funcs.c

test.c:
uilibs.c:
funcs.c:

uilibs.h:


/*###############################################*/

# makefile for CCC Compiler

OBJS    = test.o uilibs.o funcs.o
LIBS    = ../leave/leave.o ../error/error.o
          ../strlibs/strlibs.o
HDRS    = proto.h errdefs.h uilibs.h er.h
FLAGS   = -c -DCCC -DSUN
COMP    = cc

test:   $(OBJS)
        $(COMP) -o test $(OBJS) $(LIBS) -lcurses -ltermcap
```

```
test.o: test.c $(HDRS)
        $(COMP) $(FLAGS) test.c

uilibs.o: uilibs.c $(HDRS)
        $(COMP) $(FLAGS) uilibs.c

funcs.o: funcs.c $(HDRS)
        $(COMP) $(FLAGS) funcs.c

test.c:
uilibs.c:
funcs.c:

uilibs.h:
```

18.7 SELECTED REFERENCE

Material from this chapter appeared in "A Portable User Interface Using Curses." *The C User's Journal*, vol. 11, no. 4, p. 19.

19

Creating a Program Banner

When you test software, perhaps the most important issue is documenting the test itself. This is especially vital when porting is involved. Not only are the test results important, but specific information about the test programs, parameters, and environment need to be saved as well. The most accurate and foolproof method of accomplishing this is to have the test program automatically generate as much of this information as possible in a program banner. This banner should, at minimum, include such information as the program name, program version, execution date and time, operating system name and version, and the command line used to invoke the program. Any other information that is considered helpful can also be included.

19.1 PROGRAM MAINTENANCE

The program version is absolutely vital, since the code will usually change at least a little for every new platform introduced. The manner in which the program version is maintained is up to the developer. However, to avoid confusion it must be logical and straightforward. As an example, consider the following program version: (2.8e). Every time the program undergoes a major functional or structural change, the number to the left of the decimal point is incremented. The number to the right of the decimal point represents a minor change of functionality. The letter indicates a change to correct a bug.

Further revision information can be added to indicate a specific platform (e.g.: 2.8e-HP/UX). At this point the following question may arise: if the code is supposed to be portable, why have so many versions, some of which are platform-specific? The answer to this question is that the final product will be portable. However, reaching this goal will require a lot of code changes and testing on the individual platforms. It is imperative that all changes be documented and placed in a configuration management system (CMS). The particular CMS system selected is not as important as the fact that one is used.

Once a change is made, the new code must be backported. This is accomplished in one of two ways. In the first approach, once a change is identified, the change is made against the master version of the code on the primary system. This is potentially dangerous since it introduces the possibility of typographical errors and the like. Under the second option, the entire product is backported to the primary system. The second approach is by far the safest, despite the fact that it can consume a lot of time. If the change is trivial and well documented, the first approach is a viable option. In any event, the change must find its way back to the primary platform and CMS.

19.2 PRINTING THE BANNER

In this example, the program banner, generated by a routine called *banner*( ), is printed whenever the program is invoked. In fact, printing the banner is the first thing that occurs. Furthermore, in this example, calling the program as follows with the '-b' option

```
$ test -b
```

will cause the program to print the banner and then exit.

```
TEST(1.0) - Saturday, April 10, 1993. 12:03.02 AM.
NODE(CASPER) - VAX/VMS V5.4-3
test -b
```

This information is vital for documenting tests and confirming portability among different platforms. Other test efforts may have additional information requirements that can easily be added to the banner.

Calling *banner( )* from a program is also a straightforward task. In order to echo the command line used to invoke the program, the routine needs to have access to *argc* and *argv* as obtained by the main program. This chapter's version of *banner( )* allows the user the option of printing the banner to any valid file stream, a helpful feature since banner information can be sent to a stream other than *stdout,* such as *stderr* or any open file. An example of how a C program calls the banner routine is

```
banner(argc,argv,stdout);
```

This example will print the banner information to the standard output device.

The first line of the banner contains the name of the program, the program version, and the time that the command was executed. The program name and version are defined in the main program. Actually, the only restriction is that the following variables be defined prior to calling the *banner( )* routine:

```
char prog_name[STRLEN] = "test";
char prog_version[STRLEN] = "1.0";
```

These variable names are not negotiable, since *banner( )* declares them as *extern* and is looking for these specific names.

Since the program name is usually the item that is most recognizable, it is often a good practice to highlight it. The screen libraries that were previously developed work well here. In this case, the program name is bolded using the library function *do_bold( )*.

```
do_bold();
printf ("%s", strtoupper(prog_name));
do_norrmal();
```

Make sure that the text attribute is returned to normal after the program name is printed. The library function *strtoupper*( ) is used so that the program name is always printed in uppercase characters. The time is added by calling the library function *get_strtime*( ), which is placed in the string *start_time*. This variable may be made global so that it is available throughout the program.

19.3 ACCESSING INFORMATION IN ENVIRONMENT VARIABLES

The second line in the banner identifies the platform and the operating system. For example:

```
Node (CASPER); VAX/VMS V5.4-3  ;
```

To build the environment string, the following code is used:

```
char sys_id[80];
char *os_version;
char *sysname;
int sys_flag = OFF;

/* build environment string */

if ( (os_version = (char *) getenv("OS_VERSION")) == NULL) {
      sys_flag = ON;
}
if ( (sysname = (char *) getenv("NODE_NAME")) == NULL) {
      sys_flag = ON;
}

if (sys_flag == OFF) {
      strcpy (sys_id, sysname);
      strcat (sys_id, "; ");
      strcat (sys_id, os_version);
}

/* print environment string */
```

```
if (sys_flag == OFF)
        printf ("%s\n", sys_id);
```

The string pointers *sysname* and *os_version* are character pointers pointing to the strings returned by the respective calls to
getenv( ). It is possible that the environment variables are not
defined, in which case *getenv( )* returns a NULL. If this occurs,
there is no need to process the information further by building
the *sys_id* string. Indeed, if the string is operated on without
proper formats, the program could crash. Thus, it is necessary
to know if one of the variables is NULL. The flag *sys_flag* performs this function. If *getenv( )* returns a NULL, *sys_flag* is set
to ON and the system information is not printed by the banner.

19.4 ECHOING THE COMMAND LINE

The C programming language uses two arguments, *argc* and
argv, to pass command line information. A main program using
argc and *argv* is defined in the following manner:

```
int main (argc,argv)
int argc;
char **argv;
```

The integer *argc* represents the number of arguments passed to
the program. The pointer *argv* is actually a pointer list to a set
of pointers to the command line parameters. For example, the
command

```
test -a -b file.txt
```

is represented as follows:

```
argc = 5

argv[0] = "test\0"
argv[1] = "-a\0"
argv[2] = "-b\0"
argv[3] = "file.txt\0"
argv[4] = NULL
```

Note that even though *argc* is 5, there is no *argv*[5]. The variable *argc* is the actual number of parameters, while *argv* always starts at 0. In fact, *argv*[0] is always the program name. All parameters are actual strings terminated by a NULL. Finally, the list itself is terminated by a NULL.

To echo the command, the following code is executed:

```
fprintf (stream, "%s ", prog_name);

for (i=1; i<argc; i++)
  fprintf (stream, "%s ", argv[i]);
```

This structure can also be written as:

```
for (i=1; argv[i]!=NULL; i++)
  fprintf (stream, "%s ", argv[i]);
```

Even though the program name resides in *argv*[0], it is printed here using its explicit lowercase program definition. The program name in *argv*[0] contains the entire path to the program name. For example, VMS would list the string:

```
dka300:[test.exe]program.exe;2
```

Since it is desirable to print only the program name, the approach taken above is used.

19.5 USING THE BANNER LIBRARY

The test program for *banlibs* is very simple—it prints out the banner to the screen and then exits the program. This library requires the services of many other libraries. These include *scrlibs*, *timelibs*, *strlibs*, and possibly *envlibs*. The reason for including *envlibs* as a possibility is that the application program may need to set the environment variables. The only code necessary in the application is the definition of the program name and version, as well as the call to *banner*.

19.6 CONCLUSION

Generating a program banner is important when testing and porting programs. Having the program gather and print as much information as possible is a great time-saver and actually provides more integrity. The banner discussed in this chapter contains just some of the information that can be included in a banner. Whatever additional information is deemed important can also be incorporated.

```
/********************************************************

   FILE NAME    : test.c
   AUTHOR       : Matt Weisfeld

   DESCRIPTION : test file for banner routine

   ********************************************************/
#include <stdio.h>
#include "proto.h"
#include "errdefs.h"

char prog_name[STRLEN] = "TEST";
char prog_version[STRLEN] = "1.0";

main(argc,argv)
int argc;
char **argv;
{

        banner(argc,argv,stdout);

        leave(EXIT_NORMAL);

        return;
}

/*##############################################*/
```

```c
/******************************************************

   FILE NAME   : banner.c
   AUTHOR      : Matt Weisfeld

   DESCRIPTION : generate a program banner

******************************************************/

#include <stdio.h>
#include "proto.h"
#include "er.h"
#ifdef ANSI
#include <stdlib.h>
#include <string.h>
#endif
#ifdef BCC
#include <conio.h>
#endif

extern char prog_name[];
extern char prog_version[];

char *start_time;
/******************************************************

   ROUTINE NAME : banner()

   DESCRIPTION  : generate a program banner

   INPUT        : int argc
                  char **argv
                  FILE *stream

   OUTPUT       : none

******************************************************/
void banner(argc,argv,stream)
int argc;
char *argv[];
FILE *stream;
{
```

```
int i;

FILE *fp;

char sys_id[STRLEN];
char *os_version;
char *sysname;
int sys_flag = OFF;

/* build environment string */

if ( (os_version = (char *) getenv("OS_VERSION")) ==
NULL) {
        sys_flag = ON;
}
if ( (sysname = (char *) getenv("NODE_NAME")) ==
NULL) {
        sys_flag = ON;
}

if (sys_flag == OFF) {
        strcpy (sys_id, sysname);
        strcat (sys_id, "; ");
        strcat (sys_id, os_version);
}

/* print program name and version */

do_bold();
printf ("%s", strtoupper(prog_name));
do_normal();

printf ("(%s)", prog_version);

/* print time */

start_time = get_strtime();

fprintf (stream," - %s\n", start_time);

/* print environment string */
```

```
        if (sys_flag == OFF)
                printf ("%s\n", sys_id);

        fprintf (stream,prog_name);

        /* echo command line */

        for (i=1; i<argc; i++) {
                fprintf (stream, "%s ", argv[i]);
        }

        fprintf (stream, "\n");

        return;
}


/*###########################################*/


/***************************************************

   FILE NAME   : banner.h
   AUTHOR      : Matt Weisfeld

   DESCRIPTION : header file for banner.c

***************************************************/
#ifdef ANSI
void banner(int,char**,FILE *);
#else
void banner();
#endif

/*###########################################*/


/***************************************************

   FILE NAME   : er.h
   AUTHOR      : Matt Weisfeld
```

```
    DESCRIPTION : error definitions for banner
                  application.


***************************************************/


#define ER_NOOPEN    0      /* file can't be opened */
#define ER_BADPUTENV1       /* put_env failed */


/*###########################################*/


/***************************************************

  FILE NAME    : errdefs.h
  AUTHOR       : Matt Weisfeld

  DESCRIPTION : error descriptions for banner
                applications.

***************************************************/
#include "er.h"

ERROR_STRUCT error_message[] =

/* actual error messages */

{

        /* #0 */
        ER_NOOPEN, EXIT,
        "Can't open '%s'.",
        /* #1 */
        ER_BADPUTENV, EXIT,
        "put_env failed.",
        LASTERROR, EXIT,NULL,

};

/*###########################################*/
```

```
/********************************************************

    FILE NAME   : proto.h
    AUTHOR      : Matt Weisfeld

    DESCRIPTION : prototype file for the banner
                  application

*********************************************************/
#ifdef VMS
#include "[-.common]common.h"
#include "[-.leave]leave.h"
#include "[-.error]error.h"
#include "[-.envlibs]envlibs.h"
#include "[-.timelibs]timelibs.h"
#include "[-.strlibs]strlibs.h"
#include "[-.scrlibs]scrlibs.h"
#endif

#ifdef BCC
#include "..\common\common.h"
#include "..\leave\leave.h"
#include "..\error\error.h"
#include "..\envlibs\envlibs.h"
#include "..\timelibs\timelibs.h"
#include "..\strlibs\strlibs.h"
#include "..\scrlibs\scrlibs.h"
#endif

#ifdef HPUX
#include "../common/common.h"
#include "../leave/leave.h"
#include "../error/error.h"
#include "../envlibs/envlibs.h"
#include "../timelibs/timelibs.h"
#include "../strlibs/strlibs.h"
#include "../scrlibs/scrlibs.h"
#endif

#ifdef SLC
#include "../common/common.h"
#include "../leave/leave.h"
```

```
#include "../error/error.h"
#include "../envlibs/envlibs.h"
#include "../timelibs/timelibs.h"
#include "../strlibs/strlibs.h"
#include "../scrlibs/scrlibs.h"
#endif

#ifdef GCC
#include "../common/common.h"
#include "../leave/leave.h"
#include "../error/error.h"
#include "../envlibs/envlibs.h"
#include "../timelibs/timelibs.h"
#include "../strlibs/strlibs.h"
#include "../scrlibs/scrlibs.h"
#endif

#ifdef CCC
#include "../common/common.h"
#include "../leave/leave.h"
#include "../error/error.h"
#include "../envlibs/envlibs.h"
#include "../timelibs/timelibs.h"
#include "../strlibs/strlibs.h"
#include "../scrlibs/scrlibs.h"
#endif

#include "banlibs.h"

/*################################################*/

$! VMS DCL PROCEDURE
$ clr
$ if (P1.eqs."") then GOTO ALL
$ if (P1.eqs."ALL") then GOTO ALL
$ if (P1.eqs."LINK") then GOTO LINK
$ set verify
$ cc/define=VMS 'P1'
$ goto LINK
$ ALL:
$     set verify
$ cc/define=VMS test
```

```
$ cc/define=VMS banlibs
$ LINK:
$ link/executable=test test,banlibs,[-.leave]leave,
[-.error]error,-
[-.scrlibs]scrlibs,[-.strlibs]strlibs,[-.timelibs]timelibs
$ copy test.exe [weisfeld.exe]
$ set noverify

/*###############################################*/

# makefile for BCC/C++ Compiler

OBJS      = test.obj banlibs.obj
HDRS      = proto.h errdefs.h banlibs.h er.h
FLAGS     = -c -DBCC
COMP      = bcc

test:   $(OBJS)
        $(COMP) @listobjs

test.obj: test.c $(HDRS)
        $(COMP) $(FLAGS) test.c

banlibs.obj: banlibs.c $(HDRS)
        $(COMP) $(FLAGS) banlibs.c

test.c:
banlibs.c:

banlibs.h:

/*###############################################*/

# makefile for MSC/C++ Compiler

OBJS      = test.obj banlibs.obj
HDRS      = proto.h errdefs.h banlibs.h er.h
FLAGS     = /c /DMSC
COMP      = cl

test:   $(OBJS)
        $(COMP) @listobjs
```

```
test.obj: test.c $(HDRS)
      $(COMP) $(FLAGS) test.c

banlibs.obj: banlibs.c $(HDRS)
      $(COMP) $(FLAGS) banlibs.c

test.c:
banlibs.c:

banlibs.h:

/*###############################################*/

/*
LISTOBJS
*/

test.obj
banlibs.obj
..\scrlibs\scrlibs.obj
..\strlibs\strlibs.obj
..\timelibs\timelibs.obj
..\leave\leave.obj
..\error\error.obj

/*###############################################*/

# makefile for HPUX C Compiler

OBJS     = test.o banlibs.o
LIBS     = ../scrlibs/scrlibs.o ../leave/leave.o \
           ../error/error.o ../strlibs/strlibs.o \
           ../timelibs/timelibs.o
HDRS     = proto.h errdefs.h banlibs.h er.h
FLAGS    = -c -DHPUX -Aa
COMP     = cc

test.exe:  $(OBJS)
      $(COMP) -o test $(OBJS) $(LIBS)

test.o: test.c $(HDRS)
      $(COMP) $(FLAGS) test.c
```

```
banlibs.o: banlibs.c $(HDRS)
        $(COMP) $(FLAGS) banlibs.c

test.c:
banlibs.c:

banlibs.h:


/*##############################################*/

# makefile for SUN SLC C Compiler

OBJS     = test.o banlibs.o
LIBS     = ../scrlibs/scrlibs.o ../leave/leave.o \
           ../error/error.o ../strlibs/strlibs.o \
           ../timelibs/timelibs.o
HDRS     = proto.h errdefs.h banlibs.h er.h
FLAGS    = -c -DSLC
COMP     = cc

test.exe:  $(OBJS)
        $(COMP) -o test $(OBJS) $(LIBS)

test.o: test.c $(HDRS)
        $(COMP) $(FLAGS) test.c

banlibs.o: banlibs.c $(HDRS)
        $(COMP) $(FLAGS) banlibs.c

test.c:
banlibs.c:

banlibs.h:


/*##############################################*/
```

```
# makefile for SUN GCC C Compiler

OBJS      = test.o banlibs.o
LIBS      = ../scrlibs/scrlibs.o ../leave/leave.o \
            ../error/error.o ../strlibs/strlibs.o \
            ../timelibs/timelibs.o
HDRS      = proto.h errdefs.h banlibs.h er.h
FLAGS     = -c -DGCC
COMP      = gcc

test.exe:  $(OBJS)
       $(COMP) -o test $(OBJS) $(LIBS)

test.o: test.c $(HDRS)
       $(COMP) $(FLAGS) test.c

banlibs.o: banlibs.c $(HDRS)
       $(COMP) $(FLAGS) banlibs.c

test.c:
banlibs.c:

banlibs.h:


/*###########################################*/

# makefile for CCC Compiler

OBJS      = test.o banlibs.o
LIBS      = ../scrlibs/scrlibs.o ../leave/leave.o \
            ../error/error.o ../envlibs/envlibs.o \
            ../strlibs/strlibs.o \
            ../timelibs/timelibs.o
HDRS      = proto.h errdefs.h banlibs.h er.h
FLAGS     = -c -DCCC
COMP      = cc

test.exe:  $(OBJS)
       $(COMP) -o test $(OBJS) $(LIBS)
```

```
test.o: test.c $(HDRS)
        $(COMP) $(FLAGS) test.c

banlibs.o: banlibs.c $(HDRS)
        $(COMP) $(FLAGS) banlibs.c

test.c:
banlibs.c:

banlibs.h:
```

20

Debugging with Signals

An introduction to trapping signals was presented in Chapter 10. The fact that signals can be intercepted provides a programmer with a very powerful coding technique. Since one of the most vexing problems for any program is an unexpected event such as a program crash, using signals to trap crashes provides much more program integrity. Debugging is another application that benefits from the use of signals. This chapter presents a technique that combines the advantages of both trapping program crashes and debugging code.

20.1 PLATFORM DIFFERENCES

The differences among the many platforms in terms of signal handling were presented in Chapter 10. However, the major differences really do not surface until a crash is actually encountered. It is the information displayed when a crash occurs that really separates the platforms.

Revisit the example in Chapter 10 regarding

```
int level3()
{
```

```
int i;

i = i/0;

return(3);

}
```

This routine will obviously generate a "divide by zero" error. The three major platforms, DOS, UNIX, and VMS, all generate the message when this code is executed:

- **VMS**

```
%SYSTEM_F_INTDIV, arithmetic trap, integer divide
      by zero at PC=00001C0E, PSL=03C00006
%TRACE-F-TRACEBACK, symbolic stack dump follows
module name   routine name   line      rel PC        abs PC

TEST1         level1         269       00000008      00001C20
TEST          main           267       0000000E      00001C0E
```

- **UNIX**

```
Floating exception (core dumped)
```

- **DOS**

```
Divide error
```

The most glaring difference among the three approaches is that VMS provides much more information. Most programmers would agree that it is helpful for the system to report the routine where the exception occurred, as well as the calling sequence that led to the offending code. This information allows the programmer to avoid a multitude of *printf*( ) statements and a significant amount of debugging code. The goal of this discussion is to offer a portable method for generating this information.

20.2 DESIGNING STANDARD OUTPUT

The next step is to analyze the nature of the information provided by VMS, which the output generated by the libraries in this chapter is patterned after. Again, the output for the floating point exception is

```
%SYSTEM_F_INTDIV, arithmetic trap, integer divide
        by zero at PC=00001C0E, PSL=03C00006
%TRACE-F-TRACEBACK, symbolic stack dump follows
module name   routine name    line      rel PC      abs  PC

TEST1         level1          269       00000008    00001C20
TEST          main            267       0000000E    00001C0E
```

The first two lines, starting with the percent sign (%), print the VMS internal error numbers. The first line is the message stating that the error is in fact an integer divide by zero. The second line simply states that a symbolic stack dump follows. The stack dump contains the following information: module name, routine name, line-relative program counter address, and absolute program counter address.

The module name is the name of the source file. For example, if *main( )* resides in a file called *siglibs.c,* then *siglibs.c* is the module name. The routine name is the name of a function called within the program, such as *main( )* or *level1( )*. The line number refers to the line in the object code, not the source code. This is somewhat less helpful than the line number in the source code would be. The only time a programmer will use this information is if a hex dump is consulted or a debugger is entered. The program counter address falls into the same category.

For this exercise, the information to concentrate on is the module name and the routine name. A mechanism exists for including the line number of the first line of the routine name, and this will be discussed in detail later.

Consider the following program; the interrupt handler is presented later in this chapter.

```
/***
        signal.c
***/
#include <stdio.h>
#include <signal.h>

main()
{

        int i;
        char array[20];

        signal (SIGFPE,interrupt_handler);

        return;

}

/***
        level.c
***/
#include <stdio.h>
#include <signal.h>

int level1()
{

        level2();

        return(1);

}

int level2()
{

        level3();

        return(2);
}

int level3()
{
```

```
        int i;

#ifdef MSC
        volitile double d = 0.0f;
#endif

        level4();

#ifdef MSC
        i = i/0;
#endif
        d = d/0.0;
#endif

        return(3);


}
```

The floating point exception is generated in the routine *level3*. The following information will be the goal of the portable debugger. This sample is from a VMS test run:

```
###########################################
%SYSTEM_F_INTDIV, arithmetic trap, integer divide by zero
at PC=00001C0E,
PSL=03C00006
%TRACE-F-TRACEBACK, symbolic stack dump follows
###########################################
```

Routine Name	File Name	Line
LEVEL3	SYS$SYSDEVICE:[WEISFELD.SRC.SIGNAL]LEVEL.C;5	43
LEVEL2	SYS$SYSDEVICE:[WEISFELD.SRC.SIGNAL]LEVEL.C;5	29
LEVEL1	SYS$SYSDEVICE:[WEISFELD.SRC.SIGNAL]LEVEL.C;5	16
main	SYS$SYSDEVICE:[WEISFELD.SRC.SIGNAL]SIGNAL.C;3	18

Note that the file name includes more than just the name itself. VMS provides the device name and the directory, as well as the file name. UNIX and DOS simply provide the file name. The three systems will also print somewhat different message information. These issues will be discussed later in this chapter.

20.3 CREATING A PROGRAM STACK

A stack is used to accumulate the information necessary for the debugging routine. The concept is that every time a routine is entered, its name is pushed onto a stack. Then, every time the routine is exited, the routine name is popped off the stack. These tasks requires code for stack handling, which fortunately is fairly straightforward.

The logic behind a stack is simple—last-in-first-out. To implement a stack, four functions must be written: a means to initialize the stack, a means to check if the stack is empty, a means to push an item onto the stack, and a means to pop an item off the stack. The first issue in developing a stack handler, defining the structure of the stack, is done in the following manner:

```
#define STACKLIMIT 30
#define MAXARRAY   80

typedef struct {
        char routinearray[STACKLIMIT][MAXARRAY];
        char filearray[STACKLIMIT][MAXARRAY];
        int linearray[STACKLIMIT];
        int top;
} STACK;
```

This stack contains four fields. The character string *routinearray* holds the name of the routine just entered. The character string *filearray* holds the name of the file that the routine is in. The integer *linearray* holds the line number of the first line of the routine. The last field, the integer *top,* is the stack pointer. For example, if there are five items in the stack, *top* will equal four (the stack starts at zero). This pointer does not actually have to be physically located in the stack, but putting it there makes it much easier to manage when many stacks are declared in the same program. Just imagine having to keep track of 100 stack pointers, let alone even declare them.

To declare an instance of the stack named *calling_stack,* this single line of code is included:

```
STACK calling_stack;
```

The routine to initialize the stack must be called before any other stack options are performed. This code is quite simple:

```
/* initialize the stack to empty */

int init_stack(STACK *ps)
{

        (*ps).top = -1;

        return (NORMAL);

}
```

Basically, all this routine does is set the pointer to -1. This routine is important because the system cannot be relied upon to initialize the counter to zero, although in most cases this is its initial value. The following call will initialize *calling_stack:*

```
init_stack(&calling_stack);
```

Another very small and simple routine checks to see if the stack is empty:

```
/* returns true if the stack is empty */

int empty(STACK *ps)
{

        return ( (*ps).top == -1 );
}
```

By definition, the only time the stack can be empty is if the pointer is -1. This condition is important if, for example, a *pop( )* is attempted when nothing is left on the stack. Whenever a *pop( )* is performed, the following code must check for an empty stack:

```
if (empty(ps)) {
        return(UNDERFLOW);
```

This leads to the two major error conditions for a stack: under-flow and overflow. If a *pop*( ) is attempted on an empty stack, an underflow exists. Conversely, if a *push*( ) results in the stack growing larger than the stack pointer allows, an overflow exists:

```
if ((*ps).top == STACKLIMIT-1)
       return(OVERFLOW);
```

The complete codes for the *push*( ) routine and the *pop*( ) routine follow.

20.3.1 The *push*( ) Routine

```
/* push a new value on the top of the stack */

int push(char *file, char *routine, int line, STACK *ps)
{


    if ((*ps).top == STACKLIMIT-1) {
        return(OVERFLOW);
    } else {
        (*ps).top = (*ps).top + 1;
        strcpy ( (*ps).filearray[(*ps).top], file );
        strcpy ( (*ps).routinearray[(*ps).top], routine );
        (*ps).linearray[(*ps).top]= line;
    }

    return (NORMAL);

}
```

The only logic required here involves increasing the stack point-er and copying the necessary information into the stack memo-ry. Note that the pointer *ps* is always preceded by an asterisk. Without this constraint, the code would access the address of the pointer, not the value that it points to.

The call to push information onto the stack is

```
push (file,routine,line,&calling_stack);
```

The ampersand in front of the stack name is required, since it is the address of the stack that is being passed.

20.3.2 The *pop*( ) Routine

```
/* pop a value off the top of the stack */

int pop(STACK *ps, char *file, char *routine, int *line)
{

    int return_value;

    if (empty(ps)) {
        return(UNDERFLOW);
    } else {
        strcpy ( file, (*ps).filearray[(*ps).top] );
        strcpy ( routine, (*ps).routinearray[(*ps).top] );
        *line = (*ps).linearray[(*ps).top];
        (*ps).top = (*ps).top - 1;
    }

    return (NORMAL);

}
```

The *pop*( ) routine performs exactly the opposite logic from the *push*( ) routine. The contents of the stack are copied to the program variables and the stack pointer is decreased. The call to pop information onto the stack is

```
pop (&calling_stack,file,routine,line);
```

20.4 USING MACROS TO MANAGE THE STACK

With the stack routines available, the major decision left for the programmer to make is how to *push*( ) and *pop*( ) the information to and from the stack. One way would be simply to call the stack operations as follows:

```
level1()
{
```

```
        push(info);

        process...

        pop(info);

}
```

This will work, but it adds a lot of overhead to the program since two extra functions are called—actually three, because *empty( )* is called from *pop( )*—for every routine entered. This may not be a problem for some applications, but bear in mind that this information may only be necessary when a bug is actually encountered. Therefore, #ifdef's can be used to include this routine only when desired. For example:

```
level1()
{

#IFDEF DEBUG
        push(info);
#ENDIF

        process...

#IFDEF DEGUG
        pop(info);
#endif

}
```

This may be a better solution, but it makes the code more cumbersome to read.

An even better approach is to embed the stack calls in a macro. This overcomes the problem with extra function calls and keeps most of the code transparent to the programmer. The equivalent code using macros becomes

```
level1()
{
```

```
    r_enter(info);

    process...

    r_leave(info);

}
```

This approach still adds two lines of code to each routine. However, a lot of overhead is saved as a result. Actually, there is a way to eliminate even these lines, as you will see later in this chapter.

The macro for *enter* is

```
#define r_enter(routine_name) \
    if (first_pass) {\
        init_stack(&calling_stack);\
        r_set_signals();\
        first_pass=NO;\
    }\
    if
(push(routine_name,__FILE__,__LINE__,&calling_stack)==
OVERFLOW) {\
        printf ("STACK OVERFLOW\n");\
        exit(0);\
    }\
```

This macro contains a lot of new information in its two distinguishable parts. The first part pertains to the first call to *r_enter( )*. As explained earlier, before the stack can be used, you must initialize and set the appropriate signals. This code is included in the macro to alleviate the need for the programmer to generate it explicitly elsewhere. Including this code does add an *if* statement to subsequent calls. If this is a problem, then move this code out into the program itself.

The macros can be surrounded by #ifdef's if need be for use only when debugging. The call to *init_stack( )* has already been explained. The macro *r_set_signals( )* is used to set the signals. This enables all the signals that the signal handler will trap. Each system has its own, so if the intent is to port this to a platform not dealt with in this discussion, *r_set_signals*( ) is the place to inspect.

The line for *push*( ) has two bits of new information: *__FILE__* and *__LINE__*:

```
if (push(routine_name,__FILE__,__LINE__,
&calling_stack)==OVERFLOW) {\
```

These two macros represent information provided by the system and can be used in almost any situation. They can be printed out with a *printf*( ) as follows:

```
printf ("FILE = %s, LINE = %d\n", __FILE__, __LINE__);
```

The *leave*( ) routine is coded as follows:

```
#define r_leave() \
    if (pop(&calling_stack,routine_name, file_name,
    &line_num)==UNDERFLOW) { \
        printf ("STACK UNDERFLOW\n");\
        exit(0);\
    }\
```

Make sure that the lines within a macro are separated by a backslash(\). Omitting this character by mistake can cause much grief. For instance, a stack error generated in such cases explicitly causes an exit from the program, which may be unacceptable in many situations. Any stack error most likely indicates that a call to *r_leave*( ) was missed.

It is possible to redefine functions with a macro to reduce the amount of code written even further. For example, the *return*( ) function can be redefined to include the code for *r_leave*( ), thus freeing the programmer from having to remember to call *r_leave*( ). This approach requires that *return*( ) always be called, or the stack will become corrupted. Redefining a function to include *r_enter*( ) is not possible.

20.5 THE INTERRUPT HANDLER

The final order of business is to create the interrupt handler. In this case, the handler simply prints out the contents of the stack and exits the program.

The code to print the stack information is

```
for (;;) {
        if (pop(&calling_stack, file_name, routine_name,
        &line_num)==UNDERFLOW)
                break;
        printf ("%-10s  %-55s  %5d\n", file_name,
        routine_name, line_num);
}
```

In effect, an infinite loop is entered and *pop*( ) is called until the underflow condition is reached. Then a break is called.

20.6 USING THE SIGNAL DEBUGGER LIBRARY

The *traplibs* test program actually nests a few deep routines before the signal is generated by means of a divide by zero. The same portability issues apply here as with the *siglibs* library: some platforms generate a floating point divide by zero, while some generate an integer divide by zero. When the interrupt occurs, the stack is dumped to the screen with the calling path information.

Remember that only the last define in a VMS compile line is active. The keyword VMS is defined here only for documentation purposes.

To use the *traplibs* library, the *siglibs* object library must be linked to the application.

20.7 CONCLUSION

Handling signals is a powerful technique. It allows the programmer to maintain control of a program with much more certainty than would otherwise be the case. Not only are system exceptions trapped, but user intervention (such as CNTRL-C) can be trapped as well. And, as has been demonstrated, using signals can be a major aid in debugging.

```c
/****************************************************

   FILE NAME   : test.c
   AUTHOR      : Matt Weisfeld

   DESCRIPTION : test program for signal debugging
                 application.

****************************************************/
#include <stdio.h>
#include <signal.h>
#include <errno.h>
#include "proto.h"
#include "errdefs.h"

STACK calling_stack;
char file_name[STRLEN];
char routine_name[STRLEN];
int line_num;

int first_pass = YES;

int status;

#ifdef MSC
volatile double d = 0.0f;
#endif

main()
{

        r_enter("main");

        status = level5();
        status = level5();

        status = level1();
```

```
        r_leave();

        leave(EXIT_NORMAL);

        return(EXIT_NORMAL);

}

/*#############################################*/


/****************************************************

  FILE NAME   : handler.c
  AUTHOR      : Matt Weisfeld

  DESCRIPTION : interrupt handler for signal
                debugging application.

****************************************************/
#include <stdio.h>
#include <signal.h>
#include "proto.h"
#include "er.h"

extern STACK calling_stack;
extern char file_name[80];
extern char routine_name[80];
extern int  line_num;

/****************************************************

  ROUTINE NAME : interrupt_handler()

  DESCRIPTION  : process and handle a program
                 interrupt

  INPUT        : int (signal)
                 int (type)

  OUTPUT       : none

****************************************************/
```

```
void interrupt_handler(sig, type)
int sig;
int type;
{

        interrupt_message(sig,type);

        printf
        ("##############################################\n\n");
        printf ("%-10s  %-55s  %5s\n", "File Name", "Routine
        Name", "Line");
        printf ("——————————————————————————————————————————\n");

        for (;;) {
                if (pop(&calling_stack, file_name,
                routine_name, &line_num)==UNDERFLOW)
                        break;
                printf ("%-10s  %-55s  %5d\n", file_name,
                routine_name, line_num);
        }

        leave (EXIT_ERROR);

}

/**************************************************

  ROUTINE NAME : clean_up()

  DESCRIPTION  : clean-up routine for signal
                 handler library

  INPUT        : int (signal code or type)

  OUTPUT       : void

**************************************************/
void clean_up(code)
int code;
{

        switch (code) {
```

```
        case ILLSIG:
                error(ER_ILLSIG, code);
        break;
        case ILLTYPE:
                error(ER_ILLTYPE, code);
        break;

        default:
                printf ("Cleaning up!\n");
        break;

        }

        leave (EXIT_ERROR);

}


/*######################################*/


/****************************************************

  FILE NAME   : level.c
  AUTHOR      : Matt Weisfeld

  DESCRIPTION : routines to test signal debugger

****************************************************/
#include <stdio.h>
#include <signal.h>
#include <errno.h>
#include "proto.h"

extern STACK calling_stack;
extern char file_name[80];
extern char routine_name[80];
extern int line_num;

extern int first_pass;

int level1()
{
```

```
        r_enter("LEVEL1");

        level2();

        r_leave();

        return(1);

}
int level2()
{

        r_enter("LEVEL2");

        level3();

        r_leave();

        return(2);
}

int level3()
{

        int i;

#ifdef MSC
        volatile double d = 0.0f;
#endif

        r_enter("LEVEL3");

        level4();

#ifdef MSC
        d = d/0.0;
#else
        i = i/0;
#endif

        r_leave();
```

```
        return(3);

}

int level4()
{

        char array[10];

        int i;

        r_enter("LEVEL4");

        r_leave();

        return(4);
}

int level5()
{

        char array[10];

        int i;

        r_enter("LEVEL5");

        r_leave();

        return(5);

}


/*###########################################*/


/**************************************************

   FILE NAME   : stack.c
   AUTHOR      : Matt Weisfeld
```

```
    DESCRIPTION : stack support routines

*****************************************************/
#include <stdio.h>

#include <string.h>
#include "proto.h"

/* push a new value on the top of the stack */

int push(file, routine, line, ps)
char *file;
char *routine;
int line;
STACK *ps;
{


    if ((*ps).top == STACKLIMIT-1) {
        return(OVERFLOW);
    } else {
        (*ps).top = (*ps).top + 1;
        strcpy ( (*ps).filearray[(*ps).top], file );
        strcpy ( (*ps).routinearray[(*ps).top], routine );
        (*ps).linearray[(*ps).top]= line;
    }

    return (NORMAL);

}

/* pop a value off the top of the stack */

int pop(ps, file, routine, line)
STACK *ps;
char *file;
char *routine;
int *line;
{

    int return_value;
```

```
    if (empty(ps)) {
        return(UNDERFLOW);
    } else {
        strcpy ( file, (*ps).filearray[(*ps).top] );
        strcpy ( routine, (*ps).routinearray[(*ps).top] );
        *line = (*ps).linearray[(*ps).top];
        (*ps).top = (*ps).top - 1;
    }

    return (NORMAL);

}

/* initialize the stack to empty */

int init_stack(ps)
STACK *ps;
{

    (*ps).top = -1;

    return (NORMAL);

}

/* returns true if the stack is empty */

int empty(ps)
STACK *ps;
{

    return ( (*ps).top == -1 );
}

/*###########################################################*/


/*************************************************

  FILE NAME   : traplibs.h
  AUTHOR      : Matt Weisfeld
```

```
    DESCRIPTION : signal debugging header

    *****************************************************/
    #include "stack.h"

    #ifdef ANSI
    int level1(void);
    int level2(void);
    int level3(void);
    int level4(void);
    int level5(void);
    int push(char *, char *, int, STACK *);
    int pop(STACK *, char *, char *, int *);
    int init_stack(STACK *);
    int empty(STACK *);
    void list_errno(int);
    #else
    int level1();
    int level2();
    int level3();
    int level4();
    int level5();
    int push();
    int pop();
    int init_stack();
    int empty();
    void list_errno();
    #endif

    /*#############################################*/


    /*************************************************

      FILE NAME    : stack.h
      AUTHOR       : Matt Weisfeld

      DESCRIPTION : stack debugging macros

    *************************************************/
    #include <stdio.h>
    #include <stdlib.h>
```

```
#include "er.h"

#define STACKLIMIT 30

typedef struct {
    char routinearray[STACKLIMIT][80];
    char filearray[STACKLIMIT][80];
    int  linearray[STACKLIMIT];
    int top;
} STACK;

#define YES 1
#define NO  0

#define NORMAL 0
#define OVERFLOW -1
#define UNDERFLOW -2

#ifdef DBG

#define r_enter(routine_name) \
    if (first_pass) {\
        set_signals();\
        init_stack(&calling_stack);\
        first_pass=NO;\
    }\
    if (push(routine_name,__FILE__,__LINE__, \
    &calling_stack)==OVERFLOW) {\
        error (ER_OVERFLOW);\
    }\

#define r_leave() \
    if (pop(&calling_stack,routine_name, file_name, \
    &line_num)==UNDERFLOW) { \
        error (ER_UNDERFLOW);\
    }

#else

#define r_enter(routine_name) \

#define r_leave() \
```

```
#endif

/*###########################################*/


/****************************************************

   FILE NAME    : er.h
   AUTHOR       : Matt Weisfeld

   DESCRIPTION : file definitions for siglibs

****************************************************/
#define ER_ILLSIG       0    /* code not found */
#define ER_ILLTYPE      1    /* type not found */
#define ER_OVERFLOW     2    /* stack overflow */
#define ER_UNDERFLOW    3    /* stack underflow */

/*###########################################*/


/****************************************************

   FILE NAME    : errdefs.h
   AUTHOR       : Matt Weisfeld

   DESCRIPTION : error definitions for signal
                 debugger

****************************************************/
#include "er.h"

ERROR_STRUCT error_message[] =

/* actual error messages */

{

    /* #0 */
    ER_ILLSIG, EXIT,
    "Illegal signal '%d'.",
    /* #1 */
```

```
    ER_ILLTYPE, EXIT,
    "Illegal type '%d'.",
    /* #2 */
    ER_OVERFLOW, EXIT,
    "Stack overflow.",
    /* #3 */
    ER_UNDERFLOW, EXIT,
    "Stack underflow.",
    /* LAST */
    LASTERROR, EXIT,
};


/*################################################*/


/***************************************************

  FILE NAME   : proto.h
  AUTHOR      : Matt Weisfeld

  DESCRIPTION : prototype file for signal
                debugger.

***************************************************/
#ifdef VMS
#include "[-.common]common.h"
#include "[-.leave]leave.h"
#include "[-.error]error.h"
#include "[-.siglibs]siglibs.h"
#endif

#ifdef BCC
#include "..\common\common.h"
#include "..\leave\leave.h"
#include "..\error\error.h"
#include "..\siglibs\siglibs.h"
#endif

#ifdef MSC
#include "..\common\common.h"
#include "..\leave\leave.h"
```

```
#include "..\error\error.h"
#include "..\siglibs\siglibs.h"
#endif

#ifdef HPUX
#include "../common/common.h"
#include "../leave/leave.h"
#include "../error/error.h"
#include "../siglibs/siglibs.h"
#endif

#ifdef SLC
#include "../common/common.h"
#include "../leave/leave.h"
#include "../error/error.h"
#include "../siglibs/siglibs.h"
#endif

#ifdef GCC
#include "../common/common.h"
#include "../leave/leave.h"
#include "../error/error.h"
#include "../siglibs/siglibs.h"
#endif

#ifdef CCC
#include "../common/common.h"
#include "../leave/leave.h"
#include "../error/error.h"
#include "../siglibs/siglibs.h"
#endif

#include "traplibs.h"

/*###############################################*/

$! VMS DCL PROCEDURE
$ clr
$ if (P1.eqs."") then GOTO ALL
$ if (P1.eqs."ALL") then GOTO ALL
$ if (P1.eqs."LINK") then GOTO LINK
$ set verify
```

```
$ cc/define=VMS 'P1'
$ goto LINK
$ ALL:
$    set verify
$ cc/define=VMS/define=DBG test
$ cc/define=VMS/define=DBG level
$ cc/define=VMS/define=DBG stack
$ cc/define=VMS/define=DBG handler
$ LINK:
$ link/executable=test test,level,stack,handler,
[-.leave]leave,-
[-.error]error,[-.siglibs]siglibs
$ copy test.exe [weisfeld.exe]
$ set noverify

/*###########################################*/

# makefile for BCC/C++ Compiler

OBJS     = test.obj stack.obj level.obj handler.obj
LIBS     = ..\leave\leave.obj \
            ..\error\error.obj ..\siglibs\siglibs.obj
HDRS     = proto.h errdefs.h stack.h er.h
FLAGS    = -c -DBCC -DDBG
COMP     = bcc

test.exe:  $(OBJS)
     $(COMP) $(OBJS) $(LIBS)

test.obj: test.c $(HDRS)
     $(COMP) $(FLAGS) test.c

stack.obj: stack.c $(HDRS)
     $(COMP) $(FLAGS) stack.c

level.obj: level.c $(HDRS)
     $(COMP) $(FLAGS) level.c

handler.obj: handler.c $(HDRS)
     $(COMP) $(FLAGS) handler.c

test.c:
stack.c:
```

```
level.c:
handler.c:

stack.h:
sigbug.h:

/*###########################################*/

# makefile for MSC/C++ Compiler

OBJS    = test.obj stack.obj level.obj handler.obj
LIBS    = ..\leave\leave.obj \
          ..\error\error.obj ..\siglibs\siglibs.obj
HDRS    = proto.h errdefs.h stack.h er.h
FLAGS   = /c /DMSC /DDBG
COMP    = cl

test.exe:  $(OBJS)
    $(COMP) $(OBJS) $(LIBS)

test.obj: test.c $(HDRS)
    $(COMP) $(FLAGS) test.c

stack.obj: stack.c $(HDRS)
    $(COMP) $(FLAGS) stack.c

level.obj: level.c $(HDRS)
    $(COMP) $(FLAGS) level.c

handler.obj: handler.c $(HDRS)
    $(COMP) $(FLAGS) handler.c

test.c:
stack.c:
level.c:
handler.c:

stack.h:
sigbug.h:

/*###########################################*/
```

```
# makefile for HPUX C Compiler

OBJS     = test.o stack.o level.o handler.o
LIBS     = ../leave/leave.o  ../error/error.o
           ../siglibs/siglibs.o
HDRS     = proto.h errdefs.h stack.h er.h
FLAGS    = -c -DHPUX -DDBG -Aa
COMP     = cc

test:  $(OBJS)
    $(COMP) -o test $(OBJS) $(LIBS)

test.o: test.c $(HDRS)
    $(COMP) $(FLAGS) test.c

stack.o: stack.c $(HDRS)
    $(COMP) $(FLAGS) stack.c

level.o: level.c $(HDRS)
    $(COMP) $(FLAGS) level.c

handler.o: handler.c $(HDRS)
    $(COMP) $(FLAGS) handler.c

test.c:
stack.c:
level.c:
handler.c:

stack.h:
sigbug.h:

/*###############################################*/

# makefile for SUN SLC C Compiler

OBJS     = test.o stack.o level.o handler.o
LIBS     = ../leave/leave.o  ../error/error.o
           ../siglibs/siglibs.o
HDRS     = proto.h errdefs.h stack.h er.h
FLAGS    = -c -DSLC -DDBG
COMP     = cc
```

```
test:  $(OBJS)
    $(COMP) -o test $(OBJS) $(LIBS)

test.o: test.c $(HDRS)
    $(COMP) $(FLAGS) test.c

stack.o: stack.c $(HDRS)
    $(COMP) $(FLAGS) stack.c

level.o: level.c $(HDRS)
    $(COMP) $(FLAGS) level.c

handler.o: handler.c $(HDRS)
    $(COMP) $(FLAGS) handler.c

test.c:
stack.c:
level.c:
handler.c:

stack.h:
sigbug.h:

/*###########################################*/

# makefile for SUN GCC C Compiler

OBJS      = test.o stack.o level.o handler.o
LIBS      = ../leave/leave.o  ../error/error.o
            ../siglibs/siglibs.o
HDRS      = proto.h errdefs.h stack.h er.h
FLAGS     = -c -DGCC -DDBG
COMP      = gcc

test:  $(OBJS)
    $(COMP) -o test $(OBJS) $(LIBS)

test.o: test.c $(HDRS)
    $(COMP) $(FLAGS) test.c

stack.o: stack.c $(HDRS)
    $(COMP) $(FLAGS) stack.c
```

```
level.o: level.c $(HDRS)
    $(COMP) $(FLAGS) level.c

handler.o: handler.c $(HDRS)
    $(COMP) $(FLAGS) handler.c

test.c:
stack.c:
level.c:
handler.c:

stack.h:
sigbug.h:

/*###############################################*/

# makefile for CCC Compiler

OBJS    = test.o stack.o level.o handler.o
LIBS    = ../leave/leave.o  ../error/error.o
          ../siglibs/siglibs.o
HDRS    = proto.h errdefs.h stack.h er.h
FLAGS   = -c -DCCC -DDBG
COMP    = cc

test:  $(OBJS)
    $(COMP) -o test $(OBJS) $(LIBS)

test.o: test.c $(HDRS)
    $(COMP) $(FLAGS) test.c

stack.o: stack.c $(HDRS)
    $(COMP) $(FLAGS) stack.c

level.o: level.c $(HDRS)
    $(COMP) $(FLAGS) level.c

handler.o: handler.c $(HDRS)
    $(COMP) $(FLAGS) handler.c

test.c:
stack.c:
```

```
level.c:
handler.c:

stack.h:
sigbug.h:
```

21

A Command Executive

The final library developed in this book requires the services of many of the libraries created in earlier chapters. This is a very short chapter since the functionality provided here is actually a combination of previously presented libraries—a very good example of how the up-front work of creating libraries really pays off. Almost all the work done in this library is done by other libraries.

Three of these libraries relate to the invocation of commands. In this context, the command may be an internal command, an external command, or an operating system command. There are situations when it is not known ahead of time whether the command being called is internal, external, or system. Suppose that a command is parsed from an input file:

```
compare file1 file2
```

To determine how *compare* should be executed, the following logic is necessary:

```
If the command is internal,  execute it.
else
```

```
If the command external,  execute it.
else
attempt to execute a system command.
```

For a program to utilize internal functions, an internal function list must be built as described in Chapter 12. For a program to execute external commands, a directory must be set up so that all external executables reside there. This step is necessary so that the parent program can search the directory to determine if the executable does indeed exist. The child process is then called with the libraries developed in Chapter 13.

If there is no internal or external function to call, the command is assumed to be an operating system call and is invoked with the system call described in Chapter 14. Thus, after the line

```
compare file1 file2
```

is parsed and placed in a string called *command,* a check is executed to determine whether the command is internal:

```
status = internal(command);
```

If it is not internal (status == -1), the *command* is broken up into an *argv* structure by calling *strargv( )*:

```
args = strargv(command);
```

Then the command must be added to the path:

```
strcpy (file, path);
strcat (file,args[0]);
```

Next, the command is checked to determine if it is an external command. To do this, the routine must check the directory where the executables reside to see if the program is actually there. This task is done by the library *fexists( )*.

Note that some operating systems have extensions on their executables: VMS and DOS use *.exe,* while UNIX has no specific requirement. Thus, the executable for *compare* would actually be *compare.exe* for VMS and DOS. This extension must be added for the call to *fexists( )* to work:

```
#ifndef UNIX
strcat (file, ".exe");
#endif
```

After the extension is concatenated onto the command, *args*[0] must be reset:

```
args[0] = file;
```

Now *fexists( )* is called:

```
if (fexists(file)) {
        /* execute an external command */
        status = execv_lib(args);
} else {
        /* execute a system command */
        status = system(command);
}
```

If the external command is not found, the command is executed as if it were a system command. Remember that the status returned as a result of calling *system( )* only indicates that the command was invoked. It does not indicate the success or failure of the command.

21.1 USING THE COMMAND EXECUTIVE LIBRARY

The test program for *comlibs* incorporates three different command types: internal, external, and system. After each call to the *command( )* library function, the status returned is passed to a routine called *check_status( )* that reports the completion status of the command.

Using this libary requires linking the *intlibs, execlibs, statlibs,* and *comlibs* object libraries with the application.

21.2 CONCLUSION

This is the last library developed in this book. It is a perfect example of the advantages gained from developing libraries. This library was developed using the functionality built in previous libraries. It is this reusability that makes the libraries so powerful. Using the *comlibs* library makes calling various types of commands from within a program transparent. With just one call, a programmer can invoke an internal command, an external command, or a system command.

```
/**************************************************

   FILE NAME   : test.c
   AUTHOR      : Matt Weisfeld

   DESCRIPTION : test file for command choice

**************************************************/
#include <stdio.h>
#include <stdlib.h>
#include <string.h>
#include "proto.h"
#include "errdefs.h"

#ifdef VMS
char path[20] = "[weisfeld.exe]";
#endif

#ifdef DOS
char path[20] = "c:\\exe\\";
#endif

#ifdef UNIX
char path[20] = "../../bin/";
#endif

#ifdef ANSI
void check_status(int);
#else
void check_status();
#endif
```

```
main()
{
        int i;
        int status;
        char command[STRLEN];

        printf ("\nTEST INTERNAL COMMAND\n");

        strcpy (command, "comp one two");
        status = comexec(command);

        check_status(status);

        printf ("\nTEST EXTERNAL COMMAND\n");

        strcpy (command, "hello");

        status = comexec(command);

        check_status(status);

        printf ("\nTEST SYSTEM COMMAND\n");

#ifdef VMS
        strcpy (command, "dir");
#endif
#ifdef DOS
        strcpy (command, "dir");
#endif
#ifdef UNIX
        strcpy (command, "ls");
#endif
        status = comexec(command);

        check_status(status);

        leave(EXIT_NORMAL);

        return(EXIT_NORMAL);

}
```

```
/*****************************************************

   ROUTINE NAME : check_status()

   DESCRIPTION  : check status variable from
                  execv() libraries.

   INPUT        : int (status)

   OUTPUT       : none

*****************************************************/
void check_status(status)
int status;
{

      switch(status) {

            case BADFORK:
                  error(ER_BADFORK);
            break;

            case BADEXEC:
                  error(ER_BADEXEC);
            break;

            case BADWAIT:
                  error(ER_BADWAIT);
            break;

            case BADPATH:
                  error(ER_BADPATH);
            break;

            case BADMALLOC:
                  error(ER_BADMALLOC);
            break;

            default:
                  printf ("Child status = %d\n", status);
            break;
```

```
        }

        return;

}

/*###########################################*/


/***************************************************

   FILE NAME    : comlibs.c
   AUTHOR       : Matt Weisfeld

   DESCRIPTION : test file for command libraries

***************************************************/
#include <stdio.h>
#include <stdlib.h>
#include <string.h>
#include "proto.h"
#include "funcs.h"

extern char path[];

int comexec(command)
char *command;
{

        int i;
        int status;

        char file[STRLEN];

        char **args;

        /* attempt to execute an internal command */

        status = internal(command);

        /* if it is not an internal command, go on */
```

```
        if (status == -1) {

                /* turn command into argv structure */

                args = strargv(command);

                /* build the command, with the path */

                strcpy (file,path);
                strcat (file,args[0]);
#ifndef UNIX
                strcat (file, ".exe");
#endif

                args[0] = file;


                /* see if the file is in the path directory */

                if (fexists(file)) {
                        /* execute an external command */
                        status = execv_lib(args);
                } else {
                        /* execute a system command */
                        status = system(command);
                }
        }

        return(status);

}



/*##########################################*/


/**************************************************

  FILE NAME    : func.c
  AUTHOR       : Matt Weisfeld
```

```
   DESCRIPTION : test routines for internal
                 library.

****************************************************/
#include <stdio.h>
#include "proto.h"

/* internal function p_comp */

int p_comp(count, argv)
int count;
char **argv;
{

      int i;

      printf ("\nCOMP\n");

      for (i=0; i<count; i++)
            printf("argv[%d] %s\n", i, argv[i]);

      return(EXIT_NORMAL);
}

/* internal function p_list */

int p_list(count, argv)
int count;
char **argv;
{

      int i;

      printf ("\nLIST\n");

      for (i=0; i<count; i++)
            printf("argv[%d] %s\n", i, argv[i]);

      return(EXIT_NORMAL);
}
```

```
/* internal function p_clear */

int p_clear(count, argv)
int count;
char **argv;
{

      int i;

      printf ("\nCLEAR\n");

      for (i=0; i<count; i++)
            printf("argv[%d] %s\n", i, argv[i]);

      return(EXIT_NORMAL);
}


/* internal function p_pause */

int p_pause(count ,argv)
int count;
char **argv;
{

      int i;

      printf ("\nPAUSE\n");

      for (i=0; i<count; i++)
            printf("argv[%d] %s\n", i, argv[i]);

      return(EXIT_NORMAL);
}
#include <stdio.h>
#include "proto.h"

main()
{
      printf ("hello world\n");
```

```
        exit(EXIT_NORMAL);
}

/*#########################################*/


/*************************************************

   FILE NAME   : comlibs.h
   AUTHOR      : Matt Weisfeld

   DESCRIPTION : header file for commands
                 application.

*************************************************/
#ifdef ANSI
int comexec(char *);
#else
int comexec();
#endif

/*#########################################*/


/*************************************************

   FILE NAME   : funcs.h
   AUTHOR      : Matt Weisfeld

   DESCRIPTION : internal function definitions

*************************************************/
/* current internal commands */


int    p_comp ();
int    p_list();
int    p_clear();
int    p_pause();

/* This is the array structure used to hold voidernal
commands */
```

```
INFUNCS infuncs[] = {
      {"comp", p_comp},
      {"list", p_list},
      {"clear", p_clear},
      {"pause", p_pause},
      {NULL, NULL}
};
```

```
/*##############################################*/
```

```
/*****************************************************

  FILE NAME    : er.h
  AUTHOR       : Matt Weisfeld

  DESCRIPTION  : error definitions for commands
                 application.

*****************************************************/
```

```
#define ER_BADFORK    0      /* fork failed */
#define ER_BADEXEC    1      /* execv failed */
#define ER_BADWAIT    2      /* wait failed */
#define ER_BADPATH    3      /* calling path is invalid */
#define ER_BADMALLOC  4      /* malloc failed */
#define ER_BADPUTENV  5      /* put_env failed */
#define ER_INVARGS    6      /* invalid number of arguments */
```

```
/*##############################################*/
```

```
/*****************************************************

  FILE NAME    : errdefs.h
  AUTHOR       : Matt Weisfeld

  DESCRIPTION  : error descriptions for commands
                 application.

*****************************************************/
```

```
#include "er.h"

ERROR_STRUCT error_message[] =

/* actual error messages */

{

        /* #0 */
        ER_BADFORK, EXIT,
        "An attempt to fork() failed.",
        /* #1 */
        ER_BADEXEC, EXIT,
        "An attempt to execv() failed.",
        /* #2 */
        ER_BADWAIT, EXIT,
        "A wait() operation failed.",
        /* #3 */
        ER_BADPATH, EXIT,
        "A calling path is invalid.",
        /* #4 */
        ER_BADMALLOC, EXIT,
        "An attempt to obtain space failed.",
        /* #5 */
        ER_BADPUTENV, EXIT,
        "A put_env() failed.",
        /* #6 */
        ER_INVARGS, EXIT,
        "Invalid number of arguments.",
        LASTERROR, EXIT,NULL,
};


/*#############################################*/


/***************************************************

   FILE NAME   : proto.h
   AUTHOR      : Matt Weisfeld

   DESCRIPTION : prototype file for commands

***************************************************/
```

```
#ifdef VMS
#include "[-.common]common.h"
#include "[-.leave]leave.h"
#include "[-.error]error.h"
#include "[-.intlibs]intlibs.h"
#include "[-.timelibs]timelibs.h"
#include "[-.statlibs]statlibs.h"
#include "[-.execlibs]execlibs.h"
#include "[-.argvlibs]argvlibs.h"
#endif

#ifdef BCC
#include "..\common\common.h"
#include "..\leave\leave.h"
#include "..\error\error.h"
#include "..\intlibs\intlibs.h"
#include "..\timelibs\timelibs.h"
#include "..\statlibs\statlibs.h"
#include "..\execlibs\execlibs.h"
#include "..\argvlibs\argvlibs.h"
#endif

#ifdef MSC
#include "..\common\common.h"
#include "..\leave\leave.h"
#include "..\error\error.h"
#include "..\intlibs\intlibs.h"
#include "..\timelibs\timelibs.h"
#include "..\statlibs\statlibs.h"
#include "..\execlibs\execlibs.h"
#include "..\argvlibs\argvlibs.h"
#endif

#ifdef SLC
#include "../common/common.h"
#include "../leave/leave.h"
#include "../error/error.h"
#include "../intlibs/intlibs.h"
#include "../timelibs/timelibs.h"
#include "../statlibs/statlibs.h"
#include "../execlibs/execlibs.h"
#include "../argvlibs/argvlibs.h"
#endif
```

```
#ifdef GCC
#include "../common/common.h"
#include "../leave/leave.h"
#include "../error/error.h"
#include "../intlibs/intlibs.h"
#include "../timelibs/timelibs.h"
#include "../statlibs/statlibs.h"
#include "../execlibs/execlibs.h"
#include "../argvlibs/argvlibs.h"
#endif

#ifdef HPUX
#include "../common/common.h"
#include "../leave/leave.h"
#include "../error/error.h"
#include "../intlibs/intlibs.h"
#include "../timelibs/timelibs.h"
#include "../statlibs/statlibs.h"
#include "../execlibs/execlibs.h"
#include "../argvlibs/argvlibs.h"
#endif

#include "comlibs.h"

/*###########################################*/

$! VMS DCL PROCEDURE
$ clr
$ if (P1.eqs."") then GOTO ALL
$ if (P1.eqs."ALL") then GOTO ALL
$ if (P1.eqs."LINK") then GOTO LINK
$ if (P1.eqs."HELLO") then GOTO HELLO
$ set verify
$ cc/define=VMS 'P1'
$ goto LINK
$ ALL:
$     set verify
$ cc/define=VMS test
$ cc/define=VMS comlibs
$ cc/define=VMS funcs
$ goto LINK
$ HELLO:
```

```
$ set verify
$ cc hello
$ link hello
$ goto END
$ LINK:
$ link/executable=test test,comlibs,funcs,[-.intlibs]intlibs,
[-.leave]leave,-
[-.error]error,[-.timelibs]timelibs,[-.statlibs]statlibs,
[-.execlibs]execlibs,-
[-.argvlibs]argvlibs
$ copy test.exe [weisfeld.exe]
$ END:
$ set noverify


/*##############################################*/

# makefile for BCC/C++ Compiler

OBJS    = test.obj comlibs.obj funcs.obj
LIBS    = ..\leave\leave.obj \
          ..\error\error.obj ..\argvlibs\argvlibs.obj \
          ..\statlibs\statlibs.obj ..\intlibs\intlibs.obj \
          ..\execlibs\execlibs.obj ..\timelibs\timelibs.obj
HDRS    = proto.h errdefs.h comlibs.h er.h
FLAGS   = -c -DBCC
COMP    = bcc

test.exe:  $(OBJS)
       $(COMP) @listobjs

       $(COMP) $(FLAGS) hello.c
       $(COMP) hello.obj
       copy hello.exe c:\exe


test.obj: test.c $(HDRS)
       $(COMP) $(FLAGS) test.c

comlibs.obj: comlibs.c $(HDRS)
       $(COMP) $(FLAGS) comlibs.c

funcs.obj: funcs.c $(HDRS)
       $(COMP) $(FLAGS) funcs.c
```

```
test.c:
comlibs.c:
funcs.c:

comlibs.h:

/*###############################################*/

# makefile for MSC/C++ Compiler

OBJS    = test.obj comlibs.obj funcs.obj
LIBS    = ..\leave\leave.obj \
          ..\error\error.obj ..\argvlibs\argvlibs.obj \
          ..\statlibs\statlibs.obj ..\intlibs\intlibs.obj \
          ..\execlibs\execlibs.obj ..\timelibs\timelibs.obj
HDRS    = proto.h errdefs.h comlibs.h er.h
FLAGS   = /c /DMSC
COMP    = cl

test.exe:  $(OBJS)
        $(COMP) @listobjs

        $(COMP) $(FLAGS) hello.c
        $(COMP) hello.obj
        copy hello.exe c:\exe


test.obj: test.c $(HDRS)
        $(COMP) $(FLAGS) test.c

comlibs.obj: comlibs.c $(HDRS)
        $(COMP) $(FLAGS) comlibs.c

funcs.obj: funcs.c $(HDRS)
        $(COMP) $(FLAGS) funcs.c

test.c:
comlibs.c:
funcs.c:

comlibs.h:
```

```
/*#####################################################*/

/*
LISTOBJS
*/

test.obj
comlibs.obj
funcs.obj
..\leave\leave.obj
..\error\error.obj
..\argvlibs\argvlibs.obj
..\statlibs\statlibs.obj
..\intlibs\intlibs.obj
..\execlibs\execlibs.obj
..\timelibs\timelibs.obj

/*#####################################################*/

# makefile for HPUX C Compiler

OBJS    = test.o comlibs.o funcs.o
LIBS    = ../leave/leave.o \
          ../error/error.o ../argvlibs/argvlibs.o \
          ../statlibs/statlibs.o ../intlibs/intlibs.o \
          ../execlibs/execlibs.o ../timelibs/timelibs.o
HDRS    = proto.h errdefs.h comlibs.h er.h
FLAGS   = -c -DHPUX -Aa
COMP    = cc

test:   $(OBJS)
        $(COMP) -o test $(OBJS) $(LIBS)

        $(COMP) $(FLAGS) hello.c
        $(COMP) -o hello hello.o
        cp hello ../../bin


test.o: test.c $(HDRS)
        $(COMP) $(FLAGS) test.c

comlibs.o: comlibs.c $(HDRS)
        $(COMP) $(FLAGS) comlibs.c
```

```
funcs.o: funcs.c $(HDRS)
        $(COMP) $(FLAGS) funcs.c

test.c:
comlibs.c:
funcs.c:

comlibs.h:


/*###########################################*/

# makefile for SUN SLC C Compiler

OBJS    = test.o comlibs.o funcs.o
LIBS    = ../leave/leave.o \
            ../error/error.o ../argvlibs/argvlibs.o \
            ../statlibs/statlibs.o ../intlibs/intlibs.o \
            ../execlibs/execlibs.o ../timelibs/timelibs.o
HDRS    = proto.h errdefs.h comlibs.h er.h
FLAGS   = -c -DSLC
COMP    = cc

test:   $(OBJS)
        $(COMP) -o test $(OBJS) $(LIBS)

        $(COMP) $(FLAGS) hello.c
        $(COMP) -o hello hello.o
        cp hello ../../bin


test.o: test.c $(HDRS)
        $(COMP) $(FLAGS) test.c

comlibs.o: comlibs.c $(HDRS)
        $(COMP) $(FLAGS) comlibs.c

funcs.o: funcs.c $(HDRS)
        $(COMP) $(FLAGS) funcs.c

test.c:
comlibs.c:
funcs.c:
```

comlibs.h:

```
/*###########################################*/

# makefile for SUN GCC C Compiler

OBJS    = test.o comlibs.o funcs.o
LIBS    = ../leave/leave.o \
          ../error/error.o ../argvlibs/argvlibs.o \
          ../statlibs/statlibs.o ../intlibs/intlibs.o \
          ../execlibs/execlibs.o ../timelibs/timelibs.o
HDRS    = proto.h errdefs.h comlibs.h er.h
FLAGS   = -c -DGCC
COMP    = gcc

test:   $(OBJS)
        $(COMP) -o test $(OBJS) $(LIBS)

        $(COMP) $(FLAGS) hello.c
        $(COMP) -o hello hello.o
        cp hello ../../bin


test.o: test.c $(HDRS)
        $(COMP) $(FLAGS) test.c

comlibs.o: comlibs.c $(HDRS)
        $(COMP) $(FLAGS) comlibs.c

funcs.o: funcs.c $(HDRS)
        $(COMP) $(FLAGS) funcs.c

test.c:
comlibs.c:
funcs.c:

comlibs.h:


/*###########################################*/
```

```
# makefile for CCC Compiler

OBJS    = test.o comlibs.o funcs.o
LIBS    =  ../leave/leave.o \
           ../error/error.o ../argvlibs/argvlibs.o \
           ../statlibs/statlibs.o ../intlibs/intlibs.o \
           ../execlibs/execlibs.o ../timelibs/timelibs.o
HDRS    = proto.h errdefs.h comlibs.h er.h
FLAGS   = -c -DCCC
COMP    = cc

test:   $(OBJS)
        $(COMP) -o test $(OBJS) $(LIBS)

        $(COMP) $(FLAGS) hello.c
        $(COMP) -o hello hello.o
        cp hello ../../bin


test.o: test.c $(HDRS)
        $(COMP) $(FLAGS) test.c

comlibs.o: comlibs.c $(HDRS)
        $(COMP) $(FLAGS) comlibs.c

funcs.o: funcs.c $(HDRS)
        $(COMP) $(FLAGS) funcs.c

test.c:
comlibs.c:
funcs.c:

comlibs.h:
```

Index